Recollections of an Airline Pilot

When once you've tasted flight you will forever walk with your eyes turned skyward for there you have been, and there you will always long to return.

Leonardo da Vinci

by Peter M Orange

Captain KLM – retired

For Elly, my dear wife of more than twenty-five years.
She helped greatly in recovering these memories, and
is lovingly patient with an increasingly grumpy old man!

Published by Peter M Orange

ISBN 0-9551066-0-5

Produced by: Inca Creative Print Ltd

Cover image: ©2004 Francois Rétif / Rapho

All photographs are extracted from personal albums. Some are courtesy of The Boeing Company (Seattle USA) but the source of others is unknown. Apologies are offered for any inadvertent copyright infringements.

Acknowledgements

To my long deceased parents who unsuccessfully tried to persuade me to write a record of my travels, and to whom I was shamefully deceitful over my 1940 adventures.

To Kiki Farewell, my 97 year old friend who resides in a care home. We have shared memories of Cairo, Singapore, and Tehran that featured in many conversations. "You must write it down, Peter, you must write it all down". I never did, I couldn't be bothered, it was all too far away. Sadly, it is now too late for Kiki as her lucid moments have become too short.

To Leo van Maare, a newly acquired friend. In responding to his request for information on KLM'S Mauritius flights of 1948/49 I searched the attic for my old logbooks. The Mauritius data was there, but so were many other long forgotten memories.

With best wishes

Peter Ormond

06. Sept. 05 -

Peter M Orange

RAF   Royal Air Force (1940–47)

KLM   Royal Dutch Airlines (Holland – 1948–79)

UAC   United Air Carriers inc. (Jeddah, Saudi Arabia – 1979–80)

TBC   The Boeing Aircraft Company (Seattle, USA – 1980)

GIA   Garuda Indonesian Airlines (Jakarta, Indonesia – 1980–83)

Storrington UK August 2005

Contents

Introduction

Following a delayed release from the RAF in 1947, after seven years of mainly overseas service, I joined KLM (Royal Dutch Airlines), and became a foreign labourer in Holland, remaining there for the next thirty-one years. I subsequently transferred my status as a foreign labourer to Jeddah in Saudi Arabia, to the USA, and to Jakarta in Indonesia.

These are my logbook inspired recollections of forty-three years of active flying, from 1940 to 1983. A pilot's logbook forms the legal diary of his career, but usually records only the basic essentials concerning time, place, and aircraft type. Specific details of events encountered during a particular flight are not usually recorded, unless they actually alter or impede its progress. In later life, these sparse entries can do little more than trigger a few memories of long forgotten experiences.

...........................and memories, dear reader, can be faulty!

This narrative is of a purely personal nature. To my astonishment many forgotten dates and factual items could be obtained from the internet, a source of information which I had only just discovered. I therefore decided to pursue this private venture unaided, and so, without seeking access to any Company archives, any potential copyright problems might be avoided.

Various accidents are referred to in the text about which completely personal observations are sometimes advanced; these are mainly accidents which occurred during my propeller days. Those with more expert knowledge than mine on these affairs, or those who have had access to the official investigations, will no doubt dispute some of my observations.

My long service with KLM took me to many parts of the world in the cockpits of Douglas and Lockheed aircraft of the era, often with pre-war pioneers who were household names in Holland. These experiences had long faded from my mind when a request for information on a unique period of KLM's history reached me. The story of our fifteen hour flights across the Indian Ocean by Lockheed Constellation in 1948/49 was being researched by a friend in Holland, Leo van Maare.

In order to provide some information for his recently published book I recovered my long forgotten logbook from the attic, and in blowing the dust away I slowly began to rediscover many other events that had completely faded from my mind................*and once one starts looking!*

Approaching KLM's mandatory retirement, at the age of fifty-six, I started searching for a new landing ground. By pure coincidence I gained a partner in this search, a KLM stewardess who, through the whims of crew scheduling, had very seldom previously crossed my path. She and I flew and worked together for the last few years of my active flying life, and she thus features in the last few chapters of this narrative. Despite an alarming age gap of thirty years Elly and I married in 1980, and have remained very happily on course ever since.

Although my octogenarian footsteps are now less sprightly, we still enjoy the air show circuit particularly when today's "heavy metal" makes way for the nostalgic restorations from "My Last Propeller" days. We also read the aviation magazines, and are constantly amazed at how the lessons of history disappear from view. Despite all the modern devices such as GPWS (Ground Proximity Warning Systems, both aural and visual) and TCAS (Traffic Collision Avoidance Systems, both aural and visual) the occasional repetition of avoidable accidents is not prevented – accidents which are almost identical to those that have occurred in the past.

In the Beginning

In 1938, at the age of fifteen, I acquired my first uniform, an ill-fitting khaki one. This was as a cadet in the (boarding) school OTC (Officers' Training Corps), which was almost the private training ground of RSM (Regimental Sergeant Major) Solley, late of the Grenadier Guards. His stentorian voice was accompanied by much stamping of hob-nailed boots on the parade ground, but he also indoctrinated us into the arts of living under canvas during the school holidays. Tuition in field craft and map reading enabled us to find the shortest routes through scattered villages to their pubs – which were not too fussy about the age of their customers.

Officers' Training Corps 1939. Author, back row fourth from right

Handling of the Lee Enfield .303 rifle was no novelty to me, as my father had already trained me in its use. The art of deflection shooting, allowing for target movement before squeezing the trigger, had been learned at his shooting club, as had the stripping and re-assembly of various (inactive) machine guns. The signs of the coming war were there for those who cared to read them, but not everyone did.

A Year of Confusion

In June 1940 came the evacuation from Dunkirk, closely followed by the Battle of Britain, and the start of the Blitz with the bombing of London and other major cities. My family home in the country was bombed, apparently by an aircraft unable to reach London, and they joined the evacuees. Since I was over two hundred miles from home the news of these events took several weeks to reach me, as the mail was disrupted, and telephone lines were down.

Sixty-five years on, I find it impossible to recall the details, or even the sequence of events. Family circumstances apparently necessitated an end to my school days, and I was temporarily given shelter with the family of a school friend in Sheffield. It was not long before we abused our unaccustomed freedom, and illicitly managed to enrol in the RAFVR (Royal Air Force Volunteer Reserve) as air gunners – proof of age, or even identity, was not yet an enforced requirement!

Familiarity with drill and parades, and especially with firearms, soon had me assigned to a fast-track training group. By early 1941 I was embarked on a very short career as a tail gunner on Wellington bombers. I had only just become accustomed to seeing the runway unroll away from behind that lonely position, and to seeing continental rivers glinting in the moonlight, when my irregular enrolment was uncovered. Repercussions were swift and effective, all records of this adventure were deleted, and I was removed to the nearest railway station by the Military Police. My crew had planned to see me off, but had not returned from a flight to Bremen.

My war was not one of medals and public acclaim

The autumn of 1941 saw me formally enlisted in the RAFVR for pilot training. Very little flight training was done in the UK at the time, because of weather and enemy action, but the overseas training programmes were getting into full swing. After several weeks of button polishing, drill, medical examinations and general indoctrination, I was aboard a troopship bound for Durban (South Africa). The six week voyage was far from being a holiday cruise – we slept in hammocks in the hold of a former merchant ship, and used the decks for drill parades. When entering the tropics it was more comfortable to sleep on the deck – providing one was up and about before they were washed down – no mercy was shown to late sleepers! There were frequent submarine alerts during the early part of the voyage, and a number of us were assigned as duty loaders for the anti-aircraft guns since the subs could call in air attacks. One ship in the convoy was lost just before we called in at Freetown (West Africa). Our next sight of land was somewhere off the coast of South America, a truly circuitous route taken to avoid a reported German raider.

From Durban, we headed north by train to Bulawayo (Southern Rhodesia) a quite fascinating three day journey. At Bulawayo, there were more lengthy indoctrination and drill parades to endure before postings to flying stations were announced. We were, of course, expected to take part in camp guard duties during this waiting period; I was never too sure what we were supposed to be guarding against, but we did receive dire warnings about spitting cobras and scorpions. I soon found that my nose was very sensitive to the high altitude of around 4500 feet – a firm tap just before a drill parade could produce a most useful nosebleed! These parades were also frequently disrupted by the sexual activities of wild dogs that had failed to listen to advice on methods of separation when the deed was done!

At last the postings were announced, and I was once more on a train, this time to RAF Mount Hampden near Salisbury (now Harare) – this was an initial training school using Tiger Moths. I managed this start to my piloting life with considerable caution, but my later career as an RAF pilot was to be marked by a succession of hiccups – mostly of my own making, through over enthusiasm for the unorthodox!

.............................but now to pilot training, and a busy 1942

The de Havilland Tiger Moth

The Tiger Moth was a biplane of wooden and fabric construction. The upper and lower wings were braced by wires, and the pilots' seats arranged in tandem. In general appearance, it differed very little from the aeroplanes of the First World War, an appearance enhanced by the two bladed wooden propellers on the nose. The fuel tank was located within the top wing just over the pilots' head, and one could watch a stream of fuel exiting its vent pipe when in a near vertical dive – rather alarming at first sight!

First flights were usually a matter of weaving across the sky in a semi-controlled state. It took a while to learn the art of moving the nose cowling of the engine up and down in relation to the horizon, thereby adjusting the attitude of the aircraft. A distant landmark could be used in a similar fashion to assist in maintaining heading. As one got used to visual cues, so the instrument panel gradually entered the picture, but this panel was supplied with only an extremely modest number of instruments; and it took much practice to be able to fly on them alone, and a well developed sense of "feel" was also essential.

The student sat in the rear seat, and the long suffering instructor in the front. Communication between the two was by Gosport tube – a form of voice tube connecting the pilots' helmets.

For blind flying exercises the student's cockpit was covered with a canvas hood, and his very few instruments became a survival kit. When unusual attitudes developed, the Gosport tube became clogged with impolite suggestions. On the rare days when one's efforts satisfied the instructor, the hood would be removed, and he would remove his joy-stick (control stick), and wave it in the air – control was yours!! On less successful days the instructor would disembark his student at the far side of the airfield. The lengthy walk back around the perimeter to the hangars was both ignominious and tiring; the parachute was attached to a long harness so that the 'chute itself dangled against one's bottom. In the aircraft it had functioned as a seat cushion in a more comfortable manner.

The unforgettable first solo flight came as something of a surprise. I was instructed to stop by the offices after a modestly successful landing, and suddenly realized that the instructor was climbing out and removing his joy-stick. With a pat on the shoulder it was "off you go – keep the airfield in sight".

First Solo

I taxied out towards the take-off position on the grass field (we had no runways), and awaited a green light from the control van. In a dazed fashion I completed my few preparations for take-off, and suddenly became aware that a "green" was being flashed at me in a very impatient fashion – obviously I had missed the first signal!

Throttle gently open and away, trying desperately to keep straight. The tail seemed to come up a little quicker than usual, probably because the weight of the instructor was missing, which helped with the directional control. And then we were airborne, with an empty front seat, and no voice in my headset …… freedom of the air!! In my excitement, I almost forgot to turn back towards the airfield, but thankfully it was not long in reappearing. Down to a survivable landing and a warm greeting from my instructor who had had a long and anxious wait; little did I then realize that I would be experiencing very similar anxieties in the not too distant future.

> *Those who failed to make that vital step to solo went on to other forms of aircrew training – navigator, wireless operator etc. Navigation schools existed in S. Africa, but I believe other forms of training required a return to the U.K.*

Once solo, navigation exercises began in earnest. Cross country flying with a topographical map, and a primitive hand held (Dalton) computer were the sole aids to success. We naturally pre-calculated our headings and timings in accordance with the forecast winds, which were seldom very strong. The map was apt to disappear in the slipstream, or the computer fall out of reach on the cockpit floor, which was rather tiresome; soon one learned to hold the joy-stick firmly between the knees in order to examine the navigational data – such as it was. Isolated farms were usually our turning points, and a new course then had to be chosen. Our fuel load was sufficient for the intended exercise, but with very little to spare.

.............................and instruction continues

Dual instruction continued and endless blind flying exercises were part of the lesson plans. Stalling, spinning and aerobatics were regarded as fun days until stalls and spins were conducted under the blind flying hood – if one failed to recover from a spin by the assigned altitude it became a long walk back from the far side of the airfield after landing! Stopping and re-starting an engine in-flight was also an interesting experience. With the ignition switched off, the wooden propeller slowed down and shuddered to a halt. The resulting silence was broken only by the sound of the wind, and the singing of the bracing wires in the wings. Nosing over into an almost vertical dive the ignition would be switched on again, and the propeller would very reluctantly start to rotate – as the earth loomed larger and larger it would rotate faster until the engine suddenly burst into noisy life once more, and one's heart beat returned to normal.

Victoria Falls

After about two months our Tiger Moth training was finally complete, and future postings were announced. Mine was a twin engine SFTS (Service Flying Training School) equipped with Airspeed Oxfords, at RAF Heaney near Bulawayo.

The Airspeed Oxford

The twin engined Oxford was mainly constructed of wood and glued together in the time honoured fashion – whether the glue makers had considered tropical climates remained to be seen. Dual controls with the pilots seated side by side seemed to make for an ideal training aircraft. A modest cabin was located aft of the cockpit making it also very useful as a general communications aircraft.

After the rather basic Tiger Moth the Oxford seemed to be an extremely modern piece of machinery. The instrument panel had more dials than I was used to, but was obviously designed to help one around the skies rather than add to the confusion. Ahead, and between the pilots, was a modest pedestal with the engine controls etc. The engines had to be started by a brawny mechanic kneeling on the wing next to an engine, and laboriously winding a starting handle. This wound up an inertia starter which eventually turned the engine over until it burst into noisy life. To me, it seemed a much safer process than swinging the prop of a Tiger Moth, and jumping clear as the engine caught.

Powered by two Cheetah engines of some 850 HP (horsepower), which drove the two-bladed wooden propellers, it was somewhat underpowered for the Rhodesian altitude of around 4500 feet. To improve its overall performance it was later re-engined with more powerful Cheetah engines which certainly gave us a more agile aircraft, but the end results were rather disastrous!! The glue makers had not allowed for the deterioration which could occur in a tropical climate, and those aircraft which had been re-engined started falling to pieces around our ears. A hasty halt was called to the project.

.... *and my first hiccup!!*

My first solo on the Oxford came after just over three hours dual instruction – some last minute advice from the instructor, and then he exited from the rear door. Waved away by the ground crew I taxied out to the take-off area, completed my checklist, and awaited the green light from the control van. There it was, and off I went, all alone in a proper airplane, and with a wonderful sense of freedom! This demanded a little celebration, and so I immediately set course for the Matopas Hills, and some discreet low flying. In the Matopas Hills was the grave of Cecil Rhodes, marked by an inscribed granite slab, who had been the founder of Rhodesia – he had been one of my many school-day heroes.

Rhodes Grave, Matopas Hills

Joining a picnic

Descending towards my target I spotted a group of people apparently enjoying a picnic. They would probably enjoy a little excitement, I thought. So, down to tree top height when, to my horror, I recognized the Station Commander, and his family. Up and away, and back to base in rapid time, and then to await the inevitable summons to his august presence. That was not very long in coming, and I was faced with a very severe telling off – and quite deservedly so. The punishment, however, was equally severe; my status as an officer cadet was removed, and I was thus ejected from residence in the officers' mess. This resulted in my eventually being awarded pilot's "wings" with the rank of sergeant, rather than as an officer. Of more concern to me, however, was the fact that my pilot rating as "exceptional" was down graded to "average", apparently an extremely rare form of punishment.

My instructor at the time sagely remarked that I would most probably kill myself low flying; fortunately he was wrong, but only just!

Meanwhile, it was back to the training programme with dual instruction flights alternating with solo ones. The intention of the solo flights was primarily to practice the recently instructed lessons. These covered such things as instrument flying, low and medium level bombing, and formation flying, in addition to endless circuits, and landings. Our formation flying during solo missions was somewhat unorthodox. When in a "vee" formation it was considered proper to advise the leader of our closeness by bringing a propeller near enough to his aileron to actually make it tremble – and this he could actually feel on his controls. A further rather foolish trick (fortunately seldom attempted) was to tuck in so close to the leader that his cabin door handle could be flipped open with a wing tip. How we managed to survive these extra-curricula activities remains a mystery!

Wings parade, followed by training as an instructor

But survive we did, and it was time for "Wings" parade, which was the official presentation of our RAF wings. Future postings were obviously already decided, and it was hardly surprising that I drew the short straw – off to CFS (Central Flying School). So yet another train ride to join a small group of other newly qualified pilots, and a very intensive training course, designed to turn us into flight instructors.

The first requirement was to learn the "patter" – the verbal coaching that was given to each student during a particular in-flight exercise. We then had to demonstrate each exercise in conjunction with the required patter. Apart from my familiar Oxford, this had to be done on several different aircraft – even when doing "flick" rolls (a truly maximum rate of roll) on a Harvard.

On the single engined aircraft such as the Harvard our aerobatic capabilities were tuned to a very fine degree indeed, as was the formation flying in its many variations. The final check-out session with the

Central Flying School 1943. Author, back row 2nd from the left.

Chief Instructor lasted a full two hours, and seemed to include every possible exercise together with its accompanying "patter".

The CFS was based at RAF Norton, about twenty five miles west of Salisbury (Harare). Recreational facilities at the camp were few, but quite regular transport to town was provided. The bus would drop us off outside its most famous spot – Meikles Hotel. After a few enjoyable hours at the town swimming pool, which seemed to be Olympic in size, we would return to the hotel bar to await return transport, reminiscing meanwhile over all the delightful girls whom we had seen around the pool!

The students on my course were a very mixed collection of nationalities, and covered a wide range of ages. Some were "resting" from operational flying, and others were straight from the training schools with newly acquired "wings". The instructors were generally much more senior in age, and experience, and their expertise was extremely impressive; their actual flying was so precise, and accurate that one simply had to try and equal it!

The results of the course were soon posted, and I was greatly pleased to see that in addition to my B-1 instructor's qualification, my pilot rating as "exceptional" had also been restored. I was later to return to CFS to have my instructor's qualification upgraded to A-1, the highest that could be obtained.

...............................*and now an instructor, with hiccups again!*

I was fortunately posted as an instructor to an Oxford station well out of reach of the Station Commander who had previously found the need to discipline me so severely. It was not long however, before I found it necessary to demonstrate (without patter) some really serious low flying to my students. In the dry season, there were plenty of "wadis" (dry river beds) ideally suited to this purpose, and it was in one of these that I nearly came to grief. Well below the river banks it was suddenly necessary to negotiate a shallow turn – and it was then that my <u>top</u> wing-tip brushed through some tree branches!

As we carefully returned to base I busied myself with concocting a story to explain the decorations attached to my wing. Since "precautionary" (short-field) landings had been on our lesson plan, that seemed to provide the answer – we had brushed through a hedge in aiming for an early landing! On arrival at base I immediately alerted the curious ground crew to the situation; like a flash they disappeared into the nearest hedge-row, returning with armfuls of foliage. This they then tucked into the undercarriage (the wheels would have been down for a practice landing) in a very convincing manner, giving my aircraft the appearance of a true hedgecutter! By the time that the Flight Commander arrived the transformation was complete, and after a brief inspection of the damage, I was told to take more care in the future!

1943 was greeted with two welcome events, my promotion to officer status, and the arrival of a Hawker Hurricane for the use of a selected few. When time permitted we made full use of this delightful aircraft, and a great deal of "bundu bashing" resulted – low flying across very arid bush country. A challenge was unofficially invented whereby a blade of grass had to be caught in the wing tip light, without breaking the lens. There were not many takers for that, even though the grass was three feet tall.

The machine guns in the wings had been rendered inoperative, which we thought a great shame!

Operational Detachments

A few of us were sent to Tunis, and later to Bari (Southern Italy) on detachment to Hurricane Squadrons for operational experience – not a very successful move. Full of confidence in our own flying capabilities we were soon cut down to size by our reluctant hosts. They had no time or real interest in training us in combat tactics – we were there under sufferance, and needed constant guidance and protection. When we flew it was in a borrowed aircraft (from someone on leave), and returning it with battle damage – probably unnecessary – made us very unpopular with the hard pressed ground crews, let alone the other pilots. These detachments were soon discontinued as it had become very evident that even highly proficient pilots needed proper operational training.

And back to the Oxford

A further spell of instruction saw me encountering a new experience – a pilot freezing on the controls! He was a big fellow, and had been an average student when suddenly he went absolutely rigid at the controls. There was nothing that could be done to move him until in desperation I hit him on the head with the side of the fire-axe; he survived the blow, but not the subsequent investigation.

We did a great deal of night flying, practicing circuits, and landings on a grass runway marked by goose-neck (oil lamp) flares. As we became more expert these were steadily reduced in number though a floodlight still marked the touchdown zone.

The unexpected loss incurred from glue failures was added to by another sad event. A crew on a long range navigation exercise became lost, and made a (successful) forced landing in a totally barren area. Unwisely, and

Tunisia 1944

contrary to published instructions, they left their aircraft, and started walking in search of help. Even more unwisely they walked in the wrong direction – away from the solitary north/south railway line. Remnants of uniform were later recovered from the site of a native campfire, but no trace of the two trainee pilots was ever found.

The Oxford was not an approved aircraft for aerobatics, but it could be gently barrel rolled, when well away from prying eyes. Steep turns we (innocently) considered should have at least 70 degrees of bank – beyond that, unpleasant surprises could be expected. But perhaps the favourite unauthorized manoeuvre was the stall turn. This required a steep climb with full power, and then allowing the speed to decay until stall buffet was felt – at that moment one engine was throttled right back, and rudder applied on the same side. The resulting turn, and nose dive were instantaneous, and it was essential to immediately regain normal control. One unfortunate trainee was too slow in regaining control, and ended up in an unrecoverable inverted spin.

Low flying was also greatly popular, particularly when positioned in the bomb aimer's position. This involved lying prone in the nose watching the tree tops come closer and closer to the clear vision Perspex panel – a tremendous sense of speed was experienced!

..............................through the wire

We had a very varied intake of students on the courses; they came from many different countries, and from all walks of life. The Polish students were probably the most unpredictable as they appeared to be totally without fear or restraint. One particular group lost five of its members in quick succession – three collided while in close formation during a leadership change, and two went through high tension wires while waving to girlfriends at outlying farm homesteads.

..............................local hospitality

Hospitality from local people was often quite overwhelming. On one particular Christmas the population of a small local town (Plumtree, Southern Rhodesia) entertained us for the day. The wide main street was lined with tables and chairs and cooking fires were placed at intervals between them. It was a very hot summer day with scarcely a breath of wind, and the roast turkey with all the traditional trimmings was difficult going, as was the hot Xmas pudding that followed!

Many of the local people also "adopted" a serviceman for the duration of his stay in the country, making them welcome in their homes at any time. My own host family were extremely good to me, and even taught me to drive in their sedate Plymouth car. Traffic in town was very light indeed, and out of town one drove on "strip" roads almost devoid of other traffic. The strip roads consisted of two strips of tarmac laid a wheel's width apart, When meeting opposing traffic one moved aside so that you used only one strip while the oncoming car also moved on to one strip.

My first Dakota

The Douglas Dakota – or in the USAF (United States Air Force) terminology the C-47 – was the workhorse of the allied armies, carrying troops and supplies in every corner of the world. To be assigned to a conversion course, in preparation for a posting to RAF Transport Command, was an exciting prospect. After completion of the ground course we were required to become totally familiar with the cockpit controls while blindfolded. After my rather humble Oxford, this aircraft seemed enormous in size, but proved to be quite easy to fly, and responded well to the controls.

The engines could now be started from within the cockpit provided that there was a source of electrical power connected from the ground. The blades of the metal propellers could be finely adjusted for the various regimes of flight, and even turned to a fully "feathered" position (minimum drag) if an engine had to be stopped. The brakes were now hydraulic (rather than the compressed air system of the Oxford), and operated by toe movement on the rudder pedals. There was even an auto-pilot to ease the workload during a long flight. This was probably the first step on that never ending road to complete automation when the pilot was to become a highly paid programme manager.

The course included glider towing (which we were also allowed to fly), supply and paratroop dropping. Determined to take full advantage of the opportunities that existed I made several parachute jumps – a hefty shove in the back always had me first out of the door thus avoiding any unwanted hold ups! Since all the jumps were from low altitude (500 feet) there was too little time to enjoy the view, the ground came up at a rather alarming rate. When collecting our 'chutes from stores before the jump we were solemnly advised "to bring it back if it doesn't open, and we'll give you a new one" – fortunately I didn't have to follow that well meant advice. Little did we know at the time, but all this intense training was part of the preparations for Operation Market Garden (Arnhem).

..............................but first, back to instruction

With a steady demand for trained aircrew, both in Europe, and the Far East, the RAF training schools continued in full swing requiring my reluctant return to Oxford instruction. There was now more emphasis being placed on night flying which had always been an interesting aspect of training. No approach lighting to a (grass) runway existed, and it thus became very necessary to develop a sound judgement of height during the approach phase as a properly judged descent path made the ultimate landing a great deal easier.

Lining up with the runway for landing, which was fully equipped with goose-neck (paraffin lamp) flares, was the relatively easy part, but as experience was gained so the number of flares was decreased. By the time a student reached the end of his course he would be expected to land with a "Chance Light" (a restricted floodlight) illuminating the touch-down area, and two goose-necks for directional guidance marking the far end of the runway. An instructor was expected to manage without the help of a "Chance Light".

A return to Transport Command had me polishing up my own night flying capabilities, and a refresher course on low level supply dropping. This turned out to be part of the preparation for Operation Manna, which was mainly conducted by Bomber Command aircraft. I am not sure whether our Dakotas were officially assigned to the operation; it is quite possible that our Station Commander organised an unofficial participation – a not unheard of thing in those days.

Holland's "Hunger Winter" in 1944/45

Holland had been devastated by war, by invasion and occupation, by deportations to slave labour camps, by the summary execution of resistance fighters, by collaborators infiltrating the resistance movement or revealing the whereabouts of Jews in hiding, by floods created by the occupying forces to thwart advancing allied troops, and finally by the Hunger Winter of 1944/45. Little of this scenario was known to the outside world, occupied as it was with troubles of its own. With the incredibly brave rescue of shot down allied airman, and of troops escaping Arnhem, news from Holland became more generally known.

The spectre of widespread starvation in Holland had prompted the Allied governments into attempting negotiations with the Nazis. Permission was sought to air drop food supplies on what was still occupied territory. Lack of positive progress in these talks eventually prompted the RAF into making a trial drop with unarmed aircraft, since the situation was daily becoming more critical. The trial drop was made, and although the Nazi guns could be seen following our low flying aircraft, not a shot was fired. Deemed a success a massive air armada of bomber aircraft was launched, their bomb bays loaded with food panniers for dropping by free-fall. I believe that most of the allies took part in this relief operation.

Our Transport Command Dakotas were more useful in dropping loads by parachute, as a full floor area was available for stowage, and eventual exiting of the loads. Crew members also threw out handfuls of sweets for the children to find, and watched the waving people below as they hurried to gather in the bundles falling from the skies .... a sense of freedom was coming alive once more.

Sixty years later I am annually reminded of that operation. Just a mile from my home in Storrington (West Sussex) is an RAFA (Royal Air Force Association) nursing home. On the anniversary of "Operation Manna" the air buzzes to announce the airborne arrival of Dutch RAFA members – they have flown from Holland to drop flowers and rounds of cheese in grateful remembrance.

The peace-time RAF

Netherlands Government Air Transport.
Operated by KLM Crews Cairo 1946

With the final cessation of hostilities in Europe, and ultimately in the Far East, my first home leave in some five years was a significant event. Needing time to assess my future (which had to be a continuation of flying) I signed on for a further eighteen months' RAF service, and was posted to a Transport Command base at Kabrit on the edge of the Suez Canal in Egypt. Kabrit was located at the southern end of the Bitter Lakes, through which the Suez Canal passes on its route from the Mediterranean to the Red Sea.

Kabrit (Suez Canal)

The Suez Canal had control stations, at intervals, throughout its length. One such station was located just outside our airfield perimeter, with Mr. Zarb (a Maltese gentleman) in charge. Mrs Zarb was a Yugoslav lady, and there were five delightful daughters ranging in age from two months to twenty three years. Invitations to their house were eagerly sought, and I was soon on the guest list. This led to many enjoyable activities, including the mysterious stopping of an aircraft by the perimeter fence (out of sight of the control tower) when taxying out for a night-flying test. Giggling girls were hastily lifted aboard, and off we would go into the starlit sky!

.............................and some Egyptian hiccups!

The approach of Christmas 1946 saw me on a flight to Cyprus, carrying service personnel going on leave. Among these were several MPs (Military Policemen) in civilian clothes. As a Christmas present for a friend the Wing Commander had asked me to take a small dog along – cradled under my arm this would be well hidden by my coat, or so I thought!

My Dakota Crew, Kabrit 1946

Soon after arrival I was arrested by the local police for smuggling a dog into the island, and escorted to the nearby jail. One of my MP passengers had reported me! It took a visit by my Wing Commander to negotiate my release which was accompanied by a ban on any future visits to the island.

.............................fortunately this ban has disappeared over the course of time!

Returning to Kabrit I announced my arrival to the Zarb family by rattling the tiles on their house with a few low passes overhead. With my usual bad luck the Station Commander happened to see my wing-tip passing the flagpole in their garden, and called the Control Tower to demand my immediate attendance in his office after landing.

With great presence of mind they immediately sent someone down to the beach to push out an overturned canoe, keeping me informed by radio of their progress. Properly briefed by my control tower friends I appeared before the CO with the story that I had been investigating an overturned boat, and the possible presence of a body. The story was accepted, although he did consider the altitude to be unnecessarily low – the canoe was subsequently restored to its rightful owner.

.... a Christmas Party

On Christmas Eve, a party of nurses had been flown down from Cairo to join in the seasonal celebrations in our gaily decorated mess. Since I was only a modest drinker I had been scheduled to see them safely back to Cairo when the party was over. Towards the end of the evening I was propping up the bar, awaiting a sign that the returning nurses were ready to leave. I had seen the Commanding Officer looking at me a few times, but thought nothing of it. At last, off to the aircraft only to find another pilot in my cockpit seat! "Ah", he said – "the CO said you had been drinking too much, and I was to take the flight". "Nonsense Jack",

Chrismas Card 1946

I replied – "off you go". Since I outranked him he quickly disappeared.

Somewhat to my shame, that short flight to Almaza (Cairo) is almost a complete blank in my mind. I recall having difficulty maintaining level flight, since the heavily built wireless operator was walking up and down the cabin chatting up the girls, and disturbing the trim. How we ever found Almaza, and safely landed there is totally missing from my memory!

............................an impromptu swim

The following week saw me unexpectedly swimming in the Bitter Lake. Two of us had been scheduled for a qualification revalidation flight with an inspector from Transport Command Headquarters in the UK. I was sitting in the aircraft cabin awaiting my turn for test when both engines suddenly stopped, and very shortly thereafter we were "ditching" in the lake. In those days an engine failure was not simulated, it was positively stopped – and for some reason that I don't recall this exercise resulted in two stopped engines, an unhealthy situation at low altitude!

Anyway, we had time to put on our life jackets, and exit the aircraft from the rear door before it gently slid below the surface. Fortunately a very brief "Mayday" call had been made, but it took quite some time for an RAF rescue launch to find us. This was one incident for which I didn't have to answer questions!

...........................geographical lessons from the air

From Kabrit we flew scheduled flights for service personnel, and freight throughout the Mediterranean, and Middle East areas. These regions also provided a magnificent opportunity for a little discreet smuggling, for those so inclined. This practice was abruptly halted when a fully laden Dakota, inbound to Malta, lost an engine en-route. In their need to reduce the weight, and thus maintain enough height to reach the island the crew threw all the mail and freight overboard; the Military Police found this so curious that they insisted on examining the rather voluminous luggage of the crew. Surprise, surprise, it consisted mainly of smuggled cigarettes!!

> *The smuggling route started in Khartoum with the purchase of crates of tea. These were traded in Cairo for cigarettes, which were then carried to Rome via Malta. In Rome, further trading acquired silk scarves for delivery to Athens where sponges were received in exchange, and taken to Cairo – I heard that this was an extremely profitable sideline to the business of flying!!*

...........................Khartoum

My favourite route was down the Nile river to Khartoum (The "City of Elephant Trunks"), and then further southwards down the Nile until heading off to Nairobi. Along the Nile we would first stop at Wadi Halfa, near Aswan, and then indulge in some very low flying alongside the wonderful temple of Abu Simbel. It was in this region that the Aswan Dam was built which resulted in the creation of Lake Nasser. This dam construction had been a tremendous feat of international engineering, and under the auspices of UNESCO had also seen the relocation of the entire Abu Simbel temple to save it from the rising waters of the lake that then formed.

...........................along the White Nile

Further south between Khartoum and Nairobi we landed at the small trading towns of Malakal and Juba on the banks of the White Nile; these had been important centres associated with big game hunting expeditions in pre-war days. Needless to say, the many opportunities for low flying over the tremendous herds of big game were not to be missed before we set course for Nairobi at a respectable altitude!

From Khartoum, we also had flights ranging eastwards through Asmara (Eritrea), where the airfield was located at about six thousand feet altitude on the very edge of an escarpment. Our take-off weight was restricted because of the altitude, but it still felt like leaving the deck of an aircraft carrier – a certain amount of sink before a comforting speed was noted!

...........................The coastline of Yemen and of Oman

Aden was then a large British base in Yemen; located at the southern end of the Red Sea it was in an ideal position to guard the approaches to the Gulf of Suez and the Suez Canal. Underlining its importance were a considerable number of Army garrison troops, frequent movements of the Royal Navy through its port, and the presence of RAF squadrons. The RAF was mostly employed in keeping a watchful eye on dissident tribesmen, and in maintaining a communications network.

From Aden we flew along the southern coast of Yemen and the Sultanate of Oman to reach Masirah Island where another RAF base welcomed our visit, and the fresh supplies that we brought them. Near the border of Yemen and Oman we passed over the port of Salafah with the Sultan's summer palace, viewing the territory that I was to find myself exploring in the leisured years of retirement. That was to include a visit to the tomb of the prophet Job – recognised by both Christians and Muslims – and a very brief excursion into the vast emptiness of the famed Empty Quarter.

Leaving Masirah Island for the return flight a slight northward diversion gave us an opportunity to view the city of Muscat from the air before setting course once more for Aden. The landlocked harbour, protected from seaward assault by well sited forts, was quite a unique spectacle – as was the Sultan's immense palace within its crenellated walls.

..............................eastwards from Palestine

Also within our orbit of operations were Palestine and Iraq, landing at every possible (and impossible) variety of airfield or landing strip; these were frequently just compacted sand strips near a cluster of tents. How we ever found some of them was quite a mystery, and what went on in those isolated places I never really knew – guarding something or other apparently!

In Iraq the enormous RAF base at Habbanyia was always a welcome stop, accommodation was excellent, and every possible recreational facility was available – including sailing on the lake, a race course for the riding fraternity, and several tennis courts. On one visit I noticed a Transport Command Lancaster (bomber) with a yacht stowed in its bomb bay, the doors having been removed!

Habbanyia had also had a brief moment of glory during the war. Its training aircraft had been rapidly armed with machine guns and small bombs, to drive off an invading force of rebellious tribesmen. The invaders, who were largely encamped on the surrounding high ground, were successfully repelled and the base freed by the arrival of reinforcements for the defenders.

We also spread our wings over the length and breadth of the Persian Gulf, calling in at Bahrain and Sharjah. Over Dubai, I remember looking down on a modest fishing port spread along the central Creek, a far cry from the glass and concrete jungle that now covers the area. Its importance as a local trading centre has now grown into one of international repute, and its local citizens are now far outnumbered by the expatriate community from many Asian countries.

From the small dusty airfield at Sharjah we continued eastwards towards Karachi with sometimes a visit to Jask or Jiwani, both isolated fishing ports on the barren southern coast of Persia. Gazing down on this rugged coastline brought back memories of Alexander the Great, and the homeward struggle of part of his conquering army – only occasional provisions by sea could reach them on that terrible journey.

Finally, we would reach Karachi, and park in the shade of the enormous airship hanger that had been built for the arrival of the R-101, an arrival that never took place, since thunderstorms brought it down over France. I have no recollections of staying in Karachi, so it was probably a very short stop before the return flight commenced.

These far ranging flights from Kabrit, mainly at modest altitudes of around 6000 feet, were putting a geographical face to the history that I had read, and was still to read in the years to come.

Detachment to Palestine (Israel)

In early 1947 a detachment to Aquir (near Tel Aviv) in Palestine, provided another opportunity for working with the airborne troops. Glider flying and towing were again on the agenda, as were the occasional parachute jumps. These were the last days of the British Mandate, and freedom fighters (terrorists to us) were extremely active. Our camp guards were the impressive troops of the Royal

Jordanian Army. On a visit to our headquarters in the King David Hotel (Jerusalem), however, their vigilance had been eluded by the terrorists, and I joined the scramble for shelter in the garden when a bomb exploded.

> *This was the world's first terrorist attack, and among over ninety deaths were Arabs, Jews, and British. The hotel was the headquarters of the British administration, and of the various military services. The Irgun (National Military Society) under the leadership of Menachem Begin, had managed to plant bombs in the canteen under the west tower, and fitted them with a delayed action device. Begin was later to become the Prime Minister of Israel.*

Our main job was flying patrols over the sea to locate, and report to the Navy incoming ships carrying refugees to the Promised Land. Suspect ships were usually identifiable by the extremely crowded decks, and the trail of garbage floating in their wake. It was then the job of the Royal Navy to intercept and examine them, and probably turn them away from the coast of Palestine.

...............................Cobwebs and Oranges!

The detachments to Palestine were extremely popular since it was a welcome change of scenery and activity. We took our own ground crew team with us, and for them the release from our camp at Kabrit was akin to a holiday outing. On return to Kabrit we would carry a sizeable load of big juicy Jaffa oranges in hessian sacks, which were a welcome addition to our rather uninteresting rations.

These happy "smuggling" activities came to an abrupt end when a large and very venomous looking spider suddenly appeared in an aircraft after it had been unloaded at Kabrit. The culprit was found in the cockpit, happily spinning a web across the captain's control column.

Politics had never been part of service life, and media coverage of events in Europe were seldom seen, so that this activity of intercepting refugees had very little real meaning for us. What had really been happening to the Jews and other ethnic groups in Europe was hardly known or understood. Our detachment finally came to an end, and I was homeward bound from Egypt to the UK by Avro York for demobilization – a process which took quite some weeks.

Demobilization

Although the RAFVR (as distinct from the regular RAF service) had provided by far the largest number of wartime recruits, we did not appear too welcome at the demob centre. We were probably just another irritating intrusion into the sedate lives of the administrative staff. Name, rank, and number were the watchwords of the day, until we could leave with a rail ticket, and a set of civilian clothes as a parting gift.

Determined, by now, to continue with a flying career I enrolled in a London school to obtain the necessary civil pilot, and navigator licenses. Financial problems were solved by dish-washing in London hotels and restaurants, and taxi driving in my home town at weekends.

I started applying for jobs, but soon discovered that I was far too late in my hopeful applications to the British airlines, and only Indian ones remained a possibility – too many pilots had been demobilised ahead of me. An RAF club, just off Piccadilly, was always a good place to gather the latest information, either from gossip at the bar or from the notice boards near the entrance. It was there that I was carefully approached by a recruiting officer from the Israeli Air Force – would I care to fly Spitfires for them? Their information on individuals that they approached was quite complete, since the RAF had used civilian staff in the administrative offices at their bases in Palestine, and these staff had evidently copied any potentially useful records.

While vaguely considering this Israeli offer news began to circulate that KLM (who were they?) were still recruiting pilots. A quick search soon located the airline, and its country and an application was speedily on the way across the North Sea.

.............................new horizons were opening!

UK Pilot and Navigators licenses

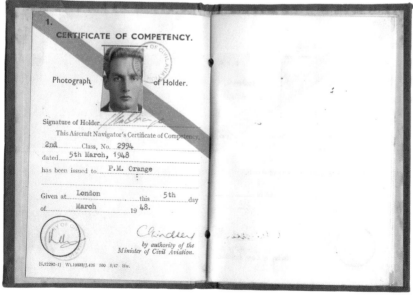

Phoenix Arises

Memories can be faulty

The following memories may not be entirely accurate after a lapse of some fifty years, but with regard to date and place they are supported by my logbook entries made at the time. It is also necessary to realize that the rules and regulations which have evolved in more recent years should not be used to criticize events that took place in a totally different era – an era in which the (Dutch) flag was being flown with unrestrained vigour, celebrating their new-found freedom from the constraints of occupation.

By the late 1940's this new-found freedom saw a slowing down of the hitherto rapid growth in aircrew numbers, though recruitment still continued for several years. Douglas Dakotas (DC-3's) were constantly opening up new routes within a battered Europe, making for some interesting night stops. It was, for example, an ornately gilded birdcage lift in our Paris hotel that started our journey to the Folie Berges, or a gas fuelled taxi that took us to a beer garden in Düsseldorf. Even internal flights within Holland made for some unusual nights out in towns such as Eindhoven or Groningen.

Lockheed Constellations were showing their uniquely beautiful shapes over the expanding routes of the Far East, and across the North Atlantic. They were supplemented by Skymasters (DC-4's and C-54's) which tended to dominate the expanding cargo, and charter services. The DC-6's were a much improved development of the Skymaster series, and were primarily in service, at their first introduction, on the South American and South African routes. My own broadening of experience as a 3rd pilot/navigator found me on the DC-6 as well as the Constellation in that role.

Dr. Albert Plesman

KLM had been founded way back in 1919, and Dr. Plesman was its first administrator and director. He was then thirty years old, but already a well-known and respected businessman with a tremendous vision and understanding of world affairs – a vision in which he saw the Dutch nation maintaining a leading role in the world of international commerce.

It was the energy and vision of Dr. Plesman that created the stimulus for the Phoenix-like awakening of the national airline. The vast expansion of KLM that then occurred was under his direction, and this direction never wavered despite several tragic crashes, one of which involved the death of his own son, Capt. Hans Plesman near Bari (Southern Italy).

I had met Dr. Plesman very briefly on two occasions. On the first I had been introduced by Capt. Van Messel outside the Schiphol terminal hall. I was left with the impression of a gruff and rather

Churchillian figure, and not over friendly to junior pilots. It was thus with great surprise that, some six months later, I heard my name called across the tarmac; Dr. Plesman knew who and what I was, and questioned me closely on my last Mauritius flight.

.... and lifting a ban that he had imposed

For an intriguing background into KLM affairs one must look back for a moment to 1939. The Boeing Aircraft Company (Seattle, USA) had unveiled a new and advanced product – a pressurized, four engined passenger aircraft of great promise, the Boeing 307. Greatly intrigued, Dr. Plesman sent two engineers to Seattle to investigate the product. One of these was the founder of the Technical Department and deputy head of KLM, Pieter Guilonard. Unfortunately, both engineers died when the prototype aircraft crashed during a test flight in which they were partaking. Deeply shocked Dr. Plesman forbade any further contact with the Boeing Company.

It was some fifteen years after his death, in 1953, that this ban was relegated to history, and negotiations opened with Boeing concerning the purchase of the "jumbo jets". There is little doubt that Dr. Plesman would have approved of this initiative.

The Boeing 307 is still alive and kicking!!! Only very few of these aircraft were actually built, as wartime requirements intervened. One, however, was purchased by the legendary Howard Hughes as a personal transport. After a succession of owners, periods of storage and hurricane damage, its intact fuselage now sails the waterways of Fort Lauderdale (Miami, Florida) as a unique plane-cum-boat, bearing the name "COSMIC MUFFIN".

When I last saw it the cockpit installation and instrumentation were almost complete, and the owner, Dave Drimmer, assured me that full completion was soon to be achieved.

The Cosmic Muffin

Across the face of history

Since it is impracticable to draw sharp dividing lines across the face of history, past events in the existence of KLM must impinge on events within the focus of my own recollection. In a similar fashion, these recollections may have a connection with happenings outside the rather loosely established time frame. For example, during the war years KLM remained very active in the air. It flew the Bristol – Lisbon services to unoccupied Portugal, and thus maintained an essential wartime link with continental Europe. That this service was maintained by unarmed Dakotas, facing the risk of interception by German fighters, does great credit to the KLM crews involved. One aircraft was indeed shot down, and among the passengers lost was Leslie Howard, the well-know actor. Some of my early KLM flights were captained by pilots from the Lisbon run.

Lisbon during the war was a hotbed of intrigue and international spies. According to rumour, the Germans had targeted that particular KLM flight believing that a senior Allied official was on board.

My 1948 Arrival

By the time that I arrived in Holland in August 1948 the ashes of war had been almost dispersed, and KLM was up and running, though not yet at full throttle. Immediately after hostilities had ceased, the industrious Dutch had started erasing the signs of war, and repairing their ravaged land. Their stupendous exertions in this reconstruction work were, to the outside world, particularly noticeable in the world of aviation.

The routes to the Far East had been strengthened and re-opened, and scheduled services across the North Atlantic had been commenced. In this latter context, Prestwick (Scotland) Shannon (Ireland), and Gander (Newfoundland) became familiar with the colours of the "Flying Dutchman" since the ability to make direct flights to New York was not yet there.

Crew Composition

Intercontinental captains on the Far East routes were primarily Dutch nationals, some with experience reaching back to quite early pioneering days. The foreign pilots who had been fairly recently recruited were generally much younger, and many of us found this age difference quite difficult to adjust to; in the RAF a pilot senior to oneself was usually only a few years older, and not the twenty or more years that we were now encountering!

On the North Atlantic routes the core group of captains seemed to be Americans, and some were actually based in New York. There were also Dutch captains flying the route, as several had been involved in the ferrying of aircraft across the "pond" during the war years; the "pond" was the nickname given to that demanding stretch of water by those who flew it.

It is also of interest to note that many of the senior F/E's (Flight Engineers) of the period were survivors from the wartime merchant navy, even of torpedoing. I met one on a Mauritius flight who had actually been torpedoed twice within two weeks. These F/E's, and their younger colleagues, had been through well respected technical training schools prior to joining KLM.

There were a few pre-war veterans who could use their status and seniority to bulldoze their way through situations which were appropriate to a more careful consideration. For example, it was sometimes alarmingly evident that the weather limits published for landing at a particular airfield were only regarded as guidance for the less experienced, or that a departure with a technical malfunction in the aircraft was best left to the (secret) discretion of the captain, and his F/E.

The senior stewards, or pursers as they became known, also numbered some former merchant navy personnel among their ranks. Trix de Wint was a pre-war stewardess who had become something of a national hero through her activities in the resistance movement, and she now became increasingly involved in the recruitment and training of a new generation of stewardesses. Strangely enough these newly graduated girls were advised to regard the F/E as the safe "father figure" in the all male crew – the gender ratio was then often at least 10:1, a difficult situation for the hatchlings. In later years this gender ratio was to become markedly reversed, and the purser then tended to usurp the "father figure" accolade. Needless to say, these policies were not always crowned with success.

And re-inventing the pilots

With very few exceptions all the newly recruited pilots were required to undergo quite extensive training in KLM's Link Trainers for instrument flying procedures, in Dakotas for various aspects of flight training, and in navigation school to obtain the necessary licence. All this was to ensure that acceptable standards were reached, and that the pilots were properly orientated towards the needs of civil aviation. Flying paying passengers around the world was a very different thing from operating military aircraft!

An essential requirement on the promotional step-ladder to intercontinental captain was the possession of a 1st Class Navigator's License. To upgrade my existing license to this standard caused me some problems. Aside from the fact that I was flying some 120 hours per month in Europe at the time this requirement loomed over me, the theoretical knowledge demanded on an astro(nomy) exam seemed beyond my reach. The theoretical knowledge required for meteorology was equally daunting. I partially solved the problem by taking private tuition from one of the "met" officers at the Schiphol meteorological office – at a pre-flight briefing he would then always quiz me relentlessly!

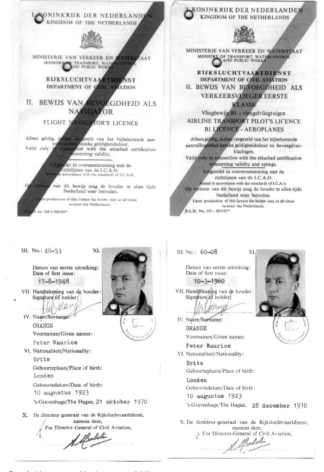

In my own case, despite several thousand hours of previous flight experience (including Dakotas), many hours were devoted to upgrading my instrument flying skills. This was followed by several months of flying as a co-pilot on the European routes before I was able to gradually regain my previous status as a captain. Further advancement was gradual as the easier routes, such as Amsterdam – Brussels, had to be flown as captain before promotion was achieved on to what were regarded as the more demanding

Dutch Licences – Navigator and Pilot

routes, for example London or Paris. Even on London one was initially confined to operating the midnight freighter service, before being let loose with a load of anxious passengers.

These midnight outings were actually rather pleasant, since they provided an opportunity for some shopping. The bundles of newspapers in the rear of the aircraft (the passenger seats had been removed), also provided some reading material for the long journey home, providing that my co-pilot was happy to watch the shop! These flights in darkened skies also stirred memories of earlier days, when we had crossed the North Sea on somewhat different missions.

.... and yet more training

An intercontinental pilot was generally qualified to fly on only a single route, the Far East or the North Atlantic for example. This led to a very rapid accumulation of the essential route knowledge, and of the seasonal weather changes. Since those were also the days of flying "through-the-weather", rather than above it, navigation was primarily a mixture of visual sightings (fixes), dead-reckoning (DR), and astro(nomical) derived positions.

DR navigation was essentially a matter of plotting on a Mercators' chart – a chart similar to those used on ships – lines to represent heading, estimated wind speed and direction, and estimated aircraft speed over the ground or sea. The result of this activity by the navigator would produce an approximate position, from which further estimates would be produced until a positive fix could be obtained. Not infrequently, such a fix located one at a fair distance from the estimated position!

Approaching destination one was sometimes fortunate enough to receive the transmission of a radio beacon, which provided final guidance towards the airfield. But beware! These beacons could be badly affected by thunderstorm conditions, and indicate a wrong direction. The navigator's task was never finished until the actual runway was in sight.

Precision final approach aids were in their infancy, and few airfields were equipped with any very up-to-date installations, and even if they were, proper maintenance and alignment were sometimes questionable. In this uncertain environment, KLM took great care in the comprehensive training of all the newly recruited pilots, regardless of previous experience. We flew endless exercises, using radio beacons, around the Amsterdam area which usually ended with a beacon approach to runway 23 at Schiphol, and this involved many final approaches across Amsterdam Central Station, and the football Stadium.

Visits to the Link Trainer (see Fluttering Wings) were also quite frequent, and instrument flying was practiced under the calm guidance of Mr. Sainsbury, the senior instructor. Many years later he was at the instructor's console on the Electra and DC-8 flight simulators when I was conducting pilot check programmes.

Link Trainer

(photo source unknown)

And getting re-acquainted with Europe

Although I was fairly familiar with Europe from RAF days, I was now destined to view it from totally different angles. Assigned as a co-pilot to experienced captains, all the major airfields that featured in the KLM timetables came into our orbit. One was airborne almost daily, flying with an absorbing variety of pilots, experiencing every possible variation of weather, and enjoying an occasional night stop in quite unfamiliar surroundings. It was indeed a Grand Tour!

Among some unusual memories of the period were the smelly armpits of the F/E's! In the RAF the two pilots had flown Dakotas accompanied by a radio operator, and possibly a loadmaster in the rear. Now the rather small cockpit space was intruded upon by a F/E, who stood between the two pilots, or sat upon a folding seat between them. When he needed to reach forward – often for quite unnecessary reasons – his armpits were unfortunately at nose level.

Some captains had rather strange ideas of flying Dakotas. One individual insisted that a landing should always be a "three pointer" – the conventional, and safest method was first to place the main wheels on the runway, and then lower the tail to land the tail-wheel. This particular individual insisted that after levelling out over the runway, a nose up attitude should be adopted allowing the main and tail wheels to land simultaneously. I felt that he was not well-pleased with my refusal to adopt his methods, as these were a recipe for disaster if a crosswind existed.

Another individual was tasked to show me the low level route through the mountains to Innsbruck, but was unfortunately not familiar with the potential agility of a Dakota. On coming up to the mountains he inadvertently entered a wrong valley, and we were faced by a rapidly approaching mountain obstacle. An abrupt reversal of course in the narrowing valley was the only option, which he immediately attempted. Since it was very obvious, to me, that the turn he was making lacked sufficient bank angle, I rapidly provided some assistance by standing the aircraft on its wing tip. With our decreased radius of turn we then just managed to clear the menace in our path!

These European events were interspersed with more navigation training and home study, with particular emphasis on astronomical requirements. I also had some brief exposure to piloting the Constellation, probably somewhat more than a second co-pilot received in later years, which was enough to familiarize me with my approaching duties as a 3rd pilot/navigator.

First Acquaintance with a Constellation

The beautiful lines of the Lockheed Constellation did not necessarily reflect the old adage – "if it looks right it will fly right". Its handling characteristics were, however, quite reasonable for the day and age. It did not really like to have its direction of flight changed too abruptly, and it thus made a rather too stable platform on an approach to landing – it was wise to make sure that your approach path did not require too many adjustments. The pilot's movements of the control column caused movement of the actual flight control surfaces through hydraulic pressure, a fairly modern concept which greatly reduced the effort needed by the pilot to manoeuvre a large aircraft. Today's "fly-by-wire" concept takes this ease of control a stage further, as will the "fly-by-light" system now coming into use on a military aircraft.

The downside of the Constellation control system – and that of other pre-jet era aircraft – was that a failure of the necessary hydraulic pumps, or of an uncontained leak of hydraulic fluid from the system, resulted in a return to pure manual control. Later hydraulic systems were more efficiently designed, so that the effects of a pump failure or a fluid leak could be quickly isolated and powered control maintained. Since control of the Connie was designed around a fully powered system, a complete

Circa 1952. Arrival of a Constellation Schiphol (East). In the background are a DC4, Convair 240 and Dakotas   (photo source unknown)

reversion to manual control was extremely demanding in terms of the sheer muscle power needed by the pilot. Flying "boost out", as it was termed, proved a very humbling experience, and demanded great anticipation, so that corrections to the flight path were initiated in good time to achieve the desired result.

The Stairway to Heaven!

To find myself suddenly living in Holland was a remarkable change in my life, akin to opening a new window on a strange, and puzzling world. The remarkably flat terrain recalled the scenery seen from above during the operations of "Market Garden", and more recently, of "Manna". In 1948 Holland was still a land of shortages in daily life; coupons were necessary for tobacco, for Dutch gin (jenever), and I think, for some foodstuffs. These were happily requisitioned by my rather acquisitive landlady and her husband; this was no problem to me as I had not yet acquired a taste for jenever, and I could easily obtain tobacco elsewhere in the world.

Many of the foreign pilots, and their wives had opted for accommodation in what was know as the "Pilotenhuis", but I felt that was nearer to community living than I wanted. A KLM staff member then took me to view different boarding houses on the outskirts of Amsterdam, and I selected one in Valeriusstraat which was convenient for catching a bus out to Schiphol airport.

I was treated most kindly by my hosts, whose status was evidently improved by acquiring a resident KLM pilot, even though only two golden stripes adorned my sleeves at that time. I stayed there for nearly two years, despite the fact that any lady visitors were subjected to a very close scrutiny as they climbed the stairs past the ever open door of my hosts' living room.

The stairs, incidentally, were nearly vertical, and my room was at the top of the building, three flights up. The room itself was quite adequately furnished, solid furniture in age darkened wood. The most unusual feature for me was an upright tubular shaped coal burning stove – know as a "pot kachel" in Holland. The coal for this fearsome, but efficient, apparatus was stacked in paper bags in the bath next door. A bath could be had by prior appointment, but I found such an arrangement too troublesome when hotels around Europe offered more trouble free facilities.

Meals "at home" could also be had by prior arrangement, but after some initial attempts I decided that the unknown contents of the various saucepans could better be left to the imagination. The café, at what is now known as Schiphol East, served recognizable food at far more convenient times. Failing that, one could always trudge across town towards the Stadionweg area, where many stewardesses had rooms, in the hope of finding an acquaintance at home that was willing to improvise a meal. Footloose, and fancy free, and for the first time, money in my pocket … credit cards were still things of the far distant future!

………………… economies of scale

Life in a single furnished room was no bad thing; one had no responsibilities beyond a care for other people's property. Personal possessions could be moved elsewhere with a maximum of two suitcases; that is until my collection of books started growing. Suitcases were but an upmarket version of the kit bag which had accompanied me on my earlier travels, to later be joined by a tin trunk when I had reached officer status.

It was into this modest life style that my very first car somewhat noisily eased its way, a Morris 10 of rather uncertain vintage. It tended to have a rather explosive rear end, but served me well for several years. Its most novel feature was, however, a remarkable on-board jacking system which I had never seen before, or since. While sitting in the car, one could use a dashboard selector to raise any wheel from the ground by means of a retractable metal leg operated by hydraulic pressure. I never had occasion to use it in anger, but it was a useful talking point.

This more stylish, and convenient mode of transport enabled me to exchange my Maarse en Kroon bus tickets for petrol coupons, and to acquire some interesting passengers. The rather explosive rear end did, however, prove too disconcerting for the more faint hearted, and those who might have had more sinister designs on the driver than was wanted were equally put off.

………………… a clash with the laws of the land

Returning to my room from Schiphol one day I stopped in an area of natural parkland. Its most attractive point was a long stretch of water with hopeful fishermen sitting on little stools along its edges, patiently watching their motionless floats on the water surface. Some appeared to be fast asleep with a finger resting on their slack fishing line, or upon their rod propped on a forked rest.

Tiring of this placid scene I entertained passing bicyclists for a while with my jacking system, until their amazed interest became too intent. It being a hot summer's day, my shirt then came off, and I lay back on a convenient grassy bank for a quiet snooze in the sun. My rude awakening was courtesy of two polished jack-boots perilously close to my side, and an irate armed policeman shouting unintelligible instructions at me.

Agitated sign language soon led me to the conclusion that the removal of my shirt in a public place was strictly unlawful, but as an ignorant foreigner I would only receive a stern warning. Proof of (foreign) identity was my pilot's license, which seemed to impress this stern upholder of the law quite considerably for his menacing jack-boots moved back a few paces!

My Landlady senses romance on the stairway

It was into this scenario that romance entered my life, for which school, and overseas RAF life had ill-prepared me. Mil was a KLM stewardess, normally flying on the North Atlantic routes in Lockheed

Constellations, but our paths crossed on a Convair 240 flight to Rome. Despite the fact that our flights were normally to totally different destinations, our off duty meetings became more frequent, and I was able to occasionally greet her Schiphol arrival in my rather noisy car.

This eventually led to an invitation to my room for a cup of tea, and to her being carefully scrutinized by my protective landlady as we climbed the stairs past her ever open door. A tea tray soon followed us up the final stairs, and at intervals we would hear her climbing up again to ask if more was needed. It was soon evident that the length of my visitor's stay was becoming unseemly.

As events progressed an introduction to her mother followed, and I learned something of other people's wars. The horror of Japanese internment camps in the Dutch East Indies during the war years. They were both, in fact, fairly recent immigrants to Holland after a long colonial life. And it was with them that I was introduced to the Dutch ritual of afternoon tea. Cups of rather weak tea, without milk, were carefully poured into porcelain cups. The covered teapot had been sitting on a stand over a small candle since the morning, thus ensuring day long availability! I tried to arrange my subsequent visits at coffee time, which was less time expired by the time it was poured.

.... which leads to married life

A somewhat whirlwind romance led to our marriage which, due to my unsympathetic crew scheduling, was followed by a greatly delayed honeymoon. Although our union was blessed by three delightful children, our faltering course became sadly lost in the drifting sands of time. It took twenty-five years, however, before we found courage enough to separate, and then amicably divorce. We maintained very friendly contact over the ensuing years, until her untimely death closed a hidden chapter in my KLM history.

Off to Batavia (now Jakarta) in the Dutch East Indies

Late December 1948 saw the commencement of a Connie (Constellation) "tour" which was to last until February 1953. Assigned as a 3rd pilot/navigator to the crew of Captain v.d. Vaart – (who later died in the crash of the "Franeker" at Bombay) – we made an afternoon departure from Schiphol for the long haul to Batavia. Our scheduled passenger carrying flight was to take us through Cairo (a crew slip station), Basra, Karachi (crew slip), Calcutta (crew slip), and then to Batavia – no less that ten days en-route. There was some variation, it should be realized, in the crew slip stations between outbound and homebound flights.

> Any particular aircraft would make a continuous flight to its final destination, stopping at intermediate airports for refuelling, and to disembark or to uplift passengers. The crew, however, would leave the aircraft at designated "slip" stations for rest. They would then take over the next aircraft to arrive, and resume their operational duties as far as the next slip station. A crew journey out East and back could thus last some ten days, depending on the frequency of services.

Navigation equipment on these flights included topographical maps of the expected routing, all the way to the East. These were stacked in the cockpit in a series of rolls, each roll covering a specific sector of the route. On the maps was drawn a line which marked the track that would normally be flown – all very similar to the maps that we had worked with across Europe. Mercators' charts were provided for plotting our (assumed) progress along the route, and an aircraft installed device for observing the drift angle created by the existing wind. The navigator would also be provided with a Bubble Sextant for astronomical observations, and a small library of astronomical tables, which enabled him to convert his sextant readings into data that could be plotted on the Mercators' chart. The navigator personally carried his own tools-of-the-trade; namely, dividers, pencils, a compass and an eraser, and of particular importance in relation to astro sights, an extremely accurate watch with a second hand.

Our outbound flight reached its destination, Batavia, after five days on-route – an extremely interesting period of my life in regard to the flying, and also in regard to the many different lands through which we had passed. Another surprise was in store, however, we were almost immediately informed that our return flight was indefinitely delayed! Home by the turn of the year was now a pipe dream, emphasized by the fact that we were assigned a Batavia-Singapore-Shanghai flight which positioned us in Shanghai for Christmas.

.... and Christmas in Shanghai

It was very cold and damp in Shanghai with frequent snow flurries, and we had only tropical clothing with us. I was sharing a hotel room with the co-pilot, "Mac" McFarlane, a hardy Scotsman, and we decided to take a look along the famous Bund (the commercial and business centre along the waterfront) by rickshaw. The bitter cold, and another snow flurry saw us encouraging the "driver" to optimize his pedal rate back to the hotel.

A party had been organized for us that Xmas evening, by the Dutch Embassy, in a local restaurant. We rather reluctantly decided to wear our uniforms, as that was the warmest clothing we had, and boarded rickshaws for the short journey. To our great surprise all was in readiness for us, an enormous table was beautifully laid, and at intervals around it, were seated some twelve attractive Chinese girls.

It was obviously up to us to find seats, and thereby choose a partner – Mac and I looked at each other in horror, this was not our idea of a party! As soon as we could politely excuse ourselves, we hurried back to our hotel room, and fortified ourselves with the last of the whiskey. We also puzzled over the three bell pushes on the wall, since they each had a different colour. Perhaps it was as well that we were in no mood for investigation, since we learned later that a companion of the appropriate colour could be summoned by the push of a finger.

Christmas morning was decision time, and I decided to head for a church, and with nothing else to do, Mac elected to join me. With appropriate instructions from the concierge, our rickshaw was furiously pedalled churchwards. The service became too lengthy, and we were becoming too cold to await a final blessing – enough was enough, and we hurried back to the hotel for the remnants of my bottle, wondering meanwhile which colour push button would be appropriate on Christmas morning!

On December the 27th we gladly left Shanghai, and returned to the warmth of Batavia, after a brief stop in Singapore. At last we were made aware of the reason for the delay in our return home, a complex international situation had arisen to cause entrapment of our aircraft (PH-TDC), and ourselves in Baravia.

We were not then aware that events had moved along, and that a connection with Holland via the island of Mauritius was in process of being established, or certainly I don't recall being aware of that fact.

And so began the Mauritius Event

.... but first – a quick look at the historical background

In the aftermath of the World War the colonial nations of the West were facing calls for freedom, and independence by their colonies. Occupied countries had been freed, and refugees rehabilitated, so a more universal cry for freedom became a popular demand. Those countries which had no colonies, and particularly the USA, were most supportive of this freedom movement. The sub-continent of India had already gained independence in 1947, and through a tragic partition of its Hindu and Muslim peoples, the nations of India and of East and West Pakistan had evolved.

The peoples of the Dutch East Indies, the world's largest Muslim country, had fought for freedom from their Japanese invaders, and were now determined to free themselves from their Dutch masters. International approval for this demand was not hard to find, and in the forefront of their supporters was the Indian sub-continent. The government of India under Nehru was valiantly waving its flag of independence in a world of collapsing empires.

To support the people of the East Indies against their colonial masters, all Dutch aircraft were then immediately banned from landing in, or over-flying, the sub-continent – the lifeline between Holland and the East Indies was very positively cut, and KLM had to find a new route between the two places.

.... and some interim events while awaiting orders

While awaiting a solution to this problem of finding a route home for PH-TDC (which was urgently needed back at Schiphol) I was assigned as a Dakota co-pilot on several internal and inter island flights. There were many foreign pilots of KLM stationed in the East Indies who flew scheduled services around this very extensive territory. One particular flight took me to the island of Moratai, via Makassar (in the Celebes), where we landed in a rainstorm on a PSP runway. PSP was a wartime creation of interlocking perforated metal planks, laid along a flattened surface to create a runway – very slippery when wet!

The cockpit crew was accommodated in a sort of native hut on stilts, which also had tables and chairs for meals. Our solitary stewardess was given her own hut on the far side of the clearing, right underneath a palm tree laden with coconuts. Inevitably, a storm got up during the night, and the poor girl arrived on our doorstep terribly frightened by the coconuts intermittently dropping on her roof! It was a rather sleepless night for everyone, and skidding on the PSP runway, while positioning for take-off, failed to improve our mood.

A Decision has been made!

Returning from one of the inter-island flights, Capt. v.d. Vaart's crew were called together for a crew briefing. It transpired that although the Indian sub-continent was still firmly closed to all Dutch aircraft, an alternative route home had been decided upon by the powers that be. We would fly first to Bangkok for a night stop, leaving the following day with full fuel tanks for a direct flight to Sharjah via Ceylon (now Sri Lanka). Initially our heading would be slightly south of west, and once overhead Colombo in Ceylon we would turn on a more westerly heading to cross the empty waters of the immense Indian Ocean on a direct course for Sharjah, a total flying time of some fifteen hours. Following a night stop in the airfield rest house we would have another long haul flight direct to Tunis, and from there home to Schiphol.

Sharjah was one of the Trucial States, which were all under British protection, at the southern end of the Persian Gulf very close to Dubai. Most of these Trucial States were later to form the United Arab Emirates (U.A.E.). Sharjah had an airport which was in regular use by British Overseas Airways Corporation (BOAC), as a refuelling stop on its flights to Australia. The runway was of compacted sand, with a trail of oil marking its centre line, and goose-neck flares (oil lamps) marking its edges.

BOAC had turned an existing fort, built by the Trucial Scouts, into quite a comfortable rest house for its transiting passengers and crews – some overnight accommodation was also available.

> *The impending arrival, or departure, of aircraft at Sharjah was brought to the*
> *attention of the locals by a fully armed Trucial Scout sitting atop his camel.*
> *At a signal from the Station Manager he would then start blowing resounding*
> *blasts on a long flag be-decked trumpet. All eyes would soon turn skywards*
> *to spot the lights of the incoming plane, or to watch the departure.*

Our forlorn Constellation PH-TDC – unused since our Shanghai expedition – was readied for its homebound departure, and the date of January 13th was set.

.... but first to Sharjah, on the Persian Gulf

Late afternoon on 13.01.48 saw us leaving Batavia, and climbing northwards over the Thousand Islands towards Bangkok. During the flight I was aware of a great deal of discussion going on between the captain and the F/E's with fuel flow charts in their hands. The co-pilot was minding the shop, and I was immersed in navigational riddles, so the potential significance of those ongoing discussions did not then occur to me. After an otherwise uneventful flight we arrived in Bangkok for a pleasant night stop. There was even time to look at a pagoda or two, and for me to very foolishly climb into a snake pit. I was assured that the venom had been removed from them all, but then .... perhaps one had been overlooked?

Concerned as we were with our own situation, we remained unaware of the moves afoot at home towards reopening the Far East route – but perhaps it was only I that remained in blissful ignorance, shielded by an impenetrable language barrier from the surrounding conversations in Dutch. At Bangkok we made out a flight plan passing just to the east of Colombo (which was also banning our flights), and from there direct to Sharjah – as I recall it, an estimated 14hrs and 30 mins en route. The weather forecasts for the route were little short of fertile imagination – clear all the way! Our calculated flight plan was filed with Air Traffic Control in the normal way, with Bahrain given as our alternate airfield.

Airborne out of Bangkok we set off on a south easterly heading towards Ceylon, climbing to some 16,000 ft. At top of climb I was abruptly jerked out of my complacent mood by a call from the captain – "Give me a course for Rangoon"!! It was then explained to us in a sort of crew meeting that we would be flying the normal routing, namely overhead Rangoon, Calcutta and Karachi to our final destination. Whether this was a decision taken solely by the captain, or whether he was following confidential instructions from head office, I never knew. Recalling his fuel discussions with the F/E's on the previous day's flight, I tended to suspect higher hands at work! Anyway, I had never seen Rangoon by moonlight, and now perhaps was the chance.

.... and I get to see Rangoon

It seemed only a very short period of time before the waters of the Irrawaddy Delta could be seen glinting in the moonlight, but I was somewhat busy reorganizing my maps and charts to cover the new routing. Providentially, I was summoned up front for a look-see at the wonderful moonlit scenery, and there was the Golden Pagoda of Rangoon, shining proudly above the flickering lights of the town.

Crossing the dark waters of the Bay of Bengal we eventually saw the glow from the lights of Calcutta on the horizon, and the captain started a descent to 10,000 feet. It was well known that the Indian Air

Force was equipped with potent Hawker Tempest fighter aircraft; it was assumed that any patrolling fighters were most likely to be operating in and around the 20,000 feet altitude. If so, they would be most unlikely to spot us at a much lower altitude, particularly as all our lights were now switched off! It even became a no-smoking flight, as the flare of a match could perhaps be seen through a window – particularly the rather lengthy process involved in lighting the inevitable cigar of the F/E.

Lights out over India

We avoided flying directly overhead Calcutta as any prying eyes overhead might spot our silhouette against a well lit background. For the next five hours an observer was maintained as look-out from the astro dome, and since he needed my stool to stand on, I was continually standing at the navigation table. We occasionally changed position when I needed an astro sighting to fix our position – visual fixes at night were almost non-existent, the lights of Jalapur (about half way across) were too far distant in the north to be of

Capt. Viruly, Capt v.d Vaart, Stewardess Sieta van Eesteren
(photo source unknown)

much use. Finally, we passed Karachi, at a discreet distance, and a relaxation of tension was accompanied by clouds of cigar smoke from the F/E's panel.

Heading once again out over the sea it was decided to maintain our existing cruise altitude, as much stronger head winds could be expected higher up. Paralleling the southern coast of West Pakistan, and then of Iran, pinpricks of light could be seen showing the location of Jiwani, and then of Jask (I was back in familiar territory from RAF Transport Command days), and eventually the Gulf of Oman, the coastline of Oman, and preparations began for a careful descent over the mountains into Sharjah.

.... and a private sandstorm!

After nearly fourteen quite tense hours we embraced the compacted sand runway of Sharjah with enthusiasm, creating a mini sandstorm with our reverse thrust. In the process we managed to blow out many of the goose-neck flares, and obliterate much of the oil marked centre line. BOAC was not amused by our stylish arrival!

Since sleeping accommodation in the rest house was somewhat limited, most of the crew, and some of our few passengers returned to the aircraft after a good meal, and there settled down for the night.

Meanwhile I had found out that we were short of topographical maps to cover part of our next route to Tunis. The BOAC station manager immediately loaned me a very good school atlas which he appropriated from his son's room, the boy currently being en-route to school in England.

Our departure from Sharjah, heralded by trumpet blasts from the Trucial Scout on his camel, was in the evening so that some astro aviation could be done over the vast desert expanse of Saudi Arabia. By pure chance we spotted the feeble lights of Hail, then a small town about half way across our desert route, but now quite a large city, complete with a royal palace, and an impressive Mosque.

Approaching the coast, at the southern end of the Gulf of Aquaba, I was starting to consult my borrowed school atlas to confirm my DR navigation. As the Nile came into view, however, I was back in quite familiar territory, and we also were back on our topographical roll maps for more precise visual fixes.

Tunis was reached after a total of thirteen and a half hour's flight, and I presume that we must have night stopped before continuing on the last six hour journey to Schiphol. PH-TDC was back at base after nearly a month away, and as far as I knew, in good mechanical condition.

An overview of the Mauritius operation

These particular flights were unique in the annals of civil aviation at that time. Perfectly standard models of the Lockheed Constellation (the L-049 and the L-749) were used in carrying passengers, freight, and mail across the vast empty wastes of the Indian Ocean, with no external aids to navigation apart from celestial sightings. This scenario brought to mind the opening words of an RAF Manual on Air Navigation – "man is never lost".

The chosen route stretched from the small island of Mauritius to Batavia on the larger island of Java, in the Dutch East Indies. The total distance to be covered was in the region of 3000 nautical miles, equivalent to some 3500 statute (land) miles or 5500 kilometres. The Lockheed sales brochures covering the early models of the Constellation announced a maximum range of 2290 miles when carrying a full payload, or a range of 3680 miles with a restricted payload; the aircraft were thus stripped of any unnecessary equipment in an effort to reduce their weight, for there was obviously little room for error in management of the flights.

Since the aircraft would be operating uncomfortably close to their maximum range capability, the payload was thus restricted by the need to depart with full fuel tanks for every crossing; this, in turn, led to every take-off being made at a weight approaching the maximum permissible, a considerable strain on man and machine. If any passengers were carried on a particular flight I would imagine that they must have had a very high government priority.

The flight time on this route was to vary between approximately fourteen and sixteen hours, dependent upon winds which were generally fairly light in those southern latitudes, which averaged about 10 degrees south. The difference in flight time between west bound and east bound aircraft was usually quite small, but the flight management tactics of the captains did appear to have some influence on our airborne times. His readings of the sea conditions far below, of the cloud formations, and of changes in the outside air temperature (OAT) could result in a sudden order for a course or altitude change – and never mind what the navigator thought!

To reach Mauritius from Holland was also to prove an interesting exercise in long range flying and in visiting, for some crew, new territories. Cairo was to remain a crew slip station for some flights, and from there the aircraft would be routed either via Aden in the British Protectorate of Yemen, or through Khartoum in the Anglo-Egyptian Sudan. My logbook shows that we also operated some flights to Aden, or to Khartoum, direct from Schiphol in some eleven hours. Stops at either of these two places were primarily for refuelling of the aircraft. While I have vivid memories of a long delay in Khartoum I am unable to recall if this, or indeed Aden, were actually crew slip stations.

Crew on beach, Mauritius

Navigation on all these flights was a demanding exercise, particularly on the long over-water stretches. Whether or not the scheduled times of operation were chosen to give us the maximum advantage of night-time flying for celestial observations I have no idea, but it seemed to work out that way. One always felt quietly triumphant when the remote island of Mauritius was positively located or the much larger island of Java hove in sight. There were unconfirmed rumours that someone had once overshot their destination, but finally landed safely with near empty tanks.

Careful chosen stars were to become our guiding lights!

And the Constellation's human element

The maximum allowable take-off weight of a Constellation at just over forty tons paled into insignificance when compared with that of a "jumbo" jet of later years, which weighed in at around three hundred and fifty tons. The change in the number of crew members was, however, less dramatic – usually ten for the Connie, and fifteen for the jumbo.

The ten crew members of the Connie were (very) concentrated in the forward area of the aircraft. The captain and his co-pilot each had a very similar panel of flight instruments immediately in front of them, and between these panels, was a central panel carrying a number of instruments for the monitoring of parameters associated with the four engines. Between the pilots was a pedestal on which were mounted various levers for the control of engines, and other essential systems.

Behind the left hand pilot's seat, mostly occupied by the captain, was a small folding seat for an observer, this was commonly known as the "jump" seat. Behind the jump seat was the radio operator's position; seated facing aft, he had an impressive array of flickering dials and black boxes, together with a small table on which was mounted his Morse key. This "key" was his tool for tapping

(keying) out transmissions in Morse code. It is said that a radio operator can actually be recognized from his "fist" when transmitting through his key.

F/E Station in Constellation

Behind the right hand pilot's seat was the F/E's station. He usually sat facing sideways scanning an impressive array of instruments and controls which represented every system in the aircraft. For take-off and landing he would reposition his seat so that he could reach the engine controls on the pedestal between the pilots. Immediately next to the rear of his panel was an upward opening (emergency) exit door, equipped with a rolled up rope ladder.

Leading through a bulkhead doorway from the cockpit was a small rest room and the navigator's position who would, of course, seldom be resting! In the rest area were two bench type seats, separated by a small table, which was ideal for card games between those off-duty.

The navigator had his own table, a few repeater instruments and a stool. The stool was also used for standing upon, so as to reach the astro dome in the roof above the central gangway. The astro dome was of clear Perspex, with a small hook at the top from which to hang the bubble sextant.

Behind this area was another bulkhead with a door leading into the pantry, and a further door giving access to the passenger compartment. The pantry steward, often fully dressed in regulation cooks' attire, and the solitary stewardess were led by a purser. The number of cabin crew actually carried on a Mauritius flight would evidently vary according to the number of passengers (if any) on board. I can no longer recall this variation, but have the impression that there was always a girl around at coffee time.

The cockpit itself seldom had any free space; the second flight engineer continually seemed to be in consultation with his senior over technical matters, making entries in the technical log or receiving instruction. A favourite device, frequently in use, was the Ignition Analyser which enabled them to check the operation of each of the sixteen spark plugs in the four engines.

As fuel was consumed the aircraft weight also decreased, and these needed small reductions in the engine power settings at regular intervals, so that a constant cruise speed was maintained. Unfortunately, some individuals were never content, and these adjustments seemed to be

Constellation Cockpit. Capt. Vic Mans

continual. Another interesting "toy" for the F/E was a dial which featured miniature propellers. If these rotated it was an indication that the real propellers' rotation was not synchronized, creating unnecessary noise and vibration. Small adjustments were thus called for in order to obtain precise synchronization of propeller rotation – an absorbing (but necessary) game!

The off duty radio operator was about the only off duty crew member who could be expected to keep out of the way, and since he was usually in the rest area was very helpful in steadying my stool while I was in the astro dome. It was very seldom that I saw the captain or the co-pilot in the rest area.

.... environmental aspects of the "sharp end"

In the cockpit the outer metal skin of the aircraft was hidden behind a green quilted leather-like cloth, which presumably was a primitive form of sound deadening, and also concealment for a multitude of pipes and wires. It did nothing, however, to stop the condensation which inevitably occurred as we climbed to cruise altitude through falling temperatures. The continual drips from this condensation were no respecter of persons, but it was the pilots who seemed to suffer the most – perhaps because they were seated under a more sloping area of the roof line.

Air conditioning, as I remember it, was not particularly effective. In those days a non-smoking individual was something of a rarity, so that the sharp end soon developed quite a pronounced fog.

Apart from a fan, there was no air conditioning at all on the ground. In tropical temperatures the heat and humidity thus became quite a problem; the most general solution was to hang shirts over the backs of our seats, and allow them to dry out during the initial climb. By 7-8000 feet the falling temperatures prompted us into getting dressed again. The control wheels were often bound with string which provided a better grip for slippery hands.

The astro dome was regarded with some suspicion following an unusual accident in another airline – possibly Swissair, but I am unsure about that. At cruise altitude the navigator had been busy taking an astro sight through the dome; suddenly …… there was an explosive decompression, and the astro dome disappeared, as did the unfortunate navigator. Presumably, an alert bulletin went out to all operators requiring an immediate check on the security of their domes, and a check on the Perspex for undue scratching that could weaken it. I have no recollection of any temporary limit being placed on the degree of pressurization that we normally used.

For quite a while after that unusual accident, it was very noticeable that people tended to squeeze past the astro dome sideways, and certainly avoid standing directly underneath it.

………………… environmental hazards leading to the affliction of the "Golden Ring"

Continually sitting on a damp bottom for hours on end did that area no good at all! A process was started which was to dog my entire flying career ………… but being scarred for life was a small price to pay for such an interesting one.

Medical opinion is well divided, as is the human bottom. Prolonged research ultimately discovered, however, that the affliction splendidly named the "Golden Ring" was indeed a fact of aviation life. It also discovered that the greater the number of golden rings upon a sufferer's sleeve, the greater the lasting damage to be expected upon his lower cheeks. The actual width of the golden rings was also found to be significant, since the narrower rings of a F/E or a radio operator were seldom associated with this rather messy complaint. Silver ringed cabin attendants were more prone to difficulties with their extremities.

This affliction was not a matter for discussion in polite society, the sufferers preferring to remain quiet about their rather embarrassing, and potentially explosive condition. Departing the circles of polite society, a protest against inhumane working conditions was eventually organized, and put into effect.

The harassed Minister of Works received the protesters with some reluctance, and immediately demanded a valid identification of the assembled gathering. Caps off, about turn, lower trousers, came a discreet command. This bare-arsed revelation left the Minister in little doubt of the situation, but not to be outdone, he instantly counted the number of golden rings upon the sleeves of the worst afflicted. Then, with a curt "Re-dress" command, he announced that the costs of this particular research had been vindicated by reaching the very bottom of the rumours that had been circulating through the corridors of the medical examination centre…………action would be forthcoming!

"Thank You Gentlemen"……….. to your cockpits".

A quarter of a century later, after intensive discussions related to cost effectiveness, the pilots seats were furnished with sheepskin covers. They certainly improved comfort, but whether they actually stopped the rot I have no idea – I was not around long enough to find out.

Some Navigational Notes

A 16th century Flemish mapmaker developed a map which became known as the Mercator projection. It showed lines of latitude and longitude, rather distorted outlines of land masses, and the first means of plotting positions with some accuracy. Its nautical use was taken over by the first long distance airmen, and has been in use ever since in areas not associated with polar flights.

Accurate measurements of distances on the Mercator's projection brought into use the nautical mile as a unit of distance. This in turn led to the speed indicators on all aircraft, in nearly every country, being calibrated in nautical miles giving rise to the term "knots" – a unit of speed in nautical miles per hour.

.... Dead Reckoning

Using available on-board data, in a ship or in an aircraft, the navigator would record headings, speeds and distances, and maintain a plot of these on his Mercator's chart. Estimated current or wind effect was vital to the plottings as was the effect of magnetic variation on compass headings.

From this accumulated data the navigator could produce an estimated position at any time. From this estimated position – known as a dead-reckoning position – the plot would be continued until such time as an accurate position could be obtained. This might be from radio bearings, celestial sightings (or a mixture of them) or from a visual fix.

.... Astro Navigation

The navigator first had to learn the star constellations, for both the northern and southern hemispheres, and their seasonal movement across the skies. Certain easily recognizable stars in the major constellations were designated as navigational stars, and these had to be memorized. The position of various planets or of the moon, were always available from his on-board library.

Equipped with some form of sextant, the altitude of a heavenly body above the horizon could then be accurately measured. This data was then used in interpolating Astronomical Tables to derive information which allowed a position line to be drawn on a plotting chart.

> *As one moves across the earth the altitude of a heavenly body will remain unchanged for any given instant of time. The position line drawn from an observation will thus give a line of position, and not a single location.*

A complete astro position required three sightings for optimum accuracy, so that three resulting position lines crossed to form a "cocked hat". The centre of the cocked hat (the smaller the better) was taken as being the fix. Careful selection of stars etc. would provide position lines that crossed at acute angles to improve fix accuracy. The total time taken in obtaining three sightings, and plotting the results, could be some fifteen to twenty minutes, by which time the aircraft would probably be some seventy miles further on. Nevertheless, the DR plot could be restarted from a position of accuracy, and various flight information updated accordingly.

We were using a Bubble Sextant in the Constellation that produced quite accurate sightings. An eye-piece allowed one to look through the lens at the chosen celestial body, and the sighting was taken by adjusting two features – a small air bubble had to be moved to a central position within the sighting areas, and the object on which the sight was aligned had to be centrally positioned within the bubble. Assuming that that was all correctly done, and that you were looking at the correct star, the altitude was read, and averaged over a period of two minutes. With the final reading one went to the Astro Tables, and then to the plotting chart!

But can we get there??

Two requirements of any long range flight, particularly when they crossed large uninhabited territories, were the calculation of a "Point-of-no-return" (PNR), and a "How-goes-It".

The PNR gave that point in the flight where time to destination was equal to the time which would be needed to return to the departure point. The main feature in this calculation was the effect of the prevailing winds, either actual or estimated. For example, if a head wind existed on the outbound flight, then a tail wind would exist if course was reversed – the time to return to the departure point would be correspondingly shorter. After passing the PNR, the flight had no option but to continue.

The "How-goes-it" was a graphical presentation of fuel burn (used) against time en-route, and so showed an immediate picture of fuel available against estimated flight time remaining. Depending upon how the picture developed, tension was either raised or diminished in the cockpit!

Navigating around Batavia

For our early crew slips in Batavia we enjoyed the very colonial style luxury of the Hotel des Indes; it was there that I enjoyed my first "rysttafel" – a traditional East Indies dish based around a central portion of rice, and a truly tremendous selection of spicy dishes to accompany it.

Capt. v.d. Vaart had gathered the whole crew to celebrate our long delayed departure for home, and we were all seated around a large table. About twelve waiters, all beautifully dressed in long white robes with red sashes, and red tasselled fez's, stood at a discreet distance behind us; each carried one or more dishes of mysterious spicy food with which to supplement our rice. It took several years to acquire some familiarity with the varied dishes which comprised such a meal, and just as long to actually develop a taste for it.

Our hotel rooms were well separated from the main reception area and restaurant, and opened out on to a tropical garden. The doors to the room were actually two swing doors of half normal size, and with no locks or catches. I soon discovered that the correct drill was to hang a towel across both halves if one wished to remain undisturbed. If a servant was wanted, then the towel should be hung over one half only. Probably there were many more such signs, but that was enough for starters!

Servants glided around the garden paths carrying covered trays to rooms which displayed the correct signs, and gardeners squatted on their haunches carefully weeding or gently brushing the grass clear of fallen leaves. It was all very restful and idyllic …………..

………………… and a little wheeling and dealing

Ambling around the city streets or being pedalled in a rickshaw brought into focus the novel sights of eastern life. Clouds of rickshaws jostled for position on the roads, some travelling at breakneck speeds, and others gently drifting along. Their occupants were quite a mixture of well dressed Europeans and of local people – pedal power being supplied by thin wiry individuals in somewhat ragged clothing, but always with some form of headscarf. Very few cars were in evidence, and those that were often sported a pennant flying on the bonnet – ambassadorial types!

At some spots along the canals, steps led down to the rather murky water. At such spots there were always gathered washerwomen, and those engaged in some form of daily ablutions – I sometimes wondered if this was where my new shirt was being refreshed! Various stalls selling fast food or trinkets were also positioned along the canals, obviously very important trading areas.

It was the main markets that really held me spellbound. Stalls piled high with every possible and impossible item, wonderful displays of fruit and vegetables which to me were mostly still unidentifiable; stalls of old car parts or of radio equipment (which appeared to be of military origin), and endless arrays of clothing or of shoes and slippers.

Canal in Batavia

Many crews flying the Batavia run in those days appeared to be engaged in a mysterious exchange of goods. Extra suitcases were carried outbound, the contents destined for relatives and friends; the same suitcases were seen returning homebound, filled with various household shopping. Apparently, many items were available in Batavia which were not yet obtainable in Holland. Conditions of inflation following independence were probably responsible for flooding the market with unwanted, and unsold luxury goods. I can certainly remember acquiring books at knock down prices.

Hotel des Indes, Batavia

Such prices were not in evidence, however, the night that our cockpit crew had to supply beer for another entire Connie crew. They had been on the beach resort near the harbour when we were taking off from Kemarojan (Batavia airport) homeward bound. At lift-off an outer engine failed – somewhat panic-stricken un-commanded dumping (of fuel) had then doused them with untold quantities of aviation fuel as we floundered overhead at low altitude. With a propeller still wind-milling, creating tremendous drag, somebody seemed to have got their priorities very wrong!!

.... and a look at Karachi

In strong contrast to Batavia were the crew slips in Karachi. The entire male crew was accommodated in a large Nissan type hut, beds lining the walls with near military precision. The captain's bed would be nearest the door, and thus furthest from the ablutions – but it also provided a quick exit towards the crew bar!

The stewardess disappeared to join other transient colleagues at a distant location over which, or so rumour had it, a guard was discreetly mounted.

The crew bar, which seemed to be continuously open, was well equipped with cards, a dart board, and a full sized snooker/billiard table. This occasionally posed a problem when "calling time" for departure approached. Even if a billiard game could be left unfinished, and glasses unemptied, the occasional need to help a captain and senior F/E complete a midnight dressing and packing exercise still remained essential. This usually required careful diplomacy when a 02.00hrs departure was the target. Ensuring that all passengers were otherwise engaged enabled us to eventually get them quietly aboard, strapping the amenable captain into the right hand seat, and the equally amenable F/E into a seat in the rest area.

With them safely settled out of passenger sight, and in a non-interfering posture, the well qualified co-pilot and 2nd F/E handled the pre-flight proceedings, and eventually the departure for the next destination. Since this was followed by many hours of relatively leisurely flight, a very useful rest period was available for those in need.

Part of the pre-flight briefing that should be mentioned was a compulsory visit by at least one pilot and the radio officer to the airfield met(eorological) office for a weather briefing. We tended to regard this as an unavoidable nuisance. Weather reports from other airfields were invariably many hours old, while the en-route weather data was many years old! Upper air charts, depicting the atmospheric pressures and temperatures, used in the briefing were charts from yesteryear. We were confidently told that variations in the monsoon weather pattern never occurred, apart from the date of its actual commencement at any particular point. Very near the truth I soon learned, but still ....!

In Cairo with Commodore Moll

Slipping once again into Cairo recalled many memories; only in the absence of uniforms did it differ from wartime days, and the fact that Shepherd's Hotel had then been off-limits for junior personnel. Gezira Island sporting club was still an oasis of refined calm away from the chaotic city and Groppi's still dispensed every known variety of tea and coffee, together with a mouth-watering collection of pastries and cream cakes. A pen clipped in a shirt pocket still disappeared with lighting rapidity as one strolled the streets and shoes suddenly became very dirty as an insistent shoe cleaner enlisted the aid of his accomplice.

Tram in Cairo

The highlight of a stay at Shepherd's was an invitation to dine at the captains table; Commodore Moll (sporting a gold star above his stripes) was a true Anglophile, and an impressive gentleman of the old school. He had flown transatlantic ferry flights with BOAC during the war, and was a contemporary of a well known BOAC captain of that era, Capt. O.P. Jones, whom he knew well. The Commodore usually remained somewhat aloof from the more unruly members of his crew, preferring to spend his off-duty time with local dignitaries – no doubt a profitable sideline for KLM. On such occasions he would be impeccably dressed, acquiring an almost ambassadorial status. I believe that Captain Moll was awarded the title of Commodore by Dr. Plesman, in recognition of his seniority, and of his unique flare for public relations activity; the same honour was also bestowed upon Capt. Viruly.

.... checking-out

A Shepherd's breakfast brought to the room at 04.00hrs was somewhat disappointing; tea, toast and boiled eggs, the eggs extremely small and almost raw, very Egyptian.

After the crew luggage, which was often a strange mixture of bags on a homebound flight, had been assembled in the hotel lobby a taxi would be called. The Commodore would then travel in lonely state to the airfield, accompanied only by his golf clubs. The crew bus followed the command vehicle at a respectful distance. On one occasion I did actually see a fellow traveller with the Commodore, it was his golf companion, another English co-pilot.

.... and others of equal fame

Our later stops in Cairo saw us using the Palace Hotel in Heliopolis, its echoing marble halls a strange contrast to my tent at Almaza of yesteryear. The sporting club in Heliopolis was a meeting place for crews of many different airlines, and endless suitably exaggerated airline tales helped in the recovery from exertions on the tennis courts.

In 1980 I revisited the sporting club for a game of tennis. To my utter amazement I was immediately greeted by my tennis trainer of thirty years ago like a long lost friend. Our rather energetic game put me to bed for a day – completely dehydrated.

70					3ʳᵈ Pil / NAVIGATOR.	
Year 1949		**Aircraft Type**		**Route**	DAY	NIGHT
Month	**Date**					
				Totals brought forward	209:23	175.53
July	1	Constellation PH-TDH	Capt. Mans.	Schiphol - Cairo	7:28	
July	4	Constellation PH-TDG	Capt. Mans.	Cairo - Aden		6:48
July	5	Constellation PH-TDG	Capt. Mans.	Aden - Mauritius	8:00	2:05
July	6/7	Constellation PH-TDG	Capt. Mans	Mauritius - Batavia	3:35	10:00
July	9/10	Constellation PH-TDG	Capt. Mans	Batavia - Mauritius		14:31
July	12	Constellation PH-TES	Capt. Mans	Mauritius - Aden	9:00	1:05
July	13	Constellation PH-TES	Capt. Mans	Aden - Cairo (v.d.wart -Bombay)		6:50
July	21	Constellation PH-TET	Capt. Mans	Cairo - A'dam	9:57	
					35:00	41:19
July	20	Dakota PH-TBL		Rondvlucht		
			Summary July 1949			
		Tot. 79.39.		Constellation Dakota	35:00	41:19
					247:23	217:12
				Totals Carried forward		

Grand total 830 Hrs 46 min

Log book page showing a Mauritius flight with Capt. Mans

A small restaurant, on a corner almost opposite the Palace Hotel, was the setting for a memorable evening with Capt. Brugman where we were joined by Capt.v. Messel. We were delayed by the tragic crash that had occurred in Bombay, and Capt. v. Messel had arrived with a Connie severely damaged by a hail storm over the Alps.

Conversation naturally turned to aviation matters, from rotary engines to the new-fangled science of pressure pattern flying, which was really designed for over ocean flights. Its use over the Mediterranean was thus more experimental than anything. Looking back on that pleasant evening with such knowledgeable and courteous gentlemen, came the realization that not a word of Dutch had been spoken, even between themselves.

.... and some other leisure activities

Apart from tennis and swimming, enlivened by enormous jugs of iced shandy – a 50/50 mix of lemonade and Stella beer – there was plenty to do and see in and around Cairo. Trips out to the Sphinx and the Pyramids were a must, with the more active climbing those tremendous slopes. Camel rides usually produced some pretty sore lower limbs, but an evening meal in a restaurant floating on the Nile was a sure cure for such afflictions.

Cairo railway station was also a great spot for a little sightseeing. The hustle and bustle were tremendous, and the noise absolutely deafening. Preparations for the departure of the Luxor Express seemed to involve a solemn ritual of greetings between the ornately uniformed attendants, and their evidently

With KLM crew, Cairo 1949. Capt Vic Mans, 2nd from right, front row.

important passengers. These would sport a large cigar, firmly clenched between yellowed teeth, and carry an expensive coat nonchalantly draped over their shoulders. Finally, whistles blew and flags waved, thunderous noises came from the engine as it burst into noisy song; clouds of steam erupted around the whole train as the wheels slowly started turning; as it steadily drew away the windows were filled with waving handkerchiefs while the beggars turned aside to count their meagre winnings.

Confronting Schiphol Customs

Back at Schiphol we always seemed fair game for Customs officials. Since all luggage arrived by trolleys in the Customs hall, to be deposited on the zinc covered benches, a complete intermix of passengers and crew bags occurred. Some crew members became very adept at repositioning bags so that theirs acquired "clearance" status when placed between passengers.

Monetary wealth had also to be redistributed around one's person as the money control desk was approached. On a special card it had been necessary to enter any Dutch currency carried on departure, and this had to tally with that carried on arrival.

A more rigorous crew handling was introduced after a Customs officer, doing an external walk around the arrived aircraft, noticed a rope hanging from the nose-wheel well. This led to the discovery of an Indian carpet secreted in the wheel well, and presumably, much consternation in the F/E. corps! The Indian Rope trick had failed to work!!

The Convair 240 arrives

1949 also saw the introduction of the Convair 240, complete with a brass plate on the cockpit bulk head announcing that it was part of the Marshall Plan – aid to Europe from the USA. Its greater speed and agility, and its nose-wheel steering soon relegated the Dakota to the less important routes.

The year thus ended with my logbook entries recording four different aircraft types as active captain or co-pilot; maximum scheduling efficiency had been attained. From now on the crew scheduler who dealt with the pilots could assign me to any of four different aircraft types, and thus lessen his own problems considerably.

Looking around Damascus

During 1950 a constant change between European and Far East flights ensured an ever varying outlook on the world, as did the rotation between the cockpits of four quite different aircraft. Damascus had become a crew slip station, and although it groaned beneath the weight of a military presence – since its rulers were flexing untried muscles after attaining independence from France in 1946 – expeditions to the famous "The Street-called-Straight", and the Umayyad Mosque were still possible.

Crew in local dress

Of more recent historic interest, and well worth a visit was the Hejaz railway station. It was built in 1917 with the intention of assisting Muslim pilgrims to reach Mecca; the attentions of Lawrence of Arabia to the railway connection brought the project to a standstill. So Hejaz station, a handsome building with ornate Ottoman arches, became a white elephant, and served no useful purpose.

Our initial quarters were in a hotel near the town centre, but its former splendour was already in an advanced state of disrepair. Growing unrest in town soon prompted a move to an entirely more pleasant location, which had the additional advantage of direct access to the airport. Hotel Blaudin was located in the pine covered hills overlooking the sprawling city, and was something of a country estate, complete with swimming pool.

East of Damascus lay green and fertile lands which soon changed into true desert scenery. It was there that we crossed one of the world's earliest air routes; an oil strip, laid by tankers driven across the desert, had marked the route between Baghdad (Iraq) and Amman (Jordan) for the mail planes to follow in the early 1920's. In later years the oil pipe lines, with small airfields at their occasional pumping stations, provided the primary navigational aids.

It was here too that we passed near Rutbah Wells, an old fort and supply post from British military days. Interestingly enough Rutbah Wells was also the last resting place of KLM's legendary DC-2 – The "Uiver" (Stork). The "Uiver", piloted by Parmentier and Moll, had won the handicap section of the 1934 London to Melbourne race. After the race the "Uiver" was returned to normal airline service, only to crash mysteriously (late the same year) in the desert near Ruthbah Wells.

In January 2005 Rutbah Wells was again in the news following the crash of a US military helicopter with the loss of all on board. It apparently came down in a sand storm.

It was also in 1950 that my logbook had an entry recording a Constellation 3-engine ferry flight from Basra to Cairo; of this I have unfortunately no recollection. Considerable involvement in 3-engine ferry flights during the later jet years prompts many questions concerning this event – was it an "official" operation, were selected captains trained on the procedures, and were there passengers on board etc. etc.???

"Goolie chits"

Towards year's end a Dakota flight was made along the North African coast to Cairo, across Syria, Iraq, and the Persian Gulf, to Jiwani and Karachi. The passage of time had not yet obliterated the evidence of the recent desert war, burnt out tanks and lorries were still scattered around waiting salvaging for scrap.

Leaving the Persian Gulf the flight continued eastbound along the southern coast of Iran to India. I had always been rather mesmerized by that barren landscape, imagining part of Alexander the Great's army struggling back towards Persepolis. The blue of the ocean was edged with white as it met the sandy shores, clearly marking the many coves and bays that broke the shoreline. Now and again signs of life were apparent in clusters of huts, and radiating from them snail like trails into the wilderness beyond. The trails would come to a sudden halt, as though a search had ended, or continue aimlessly into the distant hills.

Over the lands adjacent to the Persian Gulf, only three years earlier, we had carried "goolie chits". These were statements written in various local dialects, and in Arabic, that promised the bearer a monetary reward in gold, if his captive was returned alive with all bodily parts properly in place. Since the crews of military aircraft carried side-arms, perhaps the need for such chits was then far greater. Anyway, this exhausting flight was much enlivened by our radio operator, a quite accomplished cartoonist. One of his most memorable cartoons portrayed our cargo of a spare engine disappearing through a hole in the floor, watched by goggle-eyed crew members.

Visual cues as landing aids

By the end of the year I had completed a grand total of twenty trips to Batavia and back, of which fifteen had been flown as a fully fledged co-pilot. This had resulted in quite an extensive experience of arrivals and departures at all our normally used airfields, in a wide variety of weather conditions.

A good knowledge of visual aids in approaching an airfield was almost essential, since they greatly helped in locating the airfield or runway when the weather was in an unkind mood. For example, the Habbanyia to Baghdad road, the Shatt-el-Arab at Basra, the port area and the enormous airship hangar at Karachi, the river bridge, and an isolated group of three trees at Calcutta, not to mention the sea of upturned faces as we thundered over the road at the runway's commencement, and a convenient group of pagodas at Bangkok. All these, and many more, were helpful in defining our location, or in assisting an approach path under a low cloud base.

Emigrant flights to Australia

In 1951, which was quite an eventful year, the DC4 flying hours that I logged exceeded those on the Constellation, and introduced some totally new experiences. Emigrant flights to Australia had commenced, animal transport flights for zoos (or for research) were frequent, and Capt. "Willem" came resolutely into view .... but more of him later.

The emigrant flights resulted from the decision of the Australian government to offset the influx of Asian nationals by luring Europeans down-under. Heavily subsided passages resulted, and many thousands of Dutch nationals alone took wing to a new life and culture.

With seven night stops en-route to Sydney, passengers and crew became a team of explorers discovering the world together. The majority of the passengers had never been outside their native land before, and had certainly never flown. The sights, sounds and smells of Baghdad or of Calcutta, for example, were totally unique.

The crew rapidly became guides and mentors to their wide assortment of charges – families with children and unattached males and females. Attachments were made, and final partings in Sydney, between some passengers and crew, were occasionally tearful. Not infrequently a would-be emigrant would seek an early return to their homeland.

Experienced captains on those outbound emigrant flights would delay boarding the aircraft until all passengers were loaded and settled. Loading could take quite some time, especially when strays had to be rounded up, and this saved the crew a lengthy wait in an incredibly hot cockpit at many stations. Return flights were usually charters of a quite different nature; collecting a ship's crew from Japan or the Philippines for a "booze cruise" home!

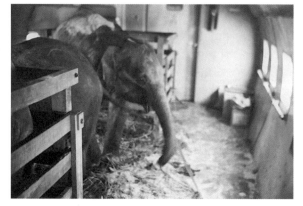

An airborne zoo

Other flights involved more exotic, but less willing emigrants, the transport of wild animals from the East, destined for zoos in

A baby elephant in a DC-4

Capt. Metz far left, Author far right

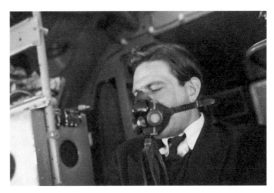

Capt. Lionel Metz

Looking for home!

Monkey cages

Europe. One such flight was made with the nose wheel doors emblazoned with the legend "Metz's Circus", announcing the name of the captain. Two animal trainers accompanied what became a full load of tigers, panthers, snakes and baby elephants.

The elephants were enclosed in waist high wooden pens immediately aft of the small crew pantry. Making a coffee one would feel a touch on the arm, and find an inquisitive trunk snaking round the corner, gently seeking out what was on offer! Visits aft ended abruptly when a panther broke loose; it was felt that the animal trainers could deal more effectively with the resulting chaos, which indeed they did.

Other flights were devoted purely to the carriage of vast quantities of caged monkeys, the noise was continuous, and the stench overpowering. On returning home everything had to go in the wash or to the cleaners.

Introducing Captain "Willem"

Capt "Willem" was a valiant survivor from the pre-war pioneering days, a larger-than-life individual who seemed the dominant figure in any gathering, whether it was a gathering of his peers or his equals made little difference. His status within KLM was gained through long years of experience, and his intimacy with those in the corridors of power – he was a law unto himself and accountable to no one. His various wartime experiences had certainly not succeeded in dampening his enthusiasm for looking around every possible corner in search of entertainment.

"Willem" seemed to be a dedicated DC-4 man, as I never encountered him on any other type of aircraft. Why this should be was not initially clear to me, but suspicions soon developed. The DC-4 was an aircraft of solid metal, the tramp of the skies in its freighter version. Solid in looks, and stolid in character, it was mechanically fairly straightforward, and not fast enough to challenge the slower decision makers in the aviation fraternity.

I first flew with "Willem" on a "search-and-seize" DC-4 flight to the Far East. I had the impression at the time (which was quite incorrect) that any cargo we uplifted was the result of on the spot negotiation rather than by pre-arrangement. Anyway, we flew east with many stops en-route, happily dispensing our load as we went and occasionally replacing it. Returning west bound through Bangkok we acquired a very full load of extremely vociferous monkeys, and continued thereafter enveloped in the ever increasing stench of their lively companionship.

Approaching Lydda (Tel-Aviv) "Willem" decided that a little cockpit company was needed, and went back to the caged load of monkeys. When he reappeared he was carrying one of these creatures under his arm, and it settled happily on his knee as he resumed his seat. Before very long, however, its inquisitive nature took over, and it disappeared behind the instrument panel, and no amount of coaxing could persuade it to come out as it completely disappeared from sight.

After landing at Lydda we were in desperate need of fresh air, and opened the cockpit sliding windows. An immediate blur of movement announced the departure of Willem's monkey friend which was last seen approaching take-off speed down the active runway.

The airport authorities were not amused, and immediately withdrew permission for a scheduled night stop. Although "Willem" handled the whole matter with restrained diplomacy, the authorities were

A DC-4 at Schiphol (East)   (photo source unknown)

adamant in their decision. Not at all put out, "Willem" immediately decided that we should make the short over water journey to Nicosia (Cyprus) where he could take advantage of a long standing agreement with a local hotel owner, a travel agent's mark up?? Certainly our greeting was effusive, and our daily allowances were saved for another day. In retrospect, I am left wondering if the whole monkey incident was carefully arranged in order to stage a meeting with an old friend!

.... where is my allowance?

Among other things, "Willem" was also somewhat notorious for his rather unorthodox handling of the crew allowances. Each crew member received a "daily allowance" to cover incidental expenses for the duration of a particular flight, and these were handed out by the captain during a trip as he thought fit. The captain collected the total of these allowances in pounds sterling before a Schiphol departure, and subsequently recorded the handouts to the crew in a pay-book. His own allowance was somewhat higher than that of other crew members as it included an entertainment addition; contrary to general opinion, it was not intended to entertain the crew, but to gain a potential passenger or to appease an existing one!!

In the distribution of these allowances certain dubious practices were noticeable. "Willem" had a system of organizing compulsory booze-ups, accompanied by compulsory deductions from the allowances, whether one attended or not. Other captains had a system of deductions for perceived misdemeanours which could only be avoided by experience.

.... are the fish biting?

It was also about this time that I learned the wisdom of making appropriate adjustments to our estimated time of arrival (ETA) when returning to Schiphol. Westbound over Germany I would calculate our arrival time, and pass it to the wireless operator for onward transmission. This would prove to be inaccurate by some fifteen minutes if I failed to make allowances for en-route diversions.

"Willem" needed time to go low flying over several favourite fishing areas in search of his rod and line friends. Once they were found it was a case of all hands to the wheel as we circled slowly around the muffled figures lining the banks of a canal or lake. Whether these antics alarmed the fishermen (or the fish) was never known, but they certainly alarmed the crew on occasions.

On Tour with Captain Tom Ekels

In between my Connie and DC-4 flights of the early 50's there was much to do in Europe, but an added attraction were several DC-6 flights with Capt. Ekels. My first and only visit to Rio de Janeiro, was as a navigator on a flight with him. To the best of my recollection a new radio station had been opened to provide long range bearings for aircraft on the South Atlantic crossing, and I was tasked with checking their accuracy by astro sightings.

Rio de Janerio

Rio itself was a novel experience. Copacabana beach, even in those days, was tastefully adorned with sun lovers who disdained the use of over protective clothing. A trip up to the gigantic figure of Christ the King on Sugar Loaf Mountain provided some enthralling views of the city, the surrounding country, and the ocean beaches.

The only memories that I have of our stopovers in Dakar (West Africa) are of rather dubious accommodation alive with monstrous cockroaches, and of even more questionable food.

Some weeks after the Rio trip, Capt. Ekels arranged for me to join him as a navigator on a flight to Capetown. I managed to enlist the aid of the stars on our Sahara desert crossing, and came up with an accurate ETA for Kano (Nigeria). After a pleasant stop over, we continued south bound for Johannesburg, and some personally dramatic events.

The clear and unpolluted air over desert regions made a visit to the astro dome a wonderful experience. Lifting one's head into the Perspex dome was like emerging into a world that contained nothing but stars; a million pinpoints of light glittered in the darkened skies with unrivalled intensity. They seemed more numerous than the grains of sand on the desert floor.

Passing over Salisbury in Southern Rhodesia (now Harare in Zimbabwe) a query came to us from Air Traffic Control (ATC) asking whether Peter Orange was on board. Tom looked at me in amazement before replying "affirmative" – "standby" came the answer, followed by a long silence. Then finally

Douglas DC-6   (photo source unknown)

a message – "please advise Peter Orange that Mary will meet him in Jo'burg". The astonished reactions from my crew were, of course, quite overwhelming in their rather indelicate suggestions.

Mary (a friend from my Rhodesian days) did indeed arrive in Johannesburg, and then there was yet another surprise. Tom declared that a navigator on the Capetown sector was totally unnecessary, and that I could remain in Johannesburg, and rejoin the north bound flight two days later. That indeed was a trip to remember.

And more tours with "Willem"

After something of a holiday interlude it was back to the tramp of the skies, and a mid-eastern meander with a DC-4 freighter – and Willem was naturally the captain. On one trip, as we left Basra bound for Teheran, heavy turbulence was encountered over the foothills of the mountains. This toppled the auto-pilot gyro, causing the AP to disconnect, and also caused a slight rearward shift of the loosely lashed cargo.

When the gyro had settled down once more the AP was re-engaged, and calm descended on the flight deck. "Willem" considered the use of an oxygen mask inappropriate, and slumbered quietly in his seat – the F/E and radio operator went aft, and busied themselves trying to tighten the cargo lashings. I meanwhile gazed awestruck (complete with oxygen mask) at the snow-covered scenery sliding majestically by. The previous night's compulsory booze-up was evidently keeping my companions at low ebb, not helped by oxygen starvation.

Cockpit of Douglas DC-6   (photo source unknown)

Under cloudless skies an early let down to more oxygen rich levels seemed a wise course of action. This decision was encouraged by a massive oil leak from No. 4 Engine. Oil leaks always tended to look worse than they were, due to light reflections on the spreading stains. The F/E was prodded into action, and helped to find the correct feather button and the emergency checklist was recovered from the floor and read. With the engine stopped, and its propeller blades turned (feathered) to minimize airflow resistance, we started a gentle descent on three engines.

Enroute to Tehran by DC-4

Enroute to Tehran by DC-4

Tehran was finally reached with a solid thump, and we taxied wearily to the parking spot where the final drops of oil seeped out. As we descended the steps, and stepped on to the tarmac the aircraft gave an audible sigh, and we watched in astonishment as it very gently settled on its tail in a prayer-like attitude. The un-installed tail support lay at the feet of an equally astonished ground crew, who were just rolling up their prayer mats.

.... a road side emergency!

En-route to the hotel we passed the familiar roughly made stone beehive structure by the road side; it was said to contain the remains of a woman stoned to death for adultery.

Later that same evening my solitary meal of caviar, toast and vodka, in a nearby garden restaurant, was rudely interrupted by the hotel manager – "pleesse, capitaine, ees need help"!!! Following his portly form towards a group of onlookers outside the hotel, I was confronted with our captain's recumbent form lying in the roadside gutter, these tended to be almost knee deep, and needed careful negotiation. With much willing help his unbroken, but bruised form was carried to his room. A hastily summoned doctor pronounced that "ees good", and helped with tucking him in bed. The doctor returned early next morning to confront a very angry "Willem", leaving again very quickly muttering "ees very good".

And "Willem" makes a diversion!!

Westbound from Calcutta to Bombay (now Mumbai) we were bouncing along one dark night through monsoon clouds, wishing that we had radar. Bombay weather was reported as torrential rain and insignificant visibility, other inbound flights were diverting elsewhere. "Willem" was giving the impression that a little flag showing was necessary, in a place which he knew so well. The flag waving idea had no appeal for me, and I suggested that a diversion would be more appropriate. Since "Willem" was quite unable to recall the last time he had diverted the novelty of it had no attraction to him. Finally, it was decided that we would divert to our alternative, Ahmadabad.

By the time we arrived my popularity was very evidently at a low ebb. The situation was not improved when it was found that we would have to spend the remains of the night on hard benches in the hall of the terminal building. Our companions were sundry sweepers, cleaners and itinerant cockroaches. I was firmly told that my place was in the "met" office to await any news of improvement in the Bombay weather.

Signs of improving weather came with the rising sun, and we tiredly set forth once more – Willem's stony silence towards me still very much in evidence. The Station Manager greeted us warmly in Bombay, and congratulated "Willem" on the wisdom of his diversion; all was forgiven as he turned to me saying "see how right we were!"

A brief European review

The landscape across Europe was undergoing significant changes for the better. The scars of war were fast disappearing, new roads were crawling over the countryside, towns and villages were being restored to normality, and the density of traffic was fast increasing. It seemed that only parts of London were still hiding their bomb damage behind wooden hoardings – the area around St. Paul's cathedral was particularly slow in this respect.

A night stop in Oslo was always a particular joy, even though the abnormally strict licensing laws demanded that one's alcoholic drink be secreted within a teapot! The morning breakfast was a delicious meal of smorgasbrood (open sandwiches), followed by an exhilarating low level flight down the fiord towards Christiansand. The early morning risers were out on their balconies having breakfast in the sun, and turned to wave as we flew by.

The Dakota night freighter flight to London was also a pleasant outing, especially for the British pilots. A night stop in a Richmond hotel gave time for some shopping or visiting before returning home with a laden aircraft, including bales of the morning papers. It took nearly two and a half hours to make the North Sea crossing – ample time for me to rescue a paper, and scan the morning news.

.... and a conflict of interests

A more alarming event occurred one foggy morning at Schiphol. I was assigned to take a Dakota up on a test flight, following an engine change, and was not best pleased to find my least favourite F/E in the cockpit. I was even less pleased to find a load of freight on board, evidently the test flight was felt to be a pure formality – such flights were usually made without load.

As our wheels left the ground on take-off the newly installed engine failed. As I struggled for control an un-commanded flurry of sweaty armpits rushed into action before the emergency checklist could be read. Since the landing gear could not be persuaded to retract, the aircraft was barely flyable, and urgent corrective action became imperative – seek, and ye shall find! Who had placed the hydraulic system selector, for powering gear movement, in the wrong position? It was located by the F/E's leg, and not directly within the pilot's reach.

In the midst of this cockpit activity the radar operator at Schiphol was trying to attract my attention. It seemed that we were on a collision course with a lofty chimney at Utrecht, and he suggested that I rapidly climb. With the gear now almost up-and-locked I could gently do that, and also slowly turn back towards the airfield. The fog had barely started to disperse, but radar guided us in to a welcome landing. Fortunately, the same F/E was not available for the re-test on the following day!

An oil crisis once more

The summer of 1951 was an extremely warm one in Europe, but I was found an even warmer location – the oil refinery at Abadan in Persia. Events in Persia were causing ripples around the world, particularly when Premier Mossadeq decided to nationalize the Anglo-Iranian Oil Company. Anglo-Iranian were then compelled to evacuate all their workers from the various oil fields, most of which were some 50 minutes flight from Abadan, and arrange for onward transportation out of Basra or Abadan.

Top: Aerial view of the Abadan refinery

Left and below: Extracts from London newspapers

Ebening Standard

MONDAY, SEPTEMBER 3 1951   Three-halfpence

OIL GANG THREATEN BRITONS

ABADAN, Monday. — A notorious Persian gang leader has threatened that a big crime wave will be directed against British property in Abadan unless the British pay "protection money," Mr. Robert Ford, British security chief, said here.

Mr. Ford said he had received the threat by way of the underworld "grapevine."

Mr. Ford said the number of thefts from the Anglo-Iranian Oil Company's refinery and British houses are mounting. Industrial thefts average £10,000 a week.

Bazaar HQ

The thieves, with headquarters in the bazaar district, have openly defied efforts to arrest them.

The Persian armed guard placed last Friday on a KLM Dakota chartered by the Anglo-Iranian Company at Abadan has been withdrawn as the result of British representations and the airplane has left Abadan for Basra, Irak and Amsterdam carrying luggage belonging to British evacuees from the oilfields.

The pilot is Peter Orange of Guildford.

The Persians had claimed the airplane as their property, on the grounds that it was a replacement for the company's chartered Bristol freighter sent home recently for overhaul.—BUP.

PLANE SEIZED
Claim by Persians

Persian armed guards were placed over a Dutch K.L.M. airliner on charter to the Anglo-Iranian Oil Company in Abadan yesterday, B.U.P. reported. This was the first hostile move against the British in Abadan since the end of the oil talks last week.

Mr. Peter Orange, of Guildford, Surrey, pilot of the K.L.M. Dakota, was told the plane would be held on technical grounds connected with clearance papers. The Persians claim the plane is their property because it was chartered to replace the company's chartered Bristol freighter, recently was sent back to England for overhaul.

The Persians assert that the Bristol freighter was included in the company's assets taken over when the industry was nationalised.

To assist in this evacuation a Dakota was chartered from KLM, and we left Schiphol in a newly painted aircraft carrying the legend "Anglo-Iranian Oil Co" on both sides of the fuselage. Having nationalized the company, the Persians had no hesitation in now nationalizing its newly arrived aircraft. PH-TDZ was rapidly removed from our care, and placed in a locked hangar under armed guard.

Some two weeks of diplomatic activity then commenced to obtain its release. Entertainment during this period was scarce, though I did manage some flights to the oil fields in a de Havilland Rapide. The most memorable episode of the period was the arrival of two Royal Navy destroyers, dressed overall[*], sailing up the Shatt-el-Arab, evidently in a move to ensure that the evacuation was peacefully carried out. Later that same evening at a bar crowded with journalists, our uninhibited F/E saw fit to commence deriding the Navy in a guttural voice – with one accord, the journalists turned upon him, and upended his stool with some gusto. One bruised and battered F/E wisely kept to his room for several days. Some weeks later I received a letter (thought at the time to be from his wife) inquiring after his well-being – did people often fall from an aircraft wing she asked!!

> *Dressed overall is a naval expression to describe a ship on which the crew are lining
> the rails in full uniform with all appropriate flags flying from the masts.

After the aircraft was finally released from custody we hopped across the river to Basra, and there awaited a renewed clearance to assist in the evacuation. When this eventually came through our return to Abadan was hardly necessary as the evacuation was almost complete. Our final departure from Abadan was then enlivened by an engine failure necessitating an arrival in Basra on half power.

Interestingly enough the F/E was the same one as on my test flight a few weeks previously, but he had certainly learned to be a little more careful in his cockpit activities. While we were kicking our heels in Basra, awaiting the arrival of a new engine, a DC-4 arrived – complete with Willem!! He and my F/E (they were old buddies) soon had their heads together in a corner in deep discussion. It soon transpired that the subject was daily allowances, and it was suggested that I was not giving the F/E his due, as after all, his seniority was considerable. Somewhat taken aback I suggested a visit to the F/E's room. It was absolutely overflowing with homebound shopping from the markets. Here was evidence of more wheeling and dealing than a normal daily allowance could possibly support. Subject closed!

Eventually we had a replacement engine, removed several rows of seats, and lashed the broken one down in their place. An uneventful return to Schiphol followed, and PH-TDZ was returned to full KLM colours.

Biak (Indonesia)

Christmas Day 1951 saw yet another of my Far East departures, to arrive in Biak on New Year's Eve. Quite why our flight went from Bangkok to Manilla, and then returned to terminate in Biak is lost in my memories. Vague memories do remain of the Biak hotel constructed in native fashion from enormously thick bamboo canes, and raised several foot above ground level, enabling empty Amstel and Heineken beer bottles to be collected underneath.

Biak came more prominently into the route network in 1957. At that time Indonesia withdrew the landing rights for Dutch aircraft. KLM was thus once again faced with developing a new Far East route which would avoid Jakarta (formerly Batavia), but still connect with Manila, Tokyo and with Sydney.

A difficult decision

In early January 1952 I returned from a Far East trip, and within a week was setting out again, this time with Capt. van Messel. My logbook notes that two weather diversions occurred during this trip, both handled with the decision and professionalism that he inevitably applied. Capt. van Messel was a joy to fly with, for he was constantly passing on information in an informal and friendly fashion. The lore of the east, its people's and their cultures was as important to him as were the technical aspects of flight through their territories. I seem to remember that he was the only intercontinental captain to address me as "captain", after I had reached that dizzy status in Europe!!

A later trip, also with a much respected captain, sadly turned out to be a considerably different experience. It was to prove the opening of the last logbook page of a veteran of the skies, and the ending of a career which had been closely involved in the pre-war history of KLM.

Outward bound for the Far East a 500 ft cloud base was encountered at Geneva, and a decision was made to fly the fairly newly installed ILS – a ground based radio beam landing device for instrument conditions which was gradually becoming more widely installed. With some apprehension I watched a corkscrew approach of increasing excursions developing before cloud base was broken, terminating in an extreme off-centre line correction being made before landing.

At various times during our journey I also became conscious of what appeared to be poor eyesight. For example, a beer bottle would be held at arm's length with the head held well back in an attempt to read the information on the label. Not an encouraging sign!

The remainder of the trip was in fine weather conditions, and flown with the captain's usual aplomb, and expertise until approaching Frankfurt homeward bound. Frankfurt weather was "on-limits" in fog, and an American operated Ground Controlled Approach (GCA) the only approach aid available. Removing his headset the captain instructed me to translate (into English), and relay the American's instructions. The results were predictable, and my concern was reflected by the operator's desperately repeated "Emergency Overshoot" instruction as we reached the minimum altitude. As the approach lights loomed at an acute angle to our approach path I blocked the captain's hopeless corrective inputs, and took over control.

As course was set for Schiphol a gracious "thank you" came from the captain – to be repeated when we later said our goodbyes.

After several days of uneasy flight leave I made a reluctant visit to the chief pilot, Capt. Snitslaar. He listened to my story with attentive care, and thanked me for drawing the matter to his attention. Some time later I heard that a check flight for the captain concerned had been scheduled, albeit with an equally senior colleague. This check was apparently passed successfully.

Not long afterwards an equally disturbing report on his instrument flying again reached the chief pilot. This veteran of the air then quietly disappeared, perhaps he had reach retirement age, which I believe was fifty in those far off days.

Different events

My first trip to Tokyo, through Manila, was made with an Australian captain. His somewhat uncouth behaviour had to be overlooked when confronted with his expertise in circumnavigating a threatening typhoon. Tokyo was, to me, rather bewildering in terms of place names and air traffic management, and also in the bustling,

At the British Embassy, Tehran

but ordered chaos of the city. The city streets were absolutely teeming with people, and the flashing neon signs were quite dazzling on the eyes. Between the many building sites I noted that space had been reserved for a golf driving range – in later years I was to find this in full use surrounded by high netting.

Midsummer saw a series of Constellation flights through Istanbul to Tehran and back; welcome opportunities for more caviar tasting, visiting the Peacock Throne, and the fascinating covered markets. Carpet shops were always a great attraction, particularly one owned by "Red", a red-headed Iranian expert on weave and texture.

An invitation to the British Embassy was always greatly appreciated; a quiet swimming pool surrounded by beautiful gardens made an oasis of peace in the turbulent city.

Although Iran was still then under the control of Mossadeq and the Shiite Muslims, a fairly tolerant attitude to dress and behaviour still existed. Having alarmed world opinion by nationalization of the oil fields, the regime was maintaining a quieter mood. Picnic expeditions into the mountain north of Tehran, even as far as the shores of the Caspian Sea, could be made without hindrance. A lively export trade was also in progress, evidenced by our cargoes of carpets and leather goods, not to mention the smelly intestines of sheep destined to become sausage skins.

A November visit by Dakota to Hull found me landing at RAF Leconfield – the site of my first UK departure some twelve years previously. Homeward bound in and out of cloud involved a near collision in our cleared airspace with an RAF transport aircraft. – it sailed serenely across our nose, close enough to read the registration letters on the fuselage side. I am unaware if any investigation ever took place over the incident.

Australian tales

Towards the end of 1952 I was again scheduled on an emigrant flight to Sydney with a DC-4, this time in the company of yet another Australian captain. To my surprise his briefcase contained nothing more than a selection of pocketbooks, and a pair of bedroom slippers – the reason for this soon became clear. After take-off, and with climb power set, he would leave his seat, replace his shoes with slippers, select a book, and retire to a seat in the passenger cabin; midway through descent he would re-appear, putting away his book and slippers, and ask for the latest weather. This sequence of events was repeated for every sector between Schiphol and Sydney, and also on the return flight. On very long sectors his head would momentarily appear at the cockpit door asking "are you fellows alright then?"

While it was very pleasing to be virtually in sole command of events it was also extremely tiring. I often wondered what prompted this individual to spend his life in the air, delegating his duties to others in such a casual fashion.

.... and Captain Ravenhill enters my world

For some long forgotten reason I was separated from my slipper-shod captain in Batavia on the return flight, and transferred to a homebound Connie crew. This brought about my first meeting with Captain Ravenhill, yet another Australian. Ray was very much a larger-than-life sort of person; his outspoken and straight-to-the-point characteristics were well concealed in a smoke cloud of diplomacy and charming manners. During the B-747 era he was our most senior captain, and we were constantly in close contact over operational issues.

In the following years he progressed to very senior positions in KLM's operational management. If my memories are correct, he retired from active flying at the mandatory age of fifty six, only to be re-employed in a managerial function – a manoeuvre not repeated for lesser mortals! It was during this managerial period that we travelled together to Amman (Jordan) on a visit to Ali Ghandour, president of Royal Jordanian Airlines. Our object was to secure a lucrative B-747 training contract if an order for the aircraft was made. Unfortunately, the order was not forthcoming, and Ray's successful powers of persuasion came to naught on this occasion.

Glimpses of Sydney and Manilla

Sydney was a city that demanded exploration unless the red light district of King's Cross was the chosen destination. Pubs were best avoided. Strict liquor laws resulted in long queues awaiting opening time, and closing time resulted in rather ferocious scuffles. The Aussie police seldom needed an invitation to become involved with anything resembling a fight.

The Harbour Bridge rose magnificently above the water, its prominence as yet still undisturbed by the arrival of the new Opera House. Near its southern foot was St. James church, a Victorian relic of days uncomfortably close to penal colony memories; beautifully restored it was a living museum. Further afield streets of terrace houses could be found, each house having a covered balcony of intricate wrought-iron construction – they brought to life the scenes found in old sepia coloured photos.

Bondi Beach was delightful, as were its resident sun worshipers. The Adonis-like figures of the life guards dominated the scenery, and were frequently practicing their prowess – much to the delight of the onlookers. Returning to the hotel after a hot and sticky day was a return to formality, requesting a pot of tea in the lounge brought the response "not without a collar and tie, mate".

Manila, on the other hand, seemed awfully brash and Americanized – every street appeared to have a "Mc'Arthurs" or "Sloppy Joe" bar. I was soon cured of solitary excursions by being relieved of my wallet (almost empty) in a shop doorway ……….. the menacing knife point looked uncomfortably sharp! To be smartly dressed seemed to require a beautifully embroidered shirt worn outside the trousers or a shirt of dazzling colours. These shirts were straight cut along their bottom edge, and always worn outside the trousers.

Much activity was still evident at Clarke Field – the American airbase – and a strong naval presence could also be seen in the surrounding waters, or by groups of noisy sailors exploring the freedom of Manila. The streets were teeming with a vast selection of gaily painted and decorated mini buses, most of which had been created from discarded jeeps and pick-up trucks after drastic treatment by inventive garages. These competed noisily for road space with the enormous chrome laden American cars of the period, and with the motorized rickshaws.

Karachi once more

A return to our slip station for the crews along the route to Batavia allowed for renewals of previous activities in Karachi. Crew transport, and picnic baskets were always available for an outing to an area known as Sandspit, which could be reached by a native sailing boat (a form of dhow) from the harbour area. That particular part of the harbour was crowded with the forlorn hulks of once proud ships of every description, but they were now being systematically reduced to unrecognizable fragments of metal by the scrap-man, and his fiercely wielded hammer and saw.

The beach would seasonally be marked by the trails of turtles, leading to the spot in the dunes where their eggs had been laid. The trails were made by the creatures' feet, and a line made by its tail dragging through he sand. The eggs themselves, laid in large clusters, were about the size of a golf

Enroute to Sandspit

ball, but with a soft outer shell. A boat was always available for these expeditions as two were permanently retained at the harbour for use by KLM crews.

"Midway" was the KLM owned rest-house just five minutes' walk from the terminal buildings of the airport. Over the years it was much changed and improved in many respects, and the original Nissan huts soon disappeared. There was quite a constant activity resulting from the intermittent arrival and departure of Constellations, Skymasters, and an occasional Dakota.

Old friends encountered on incoming crews would receive a boisterous welcome, and many parties inevitably resulted. The encounters along the route tended to underline the rather negative aspects of an airline pilot's life. It was very very seldom that I was able to meet another pilot in Holland – we were always in different parts of the world, coming and going to quite different schedules.

A quick escape from "Midway" could always be obtained by strolling across the road to the much quieter BOAC rest-house. One was always welcome there, and the latest newspapers and magazines from London provided an up-to-date source of world news. I even met a BOAC pilot who had been my flight commander during a tour of flight instruction in Southern Rhodesia many years before.

.... and a return to Calcutta

The fading colonial splendour of The Grand Hotel made us welcome in downtown Calcutta. Its central location ensured easy access to the busy streets, which simply teemed with every conceivable form of traffic. Bullock drawn carts jostled for position with hand drawn carts, rickshaws and bicycles darting in between the pedestrians, and magnificent limousines pursued their majestic way quite unperturbed. To add to the general chaos were the sacred cows which had the right of way whatever the circumstances.

Along the broken pavements were the street dwellers, complete with mattresses and lengths of cardboard to turn into shelters. Their cooking utensils lay ready to hand, and small children were transformed into seemingly disabled supplicants for alms. Amidst all the squalor smiles were readily forthcoming; this was life in the raw, but apparently accepted with the fortitude of countless generations.

Crew transport to and from the airport negotiated these randomly moving obstacles by pure horn power, though the ruminations of a sacred cow at a crossroads could cause a considerable traffic jam. Crossing the river Ganges on the rail/road bridge sometimes found us travelling alongside a slow moving train. Every conceivable hand hold was clung to by numerous figures, happily enjoying a free ride. This inevitably gave rise to some comments concerning staff passengers – we were all quite familiar with travel as staff passengers, but that did not usually involve hanging on to the wing tips!

During the monsoon season these aspects of street life became a rather different picture. The more fortunate residents crouched beneath huge umbrellas, amid scenes of abject human misery, while the water swirled around their meagre possessions. Only the bullocks seemed unaffected by the incessant rain.

Coffee by the Tigris

Baghdad was always a stop full of interest to me, since it allowed a renewal of experiences from RAF days. Initially we were accommodated in a hotel in Rashid Street in the old city centre. A busy thoroughfare lined with old fashioned shops that had their fronts decorated with pillars. Tailors' shops had shelves crowded with rolls of pinstripe and flannel material accessed by wooden ladders. Various food shops and pavement stalls were all thronged with a vociferous crowd of shoppers or curious passers-by.

The Tigris at Baghdad

The best place for a quiet coffee was at a small stall on the banks of the Tigris. From the Tigris, incidentally came a local delicacy for the fish restaurants – a mazgouf, which looked something like a carp. It proved to have a muddy flavour, and was full of tiny bones. Even in the 1950's Baghdad was showing signs of a weakening infrastructure – intermittent cuts in electricity supplies and water available only at certain hours. Smelly drains could be met everywhere.

We were soon moved to a guest house in the suburbs where the kindly owners would produce the most appetizing of evening meals – the centre piece, a mound of rice stuffed with chicken, raisins and almonds. A short taxi ride soon took us to other parts of the city, and in particular the various bridges over the Tigris to watch the astonishing variety of water traffic.

Street scene

Visits to the British Club resulted in an invitation to bring a KLM crew along for an afternoon swim – an invitation that was not repeated. Members of the club were primarily resident businessmen and diplomatic staff, and used the club for quiet relaxation – to suddenly find their swimming pool overrun by the noisy antics of strangers shouting in a strange language was altogether too much!!

Iraq at that time had been a monarchy for some thirty years, and long independent from its previous status of being a British Protectorate. Religious differences and tribal differences were strong (over one hundred different tribes then – as now – existed), but were not so much in the forefront of daily events. Conversations with businessmen at the club revealed, however, that a current of unrest existed, to finally culminate in the assassination of the royal family in 1958 leading to the beginning of military dictatorships.

These dictatorships had objectives far removed from attending to the crumbling infrastructure and welfare of the country, and their excesses led to the sad events of the 21st Century. If world leaders had studied the history unfolding in their own lifetimes, would other decisions have resulted, or would the immense difficulties of an occupation have not been realized?

The year moves relentlessly along

The remainder of 1952 was devoted to Dakota, DC-4, and Convair adventures, the Constellation having quietly disappeared from my logbook. It was not until early 1953 that it briefly reappeared, and that was only for a short flight in Europe.

.... and so does the pressure of events!

As the emigrant flights to Australia continued, I found myself scheduled for yet another trip to Sydney and Melbourne. This one, with a newly promoted captain, was to prove somewhat different when we finally turned for home. After an uneventful outbound trip to Melbourne via Sydney we were able to relax for a day, before being directed homebound via Darwin and Manila to Iwakuni in Japan.

Commencing our homebound flight through Bangkok, Calcutta and Karachi the captain came under increasing pressure from Schiphol for an early return, since apparently the aircraft was urgently needed. The pressure (on a new captain) became so intense that, despite near crew mutiny, a scheduled night stop in Damascus was rejected, and the flight continued to Rome with the captain intending to proceed directly to Schiphol. Arriving in Rome after a total flight time of over 17 hours, however, saw the captain quietly removed for medical attention while the remaining crew were transported to a hotel.

The resulting delay, awaiting the arrival of a replacement captain, rather nullified Schiphol's "come home quickly" calls.

"Willem" again, and this time it is on Safari!!

In mid summer I flew on several interesting trips across Africa to Johannesburg with that valiant workhorse the DC-4. Our modest unpressurized altitudes of 8000ft provided for some wonderful sightseeing opportunities, particularly with "Willem". When he spotted elephants or other animals in encouraging herds, a low level salute was the only possible thing – the fact that a stampede inevitably resulted was of minor importance!

Safari with "Willem"

One such flight resulted in yet another unscheduled stopover, or so I strongly suspect, at Livingstone for a visit to Victoria Falls. Admittedly our turn around in Johannesburg had been extremely brief, but I don't recall seeing any stops before Kano being mentioned in the original schedule for the trip.

As we flew with an empty aircraft northwards in the vicinity of Bulawayo, I paid a visit to the rear of the aircraft in answer to a call of nature. While there I heard an engine being shut down, a not unusual event. On returning to the cockpit I asked the F/E, since "Willem" was engrossed in an airfield chart of Livingstone, what the problem was. The mumbled reply merely mentioned a falling oil pressure, and I didn't pursue the matter. "Willem" then announced that he had decided to land at Livingstone, the airfield for Victoria Falls, and the matter would be sorted out overnight.

It soon transpired that the only suitably qualified ground engineer at the airfield was down with malaria, and I noted "Willem" and our F/E exchange quite pleased smiles at the news. We went off to the Victoria Falls hotel leaving the F/E with the aircraft to fix the problem. Barely fifteen minutes later (hardly time to open an engine cowling) he rejoined us with not an oil stain in sight. "Willem" finally finished his earnest consultations with the hotel manager (crew discount!), and after a quick handshake with the F/E we were escorted to our sumptuous rooms.

The Victoria Falls hotel was quite superb, and very much an upmarket resort in those pre-tourist days. When we later reassembled in the lobby I was rather ashamed of our somewhat scruffy appearance which was attracting quite disdainful looks. The fact that Dutch crews always seem to wear black (uniform!) socks with their khaki shorts didn't help with appearances!

It was just 10 years since my last visit, and then I was on leave from duties as an RAF flying instructor in S. Rhodesia (now Zimbabwe). This time the Zambezi River was still waiting the rainy season, but nevertheless the falls were quite spectacular. In the local language they were known as "The Smoke that Thunders".

Homeward bound through Brazzaville (Congo) and Kano (Nigeria) was followed by a welcome stopover in Tunis, and a quick visit by coastal train to Carthage. Although I had been there very briefly during the war, my most memorable visits were to come later courtesy of the Lockheed Electra, and that was still on the designer's drawing board!

Kano – crew relaxation

The Spreading Wings of KLM

By the early 1950's it was apparent that the Phoenix was regaining her full flight status. From a pre-war fleet of about forty-five aircraft the airline had now grown to a strength of some eighty aircraft, and more were on order at the insistence of Dr. Plesman. By the end of 1940 very few aircraft had survived bombardment or capture. The few survivors were scattered around the world with the exception of three that had deliberately sought refuge in Bristol (England). These DC-2 and DC-3 aircraft flew the Bristol-Lisbon line throughout the years of the European occupation by German troops.

In the background KLM was quietly preparing for the future, and the coming introduction of turbine and jet powered aircraft. The days of whirling propellers were numbered, and not before time; medical examinations had already spotted a decline in the higher tones of my hearing.

In this Phoenix-like revival of the airline it is safe to say that the many non-national pilots played an extremely important role. The Mauritius operation, for example, depended to a great extent on the navigational skills of the younger foreign and Dutch pilots; it was also their ready understanding and acceptance of more modern technology that led to many improvements in the safety of general operations. Many of the older captains tended to rely quite heavily on the younger eyes, and quicker reactions of their younger co-pilots.

In much later years, the appreciation of the non-nationals tended to diminish. By some they were seen as obstacles to promotion, and by others as grossly deficient in linguistic skills. This latter feature remained a particular drawback in the arena of social contacts with those outside the company. The vagaries of our weekly scheduling system, which in itself was subject to overnight changes, were neither understood nor appreciated by potential hosts.

The Christchurch Race

Amid the flurry of activity that marked the passage of the years, time was found in 1953 to enter a DC-6 in the London-Christchurch (New Zealand) race, and it was allocated a place in the handicap section. Since I was well acquainted with the person responsible for most of the operational planning of the flight, I had an interesting over-the-shoulder view of the preparations being made.

The navigational data, fuel consumption, precise distance calculations and expected wind conditions were all fed into the preparation of handmade flight plans. The selected aircraft also spent a considerable amount of time in the hangar being fine tuned, and much careful attention was expended on the engines to obtain first class reliability, and optimized fuel consumption.

The flight crew chosen for the race included a senior British pilot – Joe Griffiths – for the critical function of navigator. Perhaps this was partly in recognition of the part played by the non-Dutch pilots in the Phoenix revival? KLM then went on to win the handicap section of this race in grand style – a fitting reminder of the victory in the Melbourne race of 1934.

The death of Dr. Albert Plesman

In December 1953 the untimely death of Dr. Plesman somewhat subdued the national pride that the Christchurch race had fostered. His visions for KLM's future had been extraordinary; he had quietly continued planning the future of the airline throughout the war, and had maintained close contact with the American aircraft factories. He had been among the first on the scene when world peace returned, and had rapidly placed new and substantial orders.

His untimely death thus left one wondering to what extent his global visions had been achieved. It was soon evident, however, that all the stepping stones were in place for continued and successful progress, and that a line might safely be drawn under the post war restoration phase. The runway was clear, and a safe take-off into the future was assured.

Phoenix .... you are cleared for take-off!

As the increasingly crowded skies of 1953 began to fade, and amid much personal activity over the European route network, it was becoming evident that Phoenix had been restored to full flight status. KLM had fully renewed its links with the Far East, and with Indonesia in particular. World wide expansion had followed, and fleet renewal was in progress without the assistance of Marshall Aid. This plan had been a USA programme of help to war ravaged Europe, and had simultaneously been intended to block the encroachment of communism in Europe – it had come to an end in 1952.

I had now completed my first five years with KLM, and these memorable years had provided me with an incredible variety of flights and aircraft types. Those flights in unpressurized aircraft had allowed for endless sight-seeing through the pages of history, and fostered an intimacy with people and places which could never be repeated in the years to follow. In the pressurized aircraft such as the Constellation, I had seen the feeble beginnings of flight over the weather, but there was still a long way to go in an upwards direction.

Many of the places that I had visited were destined for frequent return visits in the ensuing years, and it was remarkable to see how little change occurred in some of them. Probably the most dramatic changes that I encountered were in Dubai and Bahrain, and the least evident were on the Indian sub-continent. Returning to Jakarta (Batavia) in the 1980's I felt that the changes were very largely superficial. Away from the grand hotels and shopping malls, daily life was very much the same; canals were still public ablutions, and the necessities of existence were still obtained from road side stalls.

The future, however, stretched over an almost limitless horizon, and it was to prove as intriguing as the past had been. For the moment, I was content with a great sense of achievement, and felt that I had made a substantial contribution to the resurrection of the recumbent Phoenix. The ruffled feathers had been washed and preened, flight status had been tested, and the great bird was ready to go.

Fluttering Wings

Looking at accidents in this period of 1947-61

The unusual circumstances surrounding the flights through Mauritius to the Dutch East Indies (1948/49) had come to a conclusion, and the records of that operation were already consigned to the dusty archives of the Company. The social escapades of Capt. Houba ("The Bull"), and of Capt. "Speedy" Le Good, had faded from centre stage leaving but vague memories of the crew slips on that distant island but the incredible imitation of an angry monkey, performed by Capt. Vic Mans on a table top, probably remains part of the local folklore. During that unique operation, Phoenix had firmly demonstrated the strength of her refurbished wings by epic flights of endurance but whether such a display could support the years to come was still an open question.

I feel very privileged to have been part of that venture, having made five flights to Batavia by way of Mauritius, and thus recording a total of ten Indian Ocean crossings. Sadly, in the very last week of this historic period a KLM Constellation crashed at Bombay, the circumstances of this will be discussed later. Among the passengers had been a number of important radio commentators and news reporters from the USA, and I believe that the US Government had vetoed their return home via the Mauritius route from a news gathering visit to Batavia, considering it to be too dangerous. Special clearance had thus been obtained from the Indian Government for this one flight to over-fly India, landing in Delhi and Bombay.

This particular chapter is intended to create a form of suspension bridge between the last chapter (Phoenix Arises), and the one to follow (My Last Propellers). Its span overlooks a chasm of mystery, forested with many charred question marks concerning the sad events of that decade, while its feet rest in two separate areas of progressive development. It is in this chasm that many unresolved tragic accidents occurred, and since there appears to be a commonality of background to many of those events, they are addressed from this vantage point. These events were noted in my logbook with the intention of returning to them at some future date, that date has been a long time in returning!! Some progressive improvement in the equipment that we used, particularly that of a ground based nature, is also more fully described.

The thoughts and (tentative) conclusions that arise from this viewpoint are formed by my own recollections of that far away period, although there is often a lack of detailed knowledge. Since I was an active player during the changing scenery of those years my thoughts may perhaps have some validity. Those who share that fading time with me may perhaps find my memories faulty, for which I can only apologize.

Pre-war shadows must fade away

The old guard of pilots, flight engineers, radio operators and (later) cabin staff which had pioneered KLM's route network, and forged the line to the Dutch East Indies had often become national heroes in the process. That colonial communication with the East had been maintained with frail machines, and some twenty-two possible stops were always in readiness along the way for use in case of need. Those potential en-route stops had been pre-provisioned with all manner of support material, and that alone had been a tremendous feat of organization.

Sad to say, the forging of this path to the East in the pre-war years had taken its toll in bent and broken wings. On this, and on other routes, no fewer than seven Fokker and five Douglas aircraft had fallen to the whims of nature or to the inadequacies of man. Perhaps the most notable had been the demise of the "Uiver" (a DC-2 which won the Melbourne race in 1934) at Rutbah Wells near the Syrian/Iraq border.

While technology draws ahead

It was not long before aircraft factories started rolling out new civilian planes to replace the military ones produced in thousands during the war years. These new craft included the very latest technical advances and were designed to carry passengers in comfort over increasingly long distances. Their greater size and weight led to the introduction of hydraulically powered flight controls, a rarity in wartime aircraft. Another fairly novel feature was the introduction of cabin pressurization which gave them the ability to fly (almost) above the weather. We could then fly without oxygen masks, and those then finally became items of emergency equipment with built-in microphones. Aircraft engines steadily increased in size and power output, as did the propellers which they turned but as the larger engines were thirstier the capacity of the fuel tanks had to be increased.

All these advances were quite rapid and continuous, and posed difficulties for the servicing and maintenance staff. On-the-job training was often the only way to cope with the demands made on them. To further undermine their efforts was the growing prominence of "Murphy's Law" – if it can be done wrong, it will be. The "boffins" in the design offices had not yet fully realized that there must only be one way of inter-connecting two components, whether they be by pipes, wires or chains. It was thus almost inevitable that the connections of flight controls became occasionally reversed so that the surfaces moved in the wrong direction, that the flight instruments provided erroneous readings, or that propellers failed to "feather" on demand ....a propeller was "feathered" by turning its blades (hydraulically or electrically) edgewise to the air-stream, thus minimizing aerodynamic drag when its engine had stopped.

...........................and I join the race

My own enthusiasm to join this maelstrom of aerial activity was firmly entrenched but my extended RAF service (voluntary) left me at a disadvantage. The "no vacancy for pilots" signs had already gone up by the time I was free. My acceptance by KLM seemed, at the time, a godsend but perhaps only a temporary solution – it was impossible to realize that a life-long career was about to commence.

As so often happens in life, one tends to become cocooned in one's immediate surroundings, and remain blissfully unaware of the broader picture. I was not then aware, for example, of the long history of the Company or of the various post-war tragedies that had already befallen it. I was also in blissful ignorance of the many other aviation tragedies that had occurred around the world since they received scant notice in the London newspapers – civil aviation was to be a new beginning devoid of shot and shell.

As I settled down in my new working environment, however, a fresh sense of involvement, and loyalty began to develop. I became very much aware of our tragedies when they occurred, and their impact was keenly felt. In their aftermath a steely resolution was felt among the personnel, and the unshakeable ambitions of Dr. Plesman seemed to filter down the ranks. To many of us, however, these tragic events merely served to show that there was really little difference between military and civil flying – some just did not come back. Such feelings lasted many years.

From the outline of circumstances given above I have developed my own thoughts and ideas concerning what actually took place in those turbulent years. I have tried to avoid the influence of hindsight but that is not always possible: it is certainly unlikely that all will agree on some of the tentative conclusions that I have drawn.

The post-war scenario

..............................collecting aircraft and recruiting crews

The immediate post-war years saw a wide variety of companies taking to the skies after acquiring aircraft, surplus to military requirements, at knock-down prices. Many were somewhat battered relics well beyond their best sell-by date but patched and polished to represent saleable goods. There was a profusion of Dakotas and Skymasters which could rapidly be converted for civil use. The paratroopers' canvas seating along the fuselage walls was easily removed as was the overhead static line to which their parachute release cords had been clipped.

KLM maintained a wary distance from this unseemly scramble preferring whenever possible to obtain factory-fresh examples of aircraft which had only been intended for military use. Captain Parmentier had been an early visitor to the American aircraft factories. Carrying a shopping list from Dr. Plesman he made a close study of what machines were immediately available.

Other major airline companies sought different solutions; BOAC, for example, had late model Lancaster bombers converted for civil use naming them Lancastrians. These were not very popular with their passengers who had to clamber over an internal main wing spar to reach their rather uncomfortable seats .... not yet the "world's favourite" airline!

Plenty of flight and ground crews were available to turn entrepreneurial dreams into reality. A Chief Pilot and senior Technician were easily acquired, and they quickly recruited additional personnel on an "old boy" basis from their former RAF squadrons.

An abundance of fitters (engine specialists), riggers (flight control/system specialists) and electricians were also available to swell the ranks of newly formed companies, though their expertise tended to belong to a bygone era; a fuselage with metal skinning was rather different from one with a fabric cover, and pressure bulkheads in the fuselage were something else again!

Recruitment KLM fashion

KLM followed a more measured and deliberate approach in their recruitment of pilots. A formal interview was followed by a medical examination, and then by a flight test, before an applicant received an offer of employment. It was only slowly, however, that the new recruit became aware of the unique history of KLM, and of its current phase of rebirth and renewal.

The old guard of pilots, who had spanned much of the globe pre-war, were beginning to drift away, their ranks thinned by accidents and advancing years. The new guard, destined to replace them, had first to be carefully assessed, and trained to succeed them. During this process of succession more modern and challenging equipment was being introduced which inevitably resulted in a great deal of "on-the-job" training.

...............................and the changing of the guard

In the post war years the number of stops en-route to the East decreased dramatically, and the old skills were overshadowed by new demands. Aircraft size, weight and speed were substantially increased, and their cockpits displayed a dazzling array of new dials and switches. Perhaps of even greater significance was a virtual doubling of approach and landing speeds – a quantum leap for some of the old guard.

While many of the old guard had to rapidly adjust to new conditions the new guard was already familiar with many of them. Most were veterans of wartime flying which had, by its very nature, demanded steadily increasing technology. They were thus a technical jump ahead but still waiting in the wings to take centre stage.

Inevitably, some of the new guard received early promotion but most played a very supportive role to the pioneers, particularly in their navigational needs. This supportive role was probably most evident in the Mauritius-Batavia flights of 1948/49 where familiarity with long range navigation was so essential.

The KLM cockpit, and probably that of other major airlines had thus become a meeting place of two generations. Many captains of pre-war vintage, some of whom had flown the wartime Bristol-Lisbon line or trans-Atlantic delivery flights, were now seated side by side with a much younger generation

Constellation cockpit, checklist reading

(photo source unknown)

of national and non-national pilots. I am not personally aware that these circumstances were the source of any conflict but rather that they led to the development of a degree of respect by both parties, and in some cases this led to an eager delegation of duties to younger colleagues.

With the new guard came a different approach to aviation... they had acquired a mindset as a result of their previous experiences, a mindset that perhaps tended to delay progress. We are the survivors, they said, we need no more rules or regulations – rudimentary precautions will surely suffice. Those of the old guard who had also seen wartime service were not immune to this phenomena.

Flight safety in those days was principally a matter of getting an aircraft safely up and safely down again. What happened in between these events received little attention; certainly the mindset that then existed was little disturbed. The challenge of resurrecting Phoenix was real, and was resolutely met by old guard and new alike. A respected national flag was flown from the cockpit windows of all departing, and arriving KLM aircraft, and passengers were presented with small gifts as reminders of their presence on a Dutch aircraft, ... by "Flying Dutchman" was the only way to travel!

Most memories will slowly fade as circumstances change, and so it was with this mindset that had been imperceptibly acquired.

Looking at tattered reputations

The rush for dominance in the post war skies brought an unseemly number of disasters in its wake, and KLM was certainly no stranger to the misfortunes that befell the world of civil aviation. This was an era that lacked the advantages of "black-boxes" (Flight recorders) and CVR's (Cockpit Voice Recorders) to assist in determining the reasons for a crash. Investigations were mainly limited to forming assumptions, and blame would be related to mechanical faults, to weather conditions or to pilot error or even to a mixture of all these possible factors.

Instances of CFIT (Controlled Flight into Terrain) were not unusual, neither were other forms of pilot error. The fact that a live pilot was seldom around, and thus unable to defend his actions was probably rather convenient. Very often, more effort was expended on finding someone or something to blame, rather than in seeking real causes, and taking proper steps towards preventing their repetition.

It was fortunate that terrorist activities had not yet surfaced, activities which were to hold the world to ransom, and bedevil many investigations in future years. Such activities were also to have a profound effect on all aspects of travel from a passenger's point of view.

.............................and at some of the KLM realities

Between 1946 and 1961 some eighteen KLM aircraft were badly damaged or destroyed in crashes.

In 1946 two Dakotas were lost, and yet another in 1947. This 1947 event (at Copenhagen, Denmark) received more attention than most since a famous singer was one of the casualties, as were members of the Danish royal family, and the circumstances of the crash were rather unusual.

The pilot had been Captain Gerrit Geysendorffer*, a well known figure in Holland since he had been one of KLM's very first pilots. The laden aircraft had left the ramp among waving crowds, taxied to the take-off runway, and without pause commenced its take-off run. Very shortly after lift-off it returned abruptly to earth creating a thunderous explosion. The subsequent investigation found that the external control locks on the elevators had not been removed; in the RAF these same locks had had red flags attached but whether KLM followed the same practice I cannot remember. It was very evident, however, that the pilots had not carried out a "full and free" movement of the flight controls, and that the ground crew had also grossly neglected their duties.

> *In 1972 Capt. Geysendorffer had flown the American millionaire, van Lear Black, on KLM's first intercontinental charter flight. After various stops in Europe, the flight continued to Batavia in the Dutch East Indies.*

>   ....*explosions aloft!!!!*

Turning away, for a moment, from the troubles beginning to beset KLM, mysterious events were also occurring elsewhere in the world, and some felt (with hindsight) that they were the precursors of later happenings.

In 1947 British South American Airways (BSAA) started taking delivery of Avro Tudors, an aircraft designed by Roy Chadwick of Lancaster bomber fame. The Tudor was Britain's first pressurized airliner, and thus a very late rival to Lockheed and Douglas aircraft. The fact that it was also a giant "tail-dragger" (an aircraft with a tail wheel) tended to emphasis the lateness of its appearance on the aviation scene, since nosewheels were now the fashion.

Before the year was out, two of these Tudor aircraft had silently disappeared from the skies over the South Atlantic – total silence, total mystery, and total lack of any wreckage. According to a contemporary newspaper report the be-ribboned, and highly experienced flight crews (ex-RAF) had displayed a nonchalant "piece of cake, old boy" attitude to their long-distance flights. Had Murphy's Law been an uninvited passenger?...after all, an earlier test flight had been compromised by the incorrect connection of aileron controls. Many theories were advanced in an attempt to explain the mysteries but all were discounted through lack of evidence. Whether or not the theory of explosive decompression was explored I am not sure.

A virtually untried pressurized fuselage was involved, and the insidious nature of metal fatigue was still awaiting discovery in the later Comet years. I cannot recall that KLM crews were ever trained in decompression (non-catastrophic) procedures on the DC-6 or Constellation aircraft of that era, and it is thus unlikely that the Tudor crews were either. We certainly had no "quick-don" oxygen masks available, probably because our cruise altitudes were more modest than those used in the later jets, and a decompression would thus have been less severe. However, the various wires and cable runs to the flight controls etc. would have been in more vulnerable positions than those in more advanced aircraft designs, and thus more exposed to even modest damage.

Is it possible to make a link between the Tudors and the equally mysterious demise of a KLM Constellation in the Adriatic Sea near Bari (Southern Italy) in 1949? That tragic event had also been characterized by complete radio silence, though sounds of a possible explosion had been heard from the shore, and burning debris was seen falling from the skies. The whole affair, as with the Tudors, was also the subject of rumours which included the likelihood of an autopilot malfunction. Provided that a pilot's seat was occupied, however, little credence can be given to an irreversible autopilot malfunction.

The fact that the KLM Constellation must have undergone a considerable number of pressurization cycles during its life, and the newer Tudors very few is an unaccountable feature. It is possible that an age related factor versus a first attempt product should be considered.

..............................or high ground ahead!

In 1948 two outstanding cases of CFIT (Controlled Flight into Terrain) occurred which shocked the aviation community. A BSAA Lancastrian abruptly disappeared over the Andes in South America and a KLM Constellation collided with high tension wires at Prestwick, Scotland. From a detailed reconstruction of the Lancastrian's flight path it was calculated that the pilot had descended too early into headwinds much stronger than forecast. This calculation was confirmed over fifty years later by the accidental discovery of the wreckage close to a mountain top together with the remains of the casualties.

The KLM Constellation had been flown by Capt. Parmentier, the Company's most senior pilot, who was intending to make a refuelling stop at Prestwick before continuing to New York. Actual weather conditions at Prestwick were marginal for landing with strong winds, low clouds and poor visibility. The rather rapidly changing weather conditions were a great deal worse than the forecast given to the departing crew at Schiphol, and this deterioration had been broadcast from Prestwick on a radio frequency not being used by the inbound aircraft. The captain was undoubtedly surprised by the actual conditions, and requested a last minute change of the designated landing runway. This resulted in the aircraft being too low to safely complete re-alignment for its approach. Rising ground and high tension wires on a nearby hill were both struck while flying in cloud, and all on board perished in the subsequent crash. Holland was stunned by this disaster as was Dr. Plesman who had lost not only his most senior pilot but also his Head of Engineering (Henk Veenendal) who had been travelling as a passenger.

These two events quite evidently had elements of pilot error in their destiny but it is also possible that other significant factors were involved. The unfortunate pilots, however, were not around to offer further explanations. It is of interest to note that Capt. Parmentier had actually required that warnings be published concerning the high tension wires. Their location, height and position were thus shown on the general information charts for the airfield but not on the actual runway approach charts.

Although all aspects of the tragedy were carefully examined nothing was found that could avoid a conclusion being reached of poor judgment by the captain, who had been thoroughly familiar with the airfield and its surrounds. KLM was, however, severely criticized for the poor quality of its various maps and charts of the Prestwick area. One of them was even a reproduction of an old and inaccurate USAF map.

..............................and yet more KLM fatalities

In 1949 the Dutch newspapers were again compelled to use black borders around their front pages. It was perhaps fortunate that the frenetic media coverage of disasters that developed in later years had not yet reached maturity. The intrusive antics of television crews and newspaper reporters were still to come.

In June 1949 a KLM Constellation ("Roermond") homeward bound from the Far East, under the command of Capt. Hans Plesman, crashed into the Adriatic Sea near Bari. Only very limited wreckage, and remains were recovered from the sea surface. Deep water recovery first became a possibility when hunting for the de Havilland Comet five years later. Investigation concluded, without any supporting evidence, that some mishap had happened at cruise altitude leading to an uncontrollable dive, during which the aircraft broke up. There was much unconfirmed suspicion that the autopilot had suddenly malfunctioned, which prompted the question of whether the pilots had been wearing their seat-belts. If not, they could have been thrown from their seats, and been unable to recover. The possibility of an explosive decompression was not apparently addressed.

Among the many rumours that arose following the Bari crash was one that suggested there had been no pilot actually in the cockpit at the time of the suspected autopilot malfunction. From personal experience this was quite a distinct possibility.

On long flights, a card game might develop among the off-duty crew in the rest area which could be a considerable distraction to the navigator, particularly when trying to balance on a stool under the astro dome. Noisy arguments, a crew change, a new course to calculate, and deliver up front, then pushing past an excitable "crowd", past the F/E station, and finding the pilots' seats empty!! …quickly I slip into a seat, intending to hold the fort until my course change can be implemented…and then suddenly, "Hello Orange…I was just about to take over, back to your stars"! As I vacated the pilot's seat I was careful to avoid knocking the autopilot controller with my knee. This control was located in an extremely vulnerable position on the rear of the central pedestal.

Capt. Plesman was the second of Dr. Plesman's three sons to die in the air. His eldest son had been shot down over St. Omer (France) while serving with the RAF during the war. Two former RAF pilots were also coincidently among the crew who died at Bari.

In July 1949 the hand of fate struck once more. Another KLM Constellation ("Franeker") also homeward bound from the Far East crashed on approach to Bombay (now Mumbai in India). In command was Capt. Chris v.d. Vaart, with whom I had travelled to Shanghai, and eventually returned home via Sharjah. There was ample wreckage for examination but no mechanical failure was found that could excuse the aircraft being in the wrong place at the wrong time. Actual reported weather conditions suggested that an attempt at landing was evidence of poor judgment.

KLM had no published weather minima for the airport (weather conditions below which a pilot should not attempt a landing) since Bombay was not in the normal route network, and thus also unfamiliar to its pilots. The actual weather conditions at the time of the crash were well below those used by other international airlines that regularly used the airport, and they were even below those of Air India whose crews were based there.

The aftermath of the Bombay crash was considerable, and the news and comments spread far beyond the shores of stunned Holland. On board the "Franeker" had been an influential party of leading journalists and reporters from the U.S.A. As guests of the Dutch Government they had completed an extensive tour of the Dutch East Indies. It had been hoped that they would be so favourably impressed by the methods of Dutch colonial rule that their reports would sway international opinion away from the growing clamour for freedom. Sadly these hopes were frustrated, and were replaced by questions concerning the safety of KLM.

Perhaps there was evidence of a "mindset" in these two particular crashes. Both captains were highly experienced on the aircraft, and on the routes, and both had had wartime experience. It also was a fact of life at that time that a stigma was attached to a diversion caused by weather. A pilot worth his salt should be able to land safely in the most atrocious conditions, regardless of the availability of any approach aids. Press on regardless was not an uncommon attitude, and very junior crew members seldom had all the facts on which to reasonably question a senior's decision. There was also an impenetrable language barrier on some occasions. This was by no means deliberate but it could result in a non-national pilot being left out of the loop during hurried inter-crew communications.

The start of a new decade in KLM's troubled years

...........................first the North Sea

As 1950 dawned there was a hope for better things, and that the past troubles were firmly behind us. Unfortunately, this was not to be, and February saw the silent disappearance of a KLM Dakota into the North Sea. It was outbound to London for return as a night freighter, and vanished some forty miles off the Dutch coast without any indication of trouble. Presumably, it would just about have reached a cruising altitude of around six thousand feet so perhaps the change in power setting and in-flight altitude could have triggered off some untoward event. It was extremely difficult to formulate a convincing reason for the disaster, and I have no recollection of any information being made generally available. The aircraft involved was a trusted and reliable workhorse, and had none of the complications inherent to pressurized fuselages. Were the fingers of Murphy's Law involved or had a sudden structural failure occurred which resulted in complete, and sudden loss of control, we shall never know.

I had not personally known the pilot (Alec Legg) or any of the unfortunate crew, and can recall only a very brief sense of shock, and of deep curiosity. In those days there were no Crew Bulletins published by the Company that analysed incidents/accidents for the benefit of other crews, at least I cannot remember any. In later years we constantly looked for lessons which could be passed along.

...........................then Frankfurt

After a period of freedom from untoward events, 1952 saw the crash of a KLM DC-6 at Frankfurt with forty-four fatalities. The aircraft had been homeward bound from South Africa, and was making an intermediate stoop at Frankfurt (Germany). After acknowledging clearance for descent and approach nothing more was heard from the aircraft. Reports of burning wreckage in a nearby forest finally alerted rescue services. Despite long and thorough investigation no reason for the sad accident was ever discovered. Whether they were following a false radio beam signal or whether there had been a mechanical failure remained a complete mystery.

Convair 240 (photo source unknown)

Convair 240

..............................followed by Bangkok

Only a day after the Frankfurt crash a Constellation was written off at Bangkok (Thailand) after a propeller separated from an engine, and fire broke out. Fortunately there were no casualties amongst the forty-four people on-board, despite part of the main gear collapsing on landing. It was remarkable that such a successful evacuation could be completed without inflatable slides being available – they had not yet been invented.

..............................a forced landing in the desert

In January 1953 a serious incident of pilot misjudgment, leading to a shortage of fuel, opened yet another eventful year. A KLM Skymaster (C-54) en-route from Rome to Basra arrived in the vicinity of the airport to find that the visibility was below the allowable minima for landing, as was also the visibility at the designated alternate airfield at Baghdad. The captain then attempted a diversion to Dhahran (Saudi Arabia) but ran out of fuel before the airport could be reached. A forced landing in the desert was the sole option, and this was successfully carried out. There were, remarkably, no casualties amongst the sixty-six people on board but the aircraft was substantially damaged.

..............................a Schiphol crash

In May 1953 the toll of tragic statistics underwent further growth when a Convair 240 crashed near Schiphol. Fortunately there were no on-board fatalities but two children were struck and killed on the ground. The event soon disappeared from public view as investigative reporting was not yet in fashion, and it only remained a concern for those who had been directly involved. I later came to know the pilot involved, Capt. Frank Hawkins, extremely well but I never ventured to question him about that accident. He and I were closely involved in the acceptance programme of the Lockheed Electra. Frank went on to become internationally known as KLM's acknowledged expert on cockpit layout design, and all operational matters appertaining to flight safety.

..............................again the North Sea

In August 1954 a KLM DC-6 inbound to Schiphol was seen from the coast of Holland descending slowly into the sea. Although an earlier acknowledgment of a descent clearance had been made there had been no message from the aircraft to indicate that any problem existed. It would appear that an autopilot descent had not, for some unfathomable reason, been overruled by the crew. Again it was a case of trying to solve a puzzle without clues. The most likely solution was that the crew had slowly been overcome by fumes from the cockpit heater, a fuel fed device with an ignition igniter operated from the cockpit. The heater was probably located somewhere overhead behind the cockpit lining, as I seem to remember being able to hear it come to life.

There is also a vague memory that all such heaters in the DC-4 and the DC-6 were rendered inoperative for a period of time, no doubt a maintenance follow-up for inspection and control.

The captain of the DC-6 had been a well respected American flight instructor (Chuck Harmon) on the type, and was a familiar figure at the Schiphol coffee shop accompanied by his current students. He was always immediately recognizable by the very broad brimmed hat that he constantly wore.

I recall going to his funeral, and being surprised by the number of senior pilots who attended, no doubt a last farewell from many of his students.

............................the mud flats of the Severn estuary near Bristol.

In researching a replacement for their Constellation aircraft KLM`s attention was turned to the Bristol Britannia.The origins of the Britannia lay in the Brabazon Commitee which was formed during the war to propose future civil airliners. The Britannia, in contrast to the Avro Tudor, was a nose-wheel steering aircraft, and presented a very appealing appearance. It was fully pressurized, but without fully powered flight controls. Its initial history, however, was troublesome in the extreme. Early test flights encountered problems with balancing of the flight controls, followed by an aircraft rolling on its back as a result of a flap malfunction. Too early an Introduction into BOAC service resulted in a need for some 50 engine changes within a matter of months, and then there arose an engine icing problem demanding solution. Despite all these early troubles it finally achieved great success, and its turbo-prop engines earned it the nickname of the "Whispering Giant".

In early 1954 KLM sent a team to Bristol to evaluate the aircraft, and to fly in the second production model. Among those sent was, I believe, Capt. George Malouin whom I was to meet years later during the B-747 project.The captain of the test flight was Bill Pegg, Bristol`s senior test pilot. Shortly after take off an engine failure occured, which resulted in a severe engine fire. Bill Pegg attempted to return to Filton, the departure airfield, but the fire became so severe that he was forced to pancake the aircraft onto the River Severn mudflats. This he managed extremely successfully with no casualties resulting from the impact. A successful evacuation followed but the aircraft was overwhelmed by the incoming tide, and only the faulty engine eventually recovered.

KLM's interest in the Britannia ended rather abruptly, as had its interest in in the B-307 many years previously.

............................the mudflats of the Shannon Estuary, Ireland

September 1954 produced a news bonanza for the Dutch newspapers, while the rest of the world had their attention firmly fixed on the mysteries surrounding the de Havilland Comet. Adrian Viruly, partner and then husband to the well know Dutch actress Mary Dresselyhuys, writer and reporter on aviation matters, and KLM's Chief Pilot on the North Atlantic, had pancaked his Super Constellation onto the mudflats of the Shannon estuary shortly after take-off from the airport of Foynes, destination had been New York.

Although many of those on-board survived the actual crash, most were subsequently overcome by fumes in the cabin from the ruptured fuel tanks. One crew member was able to make a long, and difficult journey across the mudflats to seek help but it then took a long time to reach the location of the crash due to the nature of the terrain.

The Irish Board of Enquiry subsequently severely criticized Commodore Viruly for his handling of the aircraft, particularly since there was a possibility that one main gear wheel had failed to completely retract. It appeared that wing flap retraction, and the setting of climb power on the engines had taken place before a proper climb attitude at the correct speed had been established. It was concluded that a lack of attention to the aircraft's behaviour, and to the flight instruments had led to an undetected flat descent onto the mud banks.

Commodore Viruly refused to accept the findings of the Board, and retired the following year at the mandatory age of fifty. Whether he ever flew again for KLM after the accident I have no idea. Although I knew the British co-pilot I never asked for his version of events, since neither I nor others were surprised at the findings of the Board.

..............................and the island of Biak (Indonesia)

In July 1957 fifty-eight people died when a KLM Super-Constellation descended into the sea near Mokmer Airport (Biak) shortly after a night take-off in fine weather conditions. Once airborne, the captain requested that the runway lights be kept on, and received permission for a low fly-past from the Control Tower. At low altitude a turn back towards the airfield was commenced but the aircraft lost height during the turn, and struck the sea breaking up on impact. Although the investigation was unable to pinpoint any cause for this occurrence, other than a suspicion of some mechanical failure, it was generally felt that the pilot had been at fault.

> *Low altitude positioning at night using only runway lights for reference is a highly dangerous manoeuvre, and very prone to misjudgment. It is essentially an instrument flight manoeuvre flown by one pilot while the other watches for visual clues.*

..............................the North Atlantic about 100 miles west of Shannon

In August 1957 a westbound Super-Constellation out of Shannon for Newfoundland disappeared from the skies over the ocean, with ninety-nine people on board. Pieces of wreckage were later found but nothing which was of help to the investigation. It was ultimately concluded that an uncontrollable propeller over-speed had occurred leading to a rapidly deteriorating flight situation which the crew would have been unable to control or correct.

Looking back over those troubled years

Seen from the standpoint of the 21st century, the unseemly toll of tragedies experienced by KLM in this briefly reviewed decade, almost defy belief. Today's media intrusion, passenger claims and insurance factors would have driven the Company out of business. Suffice to say that KLM was not alone in this arena where aviation technology was advancing faster than its prime users, the flight crews. It is also quite remarkable that this particular decade stands in complete isolation, if one considers the following decade (of the 60's) when only two serious accidents become evident and in the 70's only one.

There is little doubt that other airline companies had also acquired crews with a mindset developed from wartime flying, so perhaps there was another factor in a Dutch airline which might have a bearing on their many accidents. In speculating on this problem, perhaps the ingrained nature of some of the persons involved should be considered.

..............................did, perhaps, national characteristics play a part
– did a degree of self certainty exist in thought and action?

Each nation has perceived characteristics, which do not necessarily apply to each individual member of that nation. The Dutch are regarded as a very forthright, and outspoken people with a tendency to follow their own line of thought (and action), rather than listen carefully to other opinions. In this connection there is a possible thread of culpability that weaves among several of the crashes in those troubled years. After all, there were frequently very senior KLM captains involved who had a wealth of operating experience in their aircraft but were perhaps prone to making their own decisions, rather than making them in co-operation with their juniors. Training in crew management was still many many years away, and it would have been almost impossible to apply it in cockpits so greatly divided by age and experience.

.............................was pilot qualification on several different aircraft a significant factor?

Pilots of later years sometimes expressed surprise that we flew several different types of aircraft on a routine basis but that was quite an acceptable factor in our lives. In my own case, I was frequently flying four different types, some as captain, and some as co-pilot but they were all piston engined aircraft with inherently similar characteristics. Furthermore, there were no proficiency checks, and we had a F/E as our resident troubleshooter for technical problems.

The exception to the rule of similarity was the Dakota. It only had two engines, and it was also the last of our "tail-draggers", and thus demanded a certain respect. If, for example, the tail wheel was not straight and locked for take-off, trouble could rapidly arise. Cockpit flight instrumentation for the Dakota was not disturbingly different from that on the Constellation, the DC-4 or the DC-6. A few minutes in a "new" cockpit was sufficient to gain essential familiarity. A much easier task than swapping one of today's mobile telephones for a new one! A minimum three man flight crew was also common to all aircraft, and mutual support was thus readily available.

How many of the very senior captains actually flew more than one type of aircraft I am not too sure, probably not very many. It is certainly my firm impression, however, that captains like Parmentier (Prestwick crash) never did. He had too many office duties to permit involvement in aircraft other than the Constellation.

I can certainly recall seeing some of the senior pilots being assigned to the Convair 240 during its introductory period: the fact that it was regarded as something of a "hot ship" in comparison to the Connie or Douglas aircraft made this seem quite an unbelievable situation to us (the juniors).

There is no evidence to suggest, however, that this multiple aircraft qualification played any role in the crashes that have been briefly reviewed in this chapter. In each of those crashes the captain was well qualified on the aircraft being flown, and the real causes must thus be sought elsewhere.

.............................unavoidable deficiencies in training

Most piston engined aircraft had rather similar handling characteristics, and the modest differences in size or weight made surprisingly little difference to the pilot at the controls. The loss of an engine at take-off thrust on a Dakota had its own unique problems but on the four engined aircraft the control requirements were basically identical, even with an outboard engine failure.

It was only when very much more powerful engines came to be installed that control reactions required by the pilot started to change. The Super-Constellation, for example, demanded a more aggressive control response from the pilot, when dealing with an outboard engine failure than had the original Constellation L-049. The thrust of each individual engine had increased by 500 horse power, demanding a slight increase of rudder area in construction in order to assist in the pilot's handling of asymmetric situations.

Aircraft familiarization was, however, only one aspect of continually expanding horizons. Various ground-based radio beacons and beams were becoming more common, as were the growing tentacles of Air Traffic Control (ATC), and their need for constant radio contact with the aircraft. Fancy free flights (to visit fishing friends, for example) had gone forever! The whims of individual captains to indulge in unscheduled night stops was also a thing of the past.

.............................engine failures on take-off

Training a pilot to handle an engine failure on take-off was a problem that defied proper solution until flight simulators became available in later years. In earlier days, an engine would actually be stopped by the instructor at a suitably critical moment but this action was irreversible, and led to unnecessary accidents.

To minimize risk on training flights a simulated engine failure procedure was then introduced. The instructor would create a zero thrust condition by simply retarding an engine power lever. This tended to be rather unrealistic, since it was possible for an instructor to match a student's ability to control the developing asymmetric condition by the speed at which he retarded the power lever. I had actually seen this happen when very senior pilots were involved, so my faith in the system was not too great. A further unrealistic feature in this training procedure was also the fact that with a true engine failure the loss of thrust could be very rapid, if not instantaneous. Not something that could be properly duplicated.

.............................the uncertainties of low flight

Airfields are seldom built at ideal locations from the pilot's point of view. The approach to them can be over high terrain, even mountains, over featureless water or desert surfaces or over heavily populated areas. In the developing years there was also a severe lack of guidance available to the pilot which enabled him to easily find them or, having found them, to locate the runway for landing.

Low flying in the (hoped for) vicinity of the airfield, particularly in unfavourable weather conditions or when no distinguishing features were available for orientation, was not always a successful venture. No training could be devised to remedy this situation other than a requirement to adhere strictly to laid down weather minima. If needed these were published for the airfield in question.

A low altitude search for an airfield or runway at night............

over featureless terrain (e.g. desert) or over water............

in clear weather or in-and-out of cloud............

with the pilot visually searching for guidance............

Is always a disaster waiting to happen!

In such circumstances it is almost inevitable that the aircraft will slowly descend even without an inadvertent slight forward pressure on the control column. The pilot is desperately looking out for visual clues, leaning forwards to the window as he does so. His instruments will have become neglected. If he sees something then he calls for his colleagues to see it as well ....

I find it impossible to overlook these conditions when pondering over many of our crashes, and those of other airlines. There are very strong elements of these hazardous circumstances which relate to Prestwick, to Bombay, to Biak and to Cairo (Lockheed Electra) in 1961*. Crew management in those days was not, unfortunately, a common subject for discussion nor was the proper delegation of crew duties. Delegation could only really occur when both pilots had an equality of experience which was mutually accepted.

*The 1961 Electra crash at Cairo is reviewed in the chapter "My Last Propellers"

To fly safely in the conditions outlined it would be essential that one pilot was primarily on instruments while the other visually searched for the necessary clues as to location. If an "altitude hold" mode of the autopilot was available then its use should also be considered. In some circumstances it could be possible that only one pilot was able to see the airfield/runway lights because they were on "his" side of the aircraft. Instrument or visual duties would then need appropriate amendment.

The role of crew training

Another factor in this scenario was undoubtedly the nature and quality of actual crew training that was taking place. Ground school classes were in place to familiarize the crews with the mechanical features of any new aircraft. In the early days these tended to be somewhat slim in content but gradually developed into a format that became excessive from the pilots' point of view, leading eventually into lesson plans based on a "need-to-know" requirement.

Ground school was followed by flight training on the aircraft, which was little more than becoming familiar with any new characteristics in take-off and landing. Instrument approaches to landing could be practiced "blind" by covering the student's window with a convenient map or tray. The fact that the instructor's outside vision was then half obscured seemed of little consequence.

Other than a simulated engine failure on take-off, or an instrument failure during an approach, no exposure to emergency conditions could reasonably be given. Further familiarity with the aircraft was then gained through some flights en-route under the supervision of an experienced captain. Whether that captain actually knew anything more about the aircraft than his "student" was often debatable. In between these adventures there would be some instrument training refresher sessions in the Link Trainer.

Instrument Flight Training

.............................on bellows and things!

The Link Trainer had been in use for many years, and was certainly familiar to former RAF pilots. It had been designed for teaching pilots the essentials of instrument flight, and to train them in the use of the various radio beams which were then available to provide guidance in locating an airfield or runway. It was little more than a large wooden box. Built to resemble a small airplane mounted on a flexible base, it could revolve through 360 degrees, tilt slightly up and down and dip or raise its stubby "wings". These small movements were sufficient to activate the necessary flight instruments in response to the pilot's movement of the control column and rudder pedals.

Link Trainer and instructor's table

A basic instrument panel confronted the pilot so that he could actually "fly" the machine in accordance with an exercise programmed by the instructor. The instructor sat at a large glass covered table watching a "crab" slowly tracing in ink the "flightpath" of the student inside the box. To liven up the exercise he had controls which could introduce a crosswind component or air turbulence. Frequently both were introduced!

Concealed in the "engine room" beneath the dreaded wooden box were four bellows attached to air pumps and pulleys. These were not entirely silent in operation, and seemed to sigh with suppressed excitement or groan in despair, when rough air or turbulence was introduced. Heaves and groans made the "cockpit" quite a distracting environment!

.............................ADF (Automatic Direction Finding)

The most frequent exercises required orientation around a radio station. This sent out signals that caused a needle on a cockpit instrument to point to the station. Known as ADF it was far from being automatic, and seldom easy to use. Radio stations using different frequencies could be positioned along routes as an aid to navigation or at airfields to assist in locating them, and even close to runways to provide some approach guidance. The needle which pointed to them often fluctuated wildly, particularly when thunderstorms were in the vicinity, and considerable inspired guesswork was frequently needed.

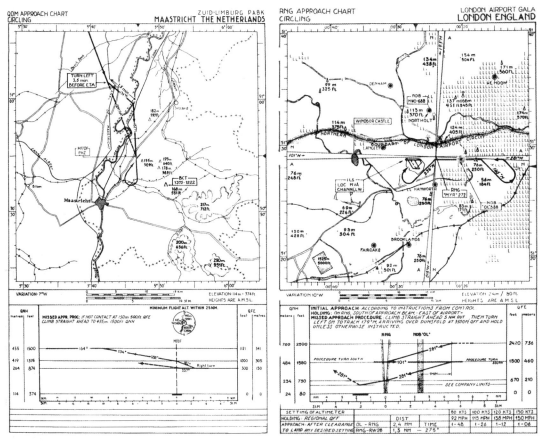

Sample of 1948 Approach charts

.............................SBA (Standard Beam Approach)

Another quite familiar device was the SBA radio beacon. This beacon transmitted a single beam (in theory) aligned with a runway in order to provide final approach guidance. The signal, in this case, was entirely aural in the pilot's headphones. When "on the beam" centre line a steady buzz would be heard, deviating to left of beam would produce a Morse code signal for the letter "A", while deviating to the right of beam would produce the letter "N". These signals were often far from being clear cut, and a sort of corkscrew flight path along the centre line was a fairly common result, the corkscrew becoming smaller as one closed in to the transmitting station.

.............................surviving the Radio Range

A more refined and confusing form of SBA was the Radio Range. This transmitted four separate beams at right angles to each other, and was intended to provide an easy means of locating the transmitting station. In practice, it produced the most complex of all exercises in orientation. The Link Trainer would be positioned at an unknown point in any of the four "sectors" between the beams and then the student had to first discover which "sector" he was in, before flying in the right direction to overhead the transmitter. Overhead the transmitter one entered a brief "cone of silence", something that I don't recall ever finding! An earful of "dots" and "dashes" combined with turbulence and crosswind soon paralysed one's will to live!

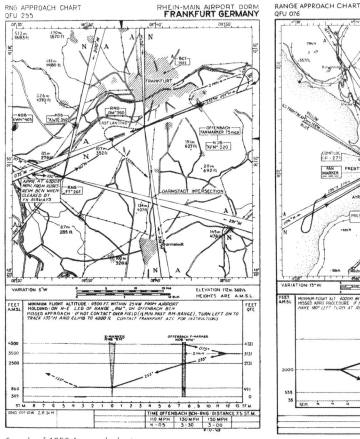
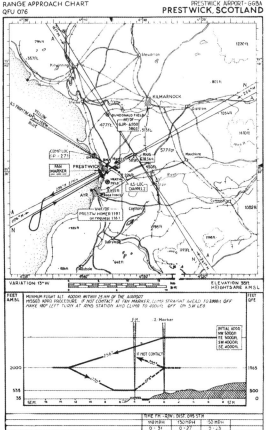

Sample of 1950 Approach charts

.... saved by the ILS (instrument landing system)

A comparatively modern radio device for that era was the introduction of the ILS. A much improved development of that device remains with us today, so improved that it now provides essential guidance for both manual approaches, and fully automatic approaches and landings.

Two radio beams were simultaneously transmitted from the runway in use, which then activated two needles on a cockpit instrument dial. One needle was used to show the pilot whether he was left or right of centre line to the runway, and the other would show whether he was above or below the correct descent path to the runway. For the pilot it thus became a (fairly simple) matter of carefully adjusting his flight path, so as to keep the needles in a central position on the dial. With a good ground installation, and a competent pilot the aircraft could be flown down to very low weather minima indeed. As flight instructors in later years we were required to demonstrate an "on centre line" approach down to fifty feet altitude – almost over the runway threshold.

.... end of session!

The Link Trainer arrangement left little room for argument at the post "flight" debriefings. The complete history of the student's "flight" lay clearly marked by the inked-in patterns on the instructor's table, the moving crab had recorded every move made, good, bad or indifferent.

These two hour sessions left one feeling quite exhausted, and sometimes a little chastened. I have no idea how many of the old guard, if any, were scheduled for these training sessions. Capt. Parmentier was an exception in this respect. It was revealed during the inquiry into the Prestwick crash that, since he was an "office" pilot, he paid quite regular visits. I have no recollection of ever seeing any senior pilots around during shift changes, and I find it difficult to imagine that they would have willingly submitted themselves to what could quite easily be a humiliating ordeal. After all, they would think the instructor is nothing more than a uniformed penguin, and is never faced with the difficult decisions that a captain must constantly make.

The accuracy of these different aids, at that time, was always open to question. They could be purchased and installed by skilled factory personnel but they demanded routine maintenance and recalibration at regular intervals. At some airfields it was unlikely that these requirements were fully met, until the system actually went "off the air" or was reported as faulty by a passing pilot.

Approaching the end of the decade

This unseemly litany of errors started to decline very noticeably as we approached the sixties, even to the extent that something was missing! A rude awakening took place in 1961 when two aircraft were lost, but happily these were to prove isolated events, and were followed by a lengthy period of extremely safe, and reliable operation.

We never knew what the reactions of the Board of Directors or of the shareholders had been to these untoward events that had persisted over a full decade. A perusal of the Company archives on this matter would probably be quite illuminating. Nevertheless, a determined investment and purchasing programme was firmly pursued which underpinned a future full of promise.

By the late fifties and early sixties a plenteous supply of new and exciting aircraft were joining the fleet. Among these were the turbine engine Vickers Viscount and Lockheed Electra, and the jet engine Douglas DC-9 and DC-8. In my opinion, however, the most significant acquisition of all was that of the flight simulators. One has only to note the very sudden and dramatic reduction of accidents which then occurred to see the reason, and this was it, a 100% improvement in crew training, and also in maintenance training through their use of "our" simulators.

The Flight Simulator arrives

The arrival of the flight simulator led to the rapid demise of the Link Trainer, and also to its rather primitive form of motion. It took some time before the initial simulators were developed into full flight simulators with freedom of motion in six-axis. That development resulted in incredibly realistic machines which, by the time visual aids were introduced, made the simulator almost indistinguishable in operation from the aircraft which it represented.

The principal advantage of the flight simulator, over every other training device, was that its cockpit truly represented, in every possible detail, the cockpit of the aircraft which it was replacing for the benefit of crew training. Each instrument would faithfully respond to pilot or F/E inputs at their various controls, the tuning-in of radio communications or of radio beacons was identical, as was the required response on the cockpit dials. Every conceivable aircraft malfunction could be programmed into a lesson plan, and the applicable emergency procedures then realistically practiced in complete safety.

Some degree of control loading was also introduced so that the pilot had a sense of "feel" when moving the control column or rudder pedals. Training sessions were scheduled to last for five hours, which included an hour of pre-flight briefing, and another hour after "flight". That left three hours to be endured in the cockpit itself. These three hours would be split between the two pilots, one of whom would be a co-pilot, and the other a captain. Concentration throughout was quite intense, leaving both instructor and students exhausted. This system also introduced another training innovation – both a captain and a co-pilot were trained to almost identical standards of proficiency, a far cry from Connie days!

I personally spent some two thousand hours giving instruction on the various simulators, often assisted by Mr. Sainsbury who had been my chief tormentor on the Link Trainer many years earlier. My simulator experience led me to believe that this was the ultimate pinnacle of efficient "aircraft" instruction, without realizing that it was a mere stepping stone in the ever onward path of future developments.

Postscript

The Link Trainers had first been housed in a humble wooden barracks at Schiphol (East) as had so many other departments that supported flight operations. With the coming of our purpose built office block it moved to more prestigious quarters. Before long, however, redundancy and dismissal became their lot – the flight simulators had arrived!

Centrally located within our office block was the "simulator hall", and my weekly schedule began to read "office/sim. instruction" – a change of venue was, rather too conveniently, just along the corridor. The flight simulators coincided with the arrival of turbine and jet powered aircraft, and became the core of our instructional activity. Even in those days, however, cost saving was an important factor: although the simulators reduced flight time on the aircraft, the cost of their operation also could be significant.

In later years, to reduce the time that a new student needed in the simulator he was first exposed to a "cockpit trainer". This was little more than an open cockpit shell equipped with panels of dummy instruments and controls which faithfully represented (by location) those which would be found in the actual aircraft cockpit. In this device many hours would be spent working through checklists and procedures until complete familiarity was obtained with the location and purpose of every control.

Transition to the real simulator was then made with no waste of valuable time, and the real training could instantly begin. By the time flight training commenced the student was completely familiar with his new aircraft and "circuits and bumps" (take-offs and landings) were the main feature of the flight programme. There then followed a period of route instruction under the watchful eye of a check pilot.

As technology advanced a dedicated Simulator Hall was built next to our office block, and this became home to the very latest developments – the Full Flight Simulators. They sat in their palatial quarters like avaricious dinosaurs awaiting the pleasure of our company. Their "legs" were gleaming pistons supporting their true cockpit cabins high in the air. Freedom of motion in six axis was their forte, and their cockpits were true replicas of the actual aircraft that they represented.

We would approach them along a metal walkway, protected with guard rails, and enter a door leading first into the instructor's station. This was awash with screens and consoles on which the "flight" exercises could be pre-programmed. Moving forward, we entered the true cockpit of our aircraft, everything in its proper place, a replica of exactitude. Settled in our seats with seatbelts fastened, checklists were read, and the engines started. The dinosaur sprang to life, and proceeded to engulf us in many hours of digestive manoeuvres.

To these flight simulators were gradually added "Visual Aids". Through the cockpit windows one could then look out upon the "real" world as it would appear by day or night. This could also be pre-programmed to display a variety of different airfields, enabling one to approach them from different directions, circle around them, or taxy along their runways. As time went on, these visual aids became increasingly realistic, and could be used to acquaint the pilots with unusual or difficult airfields such as New York or Hong Kong.

Things to come – DC8 Flight Simulator (no motion yet)   (photo source unknown)

Visual Aids in the B-747 Simulator   (photo source unknown)

It is perhaps of interest to note that the flight simulators represented the aircraft so closely that it became necessary to send a pilot, and an acceptance team, to the manufacturer's factory. There they would carry out compatibility tests as the product neared completion, and these tests would be repeated after shipping, and re-erection of the simulator at Schiphol.

.... what had the old guard missed!!

Cockpit DC8 Flight Simulator. Mr Sainsbury in foreground.   (photo source unknown)

My Last Propellers

My early days of flying had been behind a single engine, and its wooden or metal propeller. On the ground, forward view was somewhat limited. It was blocked by the engine, and aggravated by the tail down attitude of the aircraft as it rested on its skid or tail wheel. These "tail draggers" demanded constant rudder movement, swinging the nose from left to right in order to see ahead alongside the engine cowling. Tiger Moths, Cornells Harvards, and Hurricanes all had this somewhat difficult characteristic, as did many other types.

When I graduated on to twin engined aircraft – or even four engined one's – this tail down attitude on the ground became much less of a nuisance. One now sat between the engines with a far better view ahead – only the length of the nose immediately in front could somewhat restrict ground visibility. Airspeed Oxfords, Avro Ansons, Dakotas, and Lancasters all provided me with a far better ground view of events in front.

Then, at last, Lockheed produced their Constellations and Electras, and Douglas their DC-4 and DC-6 series of aircraft. These new giants of the air were fitted with four engines, and a steerable nose wheel – one was now truly in a magnificent position on the ground to view the world ahead. A small steering wheel was provided in the cockpit enabling the pilot to steer the aircraft in any direction.

Can you hear me?

Sitting behind or between very noisy propellers and engines for more than twenty years inevitably tended to raise a more personal problem. Our ears had seldom been adequately protected.

In RAF days, close fitting leather helmets with headsets were worn for radio and cockpit communication. After the war nearly all civil airlines discarded the idea of helmets, and issued headsets of rather doubtful quality to their crews. Some airlines (such as BOAC) did issue good standard padded headsets; and they also made it mandatory for all crew communication in the cockpit to be via microphone and head set.

KLM, however, allowed direct (loud!!) voice communication in the cockpit. This resulted in poor quality headsets loosely placed over the head with one ear (the inboard one) always uncovered – one ear was thought sufficient for radio communication, and one ear for cockpit talk. The long term result of this policy was the early onset of tone deafness among many pilots. Interestingly enough, this hearing defect could be seen steadily progressing at our annual medical examinations, but it was brushed aside as being a normal age related factor, and not an environmental one.

.... what would the Health and Safety Inspectors of the EU have made of that scenario?

Changing windows

As I began my last years of propeller driven flight, further very welcome improvements were occurring. In addition to nose wheel steering there was no longer the blur of a propeller disc to slightly distort the forward view, and the mountain tops had moved down to a much more comfortable level. In some aircraft cruise altitudes had increased substantially, and with that increase came pressurization of the aircraft.

Aviation was coming of age, and introducing creature comforts in the process!!!

The Zero Reader

And this coming of age was celebrated by the arrival of yet another new device to assist pilots in precision instrument flying, particularly during final approach to landing. The basic instrument panel had by now become so cluttered with dials that the ILS (Instrument Landing System) indicator was marginally outside his normal scan (of eye) pattern; this was not surprising, since an approach occupied only a small portion of any flight.

To reduce the eye scan pattern, two needles were now placed within the more centrally located AHI (Artificial Horizon Indicator), and these could be retracted when not required. When in use, these two needles used information derived from the ILS transmitters, and so the essential information for an ILS approach was provided on one instrument instead of on two. This new presentation was called the Zero Reader. The AHI which had long been the pilot's most important flight instrument (although it had not been available on the Tiger Moth), had thus suddenly grown in status.

By carefully maintaining these two additional needles within the AHI, in a central position, an ideal approach path to the runway was assured. Since the pilot was now looking at one combined instrument, pitch and roll changes were also immediately apparent. In future years speed, and altitude readings would also appear on the AHI.

.... leading to "Tunnel Vision"

The occasional result of combining different information in one instrument was the development of "tunnel vision" in a pilot. He could become so concentrated on the display within his AHI, that his normal scanning pattern was dangerously reduced; speed and height, for example, tended to receive less than their normal share of attention. The zero reader, being extremely sensitive, could demand an undue amount of pilot concentration. This situation led to the need for checking on a pilot's ability to fly a "raw data" approach – that is, an approach with the zero reader needles switched out of view. As the AHI developed, it included its own direct indications of its localizer and glideslope. These were referred to as "raw data" when the Zero Reader was not in use.

A pilot was expected to be able to fly an ILS approach down to 200 feet on "raw data" alone, and down to 100 feet with the Zero Reader needles in view. These expectations had to be met during training and proficiency checks, but could also be required during an en-route check when a suitable opportunity arose. These exercises were also routinely undertaken in conjunction with an engine failure situation, which in turn could lead to a check on a "go-around" (missed approach) procedure.

Invaded by the sea

In February 1953 I had the doubtful privilege of flying over a country invaded by the sea. The south west of Holland was devastated by floods. In a Dakota, loaded with newspaper reporters, and various officials, we flew several circuits over the stricken area looking for locations where supply drops could most successfully be made.

A combination of unusually high spring tides, and a vicious north westerly storm had resulted in an onslaught by monstrous waves against the protective dykes. In several places the dykes had broken under this battering allowing the sea to pour in across the low lying land.

> *This was a very different scenario from the Nazi created floods which I had seen during Operation Manna in 1945.*

When viewed from above the extent of the disaster became only too clear. Roofs protruding above the water, some with groups of people resignedly awaiting rescue, showed the location of isolated farms. The bodies of drowned cattle drifted aimlessly or were caught in tree tops. Several areas of coastline had almost disappeared. The streets of towns and villages had become canals, alive with a variety of small boats.

We returned to Schiphol in sombre mood, much chastened by what we had seen. In response to this overwhelming natural disaster the expertise of Dutch water engineers was rapidly put to work, old plans were dusted off, and new ones created. The Delta Plan came into being, and tremendous dykes, dams, and controllable weirs gradually made an impregnable barrier against further incursions by the sea.

> *Two of the reporters became useful acquaintances since they represented de Telegraaf and Volkskrent newspapers. At intervals they sent me aviation related photographs, particularly ones connected with KLM.*

Many years later I was able to drive through the area, visit the museum that had been created, and gain a better impression of the impressive magnitude of the task.

Collecting the Connies

In 1954 the newly arrived Super Constellations saw the introduction of the very latest in piston engine technology; the Wright "Cyclone" 18 cylinder turbo-compound engines. These were also to equip the DC-7C'a. The cost of maintenance on those highly complex engines, and their uncertainty in terms of reliability, must have provided an unwelcome financial burden.

Some twenty Super Connies eventually joined the fleet, while the older L-049's and L-749's were gradually found new homes. The ultimate demise of these graceful aircraft coincided with the world-wide introduction of various jet powered aircraft; the resulting collapse of the second-hand market for Connies and their like, led to lines of cocooned aircraft at Schiphol East – a sad sight indeed.

Henry Ford II arrives

The year of 1954 started with a flourish. January saw 120 hrs. logged in Europe, together with a Skymaster trip covering Karachi and Tehran. The following months followed a similar pattern until in June an interesting Dakota charter flight was scheduled. This entailed three weeks with Henry Ford II, his wife, and his aides touring through Europe to inspect his many factories.

The Ford family and their entourage were not only wonderful passengers, but also ensured that their crew was properly looked after. Even to a bottle of "Old Granddad" under the pillow at night stops! A stop in Helsinki allowed time for my first sauna exposure. This was at a country estate with a sauna hut positioned beside a frozen lake. The experience was wonderfully invigorating, but being

Henry Ford's Crew (photo source unknown)

The author with Mr and Mrs H Ford II (photo source unknown)

an icebreaker was not really my ambition in life! A final stop in Biarritz (France) was far more to my liking. Sunshine on beaches adorned with the beauties of nature! But it was finally time for leave taking, and we were each presented with quite an expensive item of jewellery – in my case a gold wrist watch.

Under Wiebe's wing

After the holiday flight I came under the very capable guidance of Capt. Wiebe Zijlstra for training as a Dakota instructor. Very shortly thereafter RH seat training was given on the Convair 240, enabling me to also operate as a route check pilot on that aircraft type. These two promotional events resulted in a very significant reduction in my own actual "hands-on" flying, together with a semi-permanent position in the RH seat. *In later years, fearing a decline in personal performance, I requested route flights for which no "check" activities were required. A request that was seldom honoured!

Wiebe was quite an exceptional instructor: endlessly patient, and with that rather quizzical look when you claimed an understanding, which was perhaps incomplete! In later years he was to be my chief pilot on the Electra fleet – always a wise and understanding counsellor.

> *By tradition the Captain always actually flew the aircraft from the left hand seat. When he assigned PF (pilot flying) duties to his co-pilot, then seat positions would be changed before flight, thus enabling the co-pilot to fly from the LH seat – this naturally gave him something of a captain's "feel"!*
>
> *This was far from an ideal situation as the captain seldom received adequate training in the RH seat. If the need arose for him to take over control he was at a slight disadvantage. A "fixed seat" policy would not arrive until the jets were introduced.*

A European tour guide

The mid-fifties saw a steady build up of my experience throughout Europe in every conceivable form of weather. The cockpits of Dakotas and Convairs became extremely familiar territory as did approaches into fog shrouded airports. On one occasion, over Germany, my Dakota turned into a glider for some ten minutes. We were flying parallel to a line of very black, and threatening clouds keeping in the clear air. Gradually the updraft of air associated with this line squall intensified, and we were actually gliding along at some 7000 feet for about 10 minutes. As the updraft eventually lessened then power was re-applied for level flight.

My logbook shows that the majority of these flights were as an en-route check pilot although fairly regular periods were also spent at Schiphol as a flight instructor. It was very seldom that I could break away from this routine for more adventurous DC-4 flights further afield.

One check flight to Majorca caused me quite some embarrassment. Arriving overhead the airfield, in clear weather, the "student" captain in the LH seat commenced a procedure turn and descent. The intention was to roll out from the turn, on to final approach for the runway at about 1000 ft. We had carefully discussed the necessary timing, and rate of descent required before this procedure was commenced.

Since I was in the right hand seat I was quite unable to see the airfield until the final turn in was completed. We had already received landing clearance, and I was pleased to see the runway lined up ahead of us as we rolled out from the final turn. Straight on in for a good landing, but the terminal building was surely in the wrong place, and what was that soldier doing with a rifle at the end of the runway?

Calling the control tower on the radio brought the question "Where are you?" Belatedly we realized that we had landed on a military airfield just five miles away, and with an identical runway alignment. The soldier put his rifle down, gave us a wave, and we beat a hasty retreat! Soon we were disembarking very puzzled passengers at their correct destination. It was rather unfortunate that among them were several KLM staff passengers. They departed with broad smiles on their faces. When I reported this rather sorry episode at Schiphol, the chief pilot, Capt. Ravenhill, voiced his disapproval in no uncertain manner!

Lunch in Milan

A much sought after flight was one with a morning departure from Schiphol to Milan (Malpensa). A scenic crossing of the Alps, followed by a delicious lunch at a garden style restaurant near the airfield, was a worthwhile day out. This flight did, however, introduce some quite careful calculations with regard to the Alpine passage.

Although the two engined Convair could safely negotiate the Alps under normal circumstances, the failure of an engine during the crossing could produce an unwelcome situation. The cruise altitude required to safely clear the highest ground could not be maintained on one engine. A slow loss of altitude would be inevitable. Using some specially constructed performance charts, it was necessary to pre-determine a safe course of action in the event of an engine failure during the crossing.

Depending on our location at the time of engine failure it was possible to calculate whether the flight could be continued or whether the attempt should be abandoned, and course reversed. Either solution would be accompanied by a slow loss of altitude before leaving the danger zone.

Whether or not these calculations were ever put to the test I have no idea. They certainly did not disturb my lunch of spaghetti Bolognese! With lunch completed, followed by a refreshing swim, we would climb back aboard our Convair, and indulge in a maximum rate climb before dashing across the Alps once more.

How much fuel

Even in propeller days the cost of aviation fuel could be a significant factor in an airline company's budget. The price of petrol at garages along the motorway will vary, and so did the cost of aviation fuel at different airfields.

Ordinarily one would tank sufficient fuel to fly from A to B, together with sufficient reserves to safely reach a diversion airfield. With the increasing need for economical tanking, the minimum fuel for A to B (plus reserve) could, in theory, be increased to a full tank's situation if fuel at B was the more expensive. Since, however, the actual quantity of fuel consumed en-route between A and B would increase as the aircraft became heavier, such a simple solution was seldom practicable. The actual quantity of fuel tanked would have to be balanced against the increased consumption caused by its additional weight.

These calculations were usually made by a Flight Operations officer, and then presented to the pilot with his flight plan. The pilot's decision on economical tanking was final. On many occasions I would refuse it. Usually because I considered that the increased landing weight, which could result, would be inappropriate for a destination with a short runway or one that was contaminated by snow etc. Its additional weight could also reduce my cruise altitude, putting me in the en-route bad weather rather than above it.

Proficiency checks

The years of 1955 through 1957 saw a very solid build up of experience throughout Europe, with seldom less than 100 hours in my logbook each month. Considerable instruction work on both Dakotas and Convairs was also completed. An interesting variation was carrying out "acceptance checks" on new pilot applicants to the Company. As I recall, this was frequently comparing the pilot's performance with that which he was claiming. Some very surprising mis-matches were detected!

It was in these years that the magic word "proficiency check" entered my logbook for the first time. In RAF Transport Command we had had regular in-flight handling checks on a pilot's proficiency. These were conducted by staff pilots, independent of any particular squadron. Now, ten years' later, a similar system was being introduced into civil aviation.

International agreement between the licensing authorities of many countries had resulted in a requirement for an annual proficiency check – a check of the pilot's handling abilities on the aircraft which he was qualified to fly. At the same time this was to spell the demise of multi-aircraft qualification. By the end of 1957 my own logbook was showing entries for only one aircraft type – the DC-6, instead of four, as had previously occurred. This single type qualification was also shown on my government issued pilot's license.

In the USA proficiency checks were carried out by FAA (Federal Aviation Authority) inspectors, who were qualified pilots on the relevant aircraft type. For smaller countries the supply of qualified inspectors was severely limited, and the national airlines were then required to provide them.

In Holland the RLD (State Licensing Authority) could not possibly provide pilots experienced and qualified on all the various aircraft that KLM operated. Selected flight instructors on different aircraft types, were thus requested to shoulder the mantle of the RLD, and conduct proficiency checks on their behalf. I was thus one of several KLM flight instructors who were provided with formal letters announcing that we were conducting checks on behalf of the RLD.

These checks were normally preceded by a pre-flight briefing during which the flight programme would be discussed, and the examiner could assess the candidate's knowledge of his aircraft. In later (simulator) years a multiple choice type questionnaire was introduced which permitted a more firm, and transparent marking system.

The in-flight programme usually lasted some ninety minutes. It required the close co-operation of various air traffic controllers, as our engine-out manoeuvres had to be fitted within spaces between departing, and arriving scheduled aircraft. An occasional failure of the check would result in the candidate being scheduled for further training followed by a re-check.

The cost factors involved in this system must have been considerable. An aircraft had to be made available, fuel had to be tanked, and delays from ATC had to be accepted. Fortunately, we had not yet reached a situation where noise abatement procedures were demanded by residents in the Schiphol area, though I do seem to remember that flights across Amsterdam were being restricted.

This worthwhile, but expensive system was maintained unchanged until the flight simulators arrived, and then it became a different, and more exacting story.

From Viscount to DC-6

Early in 1957 I joined a mixed group of Dutch and foreign pilots for a Viscount course at Weybridge, the home of the Vickers factory. Halfway through the course, which was run with great expertise, I was recalled to Schiphol.

A Douglas DC-6B   (photo source unknown)

A Douglas DC-6B cockpit   (photo source unknown)

From Capt. ten Duis I understood that there was an urgent need for an additional DC-6 instructor, and to underline this point I was handed an armful of manuals, and told to be ready for examination and flight instruction in ten days' time! The target was achieved, and a series of DC-6 flights around the Middle East followed, initially as co-pilot, but within a month as captain.

After a series of Middle East flights as captain I was then scheduled for flight instructor training at Schiphol. With training completed, my new status as an instructor was fully employed for the next few months. At the same time came my introduction to the DC-6 "type office". A familiar brown coloured postcard always arrived at one's home address on a Friday morning. From now, until my eventual retirement, this postcard was to regularly carry the words "type office" or "instruction", this being the assignment scheduled for the coming week. YES!. ……….. it was a week by week schedule.

My transfer to the DC-6 marked a significant change in career, and I wonder (now) whether a complete programme had been devised for my future functions within KLM's Flight Technical Department. Past RAF and KLM instructional experience seemed to be combining for future application to later, and more powerful aircraft, and a stepping stone placed for my careful introduction to an on-going "type office" environment.

The DC-6 was to provide me with some of the most satisfying flights yet experienced. As an intercontinental captain, one's personal status had grown. Ground handling staff along the routes awaited one's decisions, and many became far more than mere passing acquaintances. A personal request, unrelated to the operational factors of the moment, would invariably be met. One felt a sense of arrival on the grand scene!

The passengers that one talked to, when opportunity permitted, were usually most interesting people. Mostly businessmen, or in today's vernacular, upper class travellers, with some positive goal in mind. On occasions there would be a "King's Messenger" who carried diplomatic bags from one embassy to another, and no way could he be separated from his bags of top secret documents!

The "Type Office" story

A "type office" existed for each particular aircraft type in the KLM fleet. It was headed by a ground staff administrator who had himself attended ground school on the applicable aircraft type. He would also make an orientation flight as an observer at flexible intervals. An aircraft captain and flight engineer would then provide the operational input into actually amending or updating an existing Aircraft Operating Manual (AOM).

In the case of a new aircraft type entering the fleet, they would be responsible for producing an AOM from scratch, before the actual aircraft arrived at Schiphol. The type office pilot acquired the somewhat grandiose title of "engineering pilot", or perhaps more discretely, "technical pilot". The various type offices lay, in fact, within the domain of the Flight Technical Department at Head Office.

………………………and the Winds of Change

My first office assignment was to join an existing ground staff team in re-writing the DC-6 AOM on a "need-to-know" basis. The winds of change were sweeping through every type office, and the entire instruction school, and word had gone out that all training courses had to be shorter, and more knowledge efficient. Quite a mammoth undertaking as many ground school instructors had become very set in their ways, and were thus reluctant to consider changes.

It had become steadily evident that the very detailed information being presented to the pilots by the Ground School was creating an expensive (in time) overload situation. His cockpit had seen the disappearance of both the professional navigator, and the wireless operator. Their duties had been taken over by the pilots, which had been made possible through the rapid advances in technology. Modern radios and their control panels had been custom designed for pilot operation from his normal seat position, as had the new navigational aids.

Since my own background had also included a modest experience of giving classroom instruction, I was requested to "sit-in" as an assessor on selected lectures, and propose the changes necessary in order to achieve a "need-to-know" syllabus. Many meetings with the instructors followed, and despite some opposition gradual changes were implemented.

On the whole, the ground school instructors were quite co-operative, and began to shorten their lectures on the more intricate subjects that had formed the keystone to their lessons. For example – the fuel control of an engine. This had grown into a matter requiring many hours of classroom instruction. Beautiful cut away models and coloured diagrams took the (usually) disinterested pilot through its inner workings in minute detail. Every tiny valve or orifice that responded in sequence, or in unison, to changing power lever position, to changing temperature or pressure had to be discussed and understood. This was a typical subject that was of little importance to the actual power lever manipulator!

...........................the introduction of "need-to-know"

With the pilots now in sole charge of radio and navigational requirements, his ground school training could be safely restructured. A basic "need-to-know" knowledge of his aircraft engines and systems was judged to be sufficient. For deeper technical knowledge reliance could be placed (as always) on the F/E. The inner workings of hydraulic pumps, generators and compressors etc. were to be only the F/E's problems. The emphasis could now be placed on the pilot's full understanding of the consequences of a system failure upon further operation, and not on what might have caused the actual failure.

The ground courses for the F/E's remained very much the same, very detailed and extensive. This also allowed him to be licensed for undertaking ground repairs when no suitably qualified ground personnel were available. His presence as a crew member was a key factor in the smooth operation of KLM's global network. On charter flights in particular, airfields were visited outside the normal network, and no KLM ground staff were normally available. The F/E being licensed to repair (if necessary) faults which arose, and "sign out" the aircraft for continued operation was therefore a great operational advantage.

Many were the occasions when this oil stained, and tired individual took his place in the cockpit for a departure in which a delay had been minimized or totally avoided.

...........................watch your language

All the various operational manuals of the company were written in English, and it was mainly for this reason most of the pilots assigned to type offices were foreign pilots from English speaking countries. I also had the feeling that very few national pilots were interested in this type of work despite the fact that so many of them had an excellent command of the English language.

The Dutch ground staff in the office would ensure that the English used was of a basic nature, and readily understandable to pilots whose native language was not necessarily English. The office F/E was also very valuable in this task of monitoring language. The corrections to my draft writings were quite extensive!

The aircraft factories always supplied (ahead of the aircraft delivery) a very complete library of technical and operational manuals, together with aircraft checklists, normal and emergency. Over the years, however, KLM had developed its own format in presenting information to the crews and technical staff. American terminology and operating procedures did not fit comfortably into the pattern which KLM had evolved or into its operating philosophy which was common throughout the fleet.

A fleet-wide operating philosophy made the transition of crews from one aircraft type to another a straightforward one of adaptation to new machinery. To change this structure in any way would have a snowball effect, and the ramifications endless. A simple example – if a Power Lever was renamed a Throttle this would result in changes to all Normal and Emergency checklists, to all operating manuals, and to several explicit words of command etc. etc.

..........................*a growing library*

In addition to the various AOM's (Aircraft Operating Manual) many other publications originated from within the Company, in fact, quite a publication empire had gradually come into existence. Approach and departure charts for every significant airfield in the world were produced together with all relevant data for these airfields. These airfield charts were bound in books of increasing size and sophistication: in my opinion they were far superior to similar publications made by Jeppesen (an American Company) for world-wide airline use. Maps and charts were also produced, and various manuals dealing with specific subjects, such as the carriage of cargo or of hazardous materials. All these publications demanded an on-going, and efficient amendment service.

..........................*counting the pocket money*

The type office work in which I became increasingly involved for the remainder of my KLM career was actually only a small part of the company's publication empire. In addition to my normal pilot's salary there were incremental additions for assignment as an instructor, for assignment to be a type office pilot, and a travel allowance for actual office days. This total salary was, of course, eagerly awaited by the taxation authorities.

To obtain a break from my duties at Schiphol it was always possible to request particular route flights, and these became almost holiday outings. The downside to these circumstances was that the actual number of flight hours entered in my logbook steadily decreased in number. I began to realize what the words "office pilot" really did mean!

..........................*an unwanted event*

An early assignment as a DC-6 flight instructor produced an unwelcome surprise. I was detailed to conduct a proficiency check on a quite senior pilot, who had spent most of his career based in South America. He had returned to Schiphol from his overseas posting especially for this check. We commenced the check with a simulated outboard engine failure on take-off. To my horror he lost control of the aircraft, and I had to rapidly restore normal flight conditions, and then return for landing. We had several minutes of quiet discussion before making a second attempt at this vital exercise.

The second attempt was controlled reasonably well, so we continued with the check programme. To finish the session we then needed to make a 3-engine ILS approach. Sadly this resulted in increasing fluctuations around the ILS beam until control of the aircraft was again lost, and I had to take over control for a final landing. Inevitably the session had to be ended, and the matter referred to the Chief Pilot. I never did hear the final outcome of this sad event.

To Tehran with Mossadeq

A very interesting charter flight was made with Iranian Prime Minister Mossadeq, returning to Tehran after a meeting in The Hague. He insisted on several circuits around Istanbul, viewing that historic city from every possible angle. Approaching Istanbul from the Sea of Marmara always presented a truly wonderful picture, either from the sea or from the air. When using its Yesilkoy airport I invariably sought an approach path which would give the most scenic view of the city – and so I was well prepared for Mossadeq's request.

Further east he asked for a low level excursion over Lake Van, to see an old Armenian Monastery built on a small island. Not far from Lake Van there is also a mountainous region around the source of the Euphrates: its valleys and hillsides are home to many monasteries from Byzantine days. Most have been deliberately destroyed over the centuries, but a fragile few still remain. From recent reports it would seem that the monastery at Lake Van is now rapidly crumbling away. From Lake Van we headed northwards for a close-up of Mt. Ararat, the legendary resting place of Noah's Ark, and then a low level circuit of Tabriz. Before leaving us in Tehran, Mossadeq presented each crew member with a fistful of US dollars!! To evade Schiphol customs mine were carefully concealed within my shoulder epaulettes.

Holidays in Istanbul

Istanbul provided us with some wonderful "holiday" outings in these years. A ten days' stationing during which we flew several times a week to Tehran, and back with a night stop there. Our home base was the splendid Istanbul Hilton overlooking the Bosphorus, and a short tram ride from the old city. To my great shame I was so preoccupied with the tennis courts and swimming pool that there was little time for sightseeing. Fortunately my F/E insisted on a visit one evening to a Russian restaurant he knew, a tram ride down to the Galata Bridge; a stroll along a few alleys near the old tower brought us to an extravagant welcome, and a truly delicious stroganoff.

As political events in Iran ebbed and flowed, party time returned to Tehran under government by the Shah. Our hotel located on the outskirts of the city hosted a great number of weekend parties. A very pleasant evening could be spent in the hotel lounge just "people watching" – the fashion conscious women in evening dresses, and with elaborate hairdo's were escorted by impeccably attired escorts. A far cry indeed, from the impending regime of the Ayatollah.

The route between Tehran and Istanbul could be plagued by thunderstorm conditions, particularly in the area of Lake Van. Since our DC-6's were not equipped with weather radar, a game of "blind-man's bluff" among the towering cumulonimbus could result. By great good luck a Pan Am DC-6 frequently departed Tehran just five minutes ahead of us. The fact that he was thus assigned a higher altitude was of minor importance. The more important fact was that he was radar equipped. All the way to Istanbul he would keep us advised of the clearest paths through the cloud build-ups. Inter airline co-operation at its best!

Back to Damascus

Occasional stops in Damascus would need sometimes a crew re-positioning by road to Beirut. Syrian taxi drivers being a law onto themselves, these journeys became unforgettable events. The downward road through the mountains provided spectacular scenery of pine forests, heather and olive groves through the twists and turns.

It was standard operating procedure for the taxi driver to switch his engine off during this descent. The costs of fuel saved must have been greatly overshadowed by the cost of brake lining replacements. The smell of hot and fading brakes was extremely strong by the time the Bekka Valley was reached. The Bekka Valley, long known as the bread basket of Lebanon, was a lush area of farmlands and orchards. Later it was to gain a more sinister reputation as the stamping ground of the Hezbollah. Continuing onwards to Beirut we eventually reached the Corniche, and thankfully climbed the steps into our hotel, the Riviera, and its welcoming staff!!

Pilot discontent

1958 was also a year to feature several significant events. Firstly, there was a brief pilots' strike, and secondly there was the commencement of preparations for the introduction of the Lockheed Electra.

I.A.Aler had succeeded Dr. Plesman as President Director of KLM, and in March 1958 was confronted with the second pilots' strike of his career. With a strong military background, occasionally interrupted by appointments with KLM, Aler had displayed sound diplomacy on the international field, but within his own company such diplomacy was somewhat less evident.

I was on a "type office" schedule at the time that the momentous events of March were taking place, and thus little more than a sideline spectator – and now, at the time of writing, with little detailed memory of these events. Capt. Metz was president of the pilots' union, and negotiations were taking place with KLM management over various issues, particularly salary, and the management desire to reduce total pilot numbers. Metz was suddenly dismissed by KLM management as being a troublemaker, an instant strike by the majority of pilots resulted, and a demand for his immediate reinstatement.

Reinstatement was made, the strike called off, and negotiations resumed. Somewhere within this complex situation the foreign pilots were also seeking to obtain a formal contract of employment: a rather important subject when redundancies were being discussed. A contract was not forthcoming, and the foreign pilots decided to leave the pilots' pension fund, and set up one under their own control. KLM then paid monthly into this fund amounts exactly equivalent to those paid into the Dutch pilots' pension scheme. A fair deal, but one (through no fault of KLM) which turned out to be rather unsuccessful for foreign pilots as the years progressed, poor fund management by an internationally recognised firm being to blame.

Also at about this time a fair number of foreign pilots accepted repatriation deals to their home countries, probably with "golden handshakes"! This exodus undoubtedly resulted from personal interpretations of job security. Could KLM be trusted to handle matters of redundancy on the basis of seniority or were foreign pilots to be regarded as expendable when the need arose?

It is very possible, of course, that existing labour laws or public opinion prevented KLM from voicing a firm opinion on the matter – thus leaving the foreign pilots in complete ignorance of their potential future with the company, and therefore still without any contract of employment. A subdued sense of unease remained with a foreign pilot throughout his KLM career ………. were we expandable when the need arose or had changing labour laws worked in our favour?

From Douglas to Lockheed

In the summer of 1958 I said farewell rather reluctantly to the DC-6. This was to be my last piston engine aircraft and turbine engines (essentially jet engines with propellers) were to be my next driving force.

The DC-6 period had been relatively brief for me, but had also been greatly entertaining. It had not been a difficult aircraft to master, and could be flown with great precision. In the quite comfortable cockpit the F/E had sat facing forward between the two pilots. This had resulted in good and close crew co-operation. Each crew member was very aware of events as they progressed. The routes on which we had flown had again covered my happy hunting grounds of the Middle East and Near East. Cruise altitudes had been greater than with Dakota's and DC-4's, but the scenery and background history remained unrivalled.

My assignment was now to the newly created Lockheed Electra type office as engineering pilot for this coming KLM acquisition. Our office task was to create a complete AOM for this new aircraft type, and all the necessary documentation for cockpit use. But first we had to get thoroughly acquainted with the aircraft, its engines and propellers.

Off to the USA

The type office team set off for a grand tour of the USA, accompanied by Capt. Frank Hawkins. Frank was a key member of KLM's Research Development Department (R & D), and had been closely involved with the specification progress which accompanied KLM's order for the aircraft. He was to be instrumental in guiding me through the complexities of aircraft factories, and the detailed nature of an aircraft acceptance programme. This tuition proved invaluable when, in later years, I was to become so involved with the B-747 at Seattle. Frank's name was very well known at all major American aircraft factories, and he later was appointed a Fellow of the Royal Aeronautical Society. He was also to become KLM's acknowledged expert on ergonomics – the study of the relationship between workers, and their environment, particularly in cockpit layout.

............................*Allison Engines and Hamilton Standard Propellers*

Our first stop was at the Allison Engine Factory for a very detailed course on the turbine engine which was installed on the Electra. The detailed nature of the course – far surpassing any pilots' "need-to-know" requirement – delighted our F/E's Jan Klein and Dries Lohmeyer. Frank and I found it rather overwhelming! From the Allison Factory we continued on to the Hamilton Standard propeller factory. Since we were the first customers for this brand new propeller system, however, the instructors were not really fully prepared for us. With great aplomb and expertise Dries Lohmeyer took over the classroom. He proceeded to tell us, and the would-be instructors in grand detail how the propeller system worked!

............................*The Lockheed Factory*

With these initial training programmes completed we travelled on to the Lockheed factory at Burbank, California. Our heads were already bursting with knowledge, much of it of little use to pilots! But now it was to be a very full and complete ground course on the aircraft itself. At weekends Frank took time to introduce me to the delights of California, surfing at Laguna Beach, the homes of the movie stars, and Hollywood itself.

After one evening at a night club I was violently sick. Whether this was the result of the semi-pornographic show that we had watched or the meal we had eaten, I was not sure. It later turned out to be the beginning of a gall bladder problem which was to see me hospitalized in Zeist (Holland). The massive scar left by this episode is a source of amazement to today's keyhole surgeons.

Lockheed Electra   (photo source unknown)

Anyway, with all the ground courses completed we moved on to the aircraft acceptance programme. This reflected KLM's requirements regarding the inspection of the goods offered for sale. It had been carefully compiled by Frank and our two F/E's, and was something of a shock to Lockheed and to myself! The ground acceptance programme took several days to complete, and only then could we agree to an acceptance flight.

Interestingly enough this would be Frank's first time at the controls of the Electra, since any prior flight training would have been too expensive. It was thus under the guidance of a Lockheed captain and F/E (the aircraft was still Lockheed property) that Frank expertly conducted the acceptance flight. After a satisfactory flight of some four hours, KLM agreed to the purchase of the aircraft. We then all completed our flight training using our own aircraft, but with Lockheed instructors.

All these events took a considerable amount of time and endless travelling, so that it was not until August 1959 that we were able to commence the ferry flight to Schiphol. For me, it was to be my first experience as an active pilot in a trans-continental or trans-Atlantic crossing. Initially I was somewhat bemused by the staccato-like rapidity of the air traffic controller's instructions – very brief and to the point! By the time we reached New York for a welcome night stop the newness of it all was beginning to wear off.

...........................*across the "Pond"*

When leaving New York the following day we seemed to cause ATC considerable surprise by requesting a clearance direct to Schiphol. They were probably unaware of the range capabilities of this relatively new aircraft type. Back came the rapid staccato voice .... "Say again aircraft type, KLM" .... "say again destination, KLM" .... "say again fuel endurance, KLM", and finally, "KLM cleared for take-off, good luck"!

About half way across the pond, on a very restful flight, Frank went to the rear for a short rest before we started contacting Shannon for onward clearance. After carefully checking our weight and the wind conditions I decided to save some fuel by requesting a higher altitude. This was soon given, and we settled down at our new cruise altitude .... jet engines use less fuel at high altitudes, don't they? WRONG, not when they are driving propellers!! Frank was not best pleased with my activity in his absence.

The Electra in Europe

KLM was the only European airline to order and operate the Electra, and we thus had full time support from Lockheed, Allison and Hamilton Standard. It was an exceptionally pleasant aircraft to fly, and for its size, extremely light on the controls. The huge propeller gave it a unique short landing capability with minimum use of brakes. On landing, the blades were moved to a flat position against the existing airflow. The four great rotating discs then had a very positive decelerating effect on the aircraft.

Its own air-stairs and air conditioning ensured rapid ground handling. On aircraft test flights at Schiphol I could happily land on runway 32, sneaking low over the dyke to place my wheels exactly on the threshold markings – not a normal procedure. Runway 32 was seldom used for large aircraft unless a fair headwind existed. At 1500 meters it was considered uncomfortably short. With an Electra (on flight test) a landing could be completed in about one third of the available runway length of R/W 32, but that was at a very light aircraft weight.

Unfortunately, several early crashes in the USA brought a rapid end to the Lockheed order book. Initially the autopilot was a suspect in the crashes, and until investigation proved otherwise we were required to operate at reduced speed with the autopilot OFF. This led to the need for three pilots on some of the

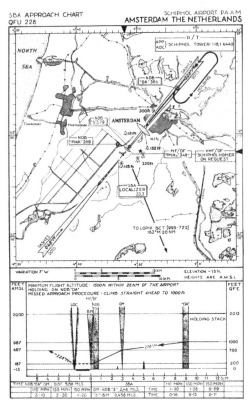

Sample of a Radio Range Approach chart

Lockheed Electra

Lockheed Electra Cockpit

longer flights. Ultimately a design fault in the engine bearers which, if only slightly damaged, could cause wing flutter and break-up was diagnosed.

An immediate modification programme was initiated demanding that all our aircraft be returned in sequence to the factory for re-work. This was conducted to a very rigid timetable which allowed for no delays in arriving at Burbank, California; some very interesting delivery flights resulted to ensure that we turned up exactly on time, mechanical saws were awaiting us!! As soon as the aircraft was parked, and before we had finished disembarking, these saws were being used to cut away the under-wing panels; no time to waste!

The simulator arrives

The arrival of the Electra at Schiphol was closely accompanied by the installation of a Flight Simulator, keeping the DC-8 simulator company in the newly built simulator hall. The following months saw me alternating between the type office, and giving instruction on the aircraft or on the simulator.

Over the following years some 1400 hours* were spent in the simulator often in the company of Mr. Sainsbury from my earlier Link Trainer days. The simulator was initially used to thoroughly train the pilot on the new aircraft type, teaching him all the normal and emergency procedures.

Simulator hours could not be entered in one's logbook as flight time hours – my recorded flight time on several aircraft types was thus unusually low.

An essential part of this training was also devoted to the constant need for proper crew coordination, solo cowboys were not required!! After simulator training was completed actual in-flight instruction commenced – delays to this period of training could frequently be caused by weather or unavailability of aircraft. Once we had become familiar with the capabilities of the simulator, its use for proficiency checks was also introduced, weather delays and aircraft availability problems became things of the past, and training expenses were greatly reduced.

.................and proficiency checks start!!

As the requirement for in-flight proficiency checks became due, these were often done in combination with a "line" (a normal passenger service) flight to Copenhagen – a cost effective operation.

The pilot due for a proficiency check would fly the Schiphol-Copenhagen-Schiphol sector as captain. During the 3 hour stop-over at Copenhagen we would then take the aircraft up to carry out a proficiency check. It was a very tense and exhausting day for the individual concerned: a full day of flying under the critical eye of an instructor. Very occasionally a failed proficiency check would require the instructor to fly the aircraft home as captain.

Finally, some "holiday" flights

As a relief from instructional or office activities some very interesting line flights could be requested. One in particular springs to mind, a sort of grand tour – via Casablanca for 3 days in Las Palmas, onward for a night in Accra (West Africa), northwards for 3 days in Tunis and so home. The beach and scenic drives in Las Palmas were great, but of more interest to me was rejoining Hannibal in Carthage, and exploring the wonderful Roman ruins in Tunisia.

Other scheduled flights also revived the activities of DC-6 days in Istanbul and Tehran, this time in a more luxurious cockpit environment, and with excellent weather radar. Past days were also revisited in Cairo and Khartoum.

At the time quite a large Greek contingent was numbered among the population of the Sudan, particularly in Khartoum. As a result, a fairly busy line developed between Khartoum and Athens, of which KLM took full advantage. So once more I could visit Government House, and the place where General Gordon had been assassinated in 1885 – or take a tour of Omdurman (once known as the largest village in

Nile paddle steamer at Khartoum

Africa) where Winston Churchill first saw active service while attached to a British army cavalry regiment. Strangely enough, there is still a memorial in Omdurman to the few British war dead of that campaign, but nothing to record the many thousands of Sudanese who died.

Khartoum airport, however, contained relics of a more recent conflict – the derelict wrecks of an old Hurricane or Blenheim bulldozed into corners. Khartoum had, in the early 1940's, been part of a re-supply route to the Cairo area of much needed aircraft for the Desert Air Force of the RAF. These were shipped in packing crates to Takoradi on the West coast of Africa, re-assembled, test flown, and despatched across the Sahara to the Nile, and then north to Cairo. Flown in small convoys, following a navigating aircraft, intermediate landings for

Approach sandstorm

re-fueling were made at remote desert landing strips; not all of those delivery flights were successful as Saharan weather tended to disrupt proceedings, and navigational errors often occurred.

The junction of the Blue and White Nile at Khartoum had always been an area of great fascination for me, the two great rivers, rising in totally different areas, and flowing through such very different countries, before uniting in their northward flow through the timeless lands of Egypt. The intrepid explorers, who had sought to locate the source of these rivers, have left travel tales of consuming interest.

Government House

At fault again

It was also on an Electra flight that I made a major error in the cockpit. South bound on a night flight from Schiphol to Casablanca we were transiting the area of Madrid Control. Gradually all radio communications faded. Much puzzlement in the cockpit until it was realised that I had programmed an incorrect heading into the auto pilot! Using the weather radar it could then be seen that we were approaching the coast to the east of Gibraltar, instead of the west. Contacting Gibraltar Control, a re-clearance to Casablanca was obtained where we landed only some ten minutes late.

Fortunately, my immediate reaction to this incident was to apologize to the crew, and write a detailed "Trip Report". The report would then stay on board the aircraft which continued on to Schiphol with another crew, while we proceeded with our scheduled trip. When we returned to Schiphol a week later my visit to the Chief Pilot brought forth the comment "stupid fool" – but also the fact that a quite uncalled for report from the Chief F/E had previously reached him, complaining about the captain's disgraceful error! Crew co-operation at its best!

Family affairs

On some Electra training flights I was able to take my 12 year old son along. His description to his friends of an Electra take-off was quite interesting. His hands simulated a backward movement of the control column to lift the nose, followed immediately by a quick movement to represent full control wheel deflection! This was all he had ever seen – "failure" of an outboard engine on take-off, which certainly demanded full aileron deflection, and a boot full of rudder!

Taking my daughter on a flight to Beirut resulted in a visit to the Casino du Leban, just up the coast from Beirut. Passing carefully through the gaming tables, crowded with high society in evening dress, we reached the stage and restaurant area, and there we were entranced by a most spectacular stage show, enlivened by stunning effects such as waterfalls complete with mermaids! A really enjoyable evening!

Lack of lights at Cairo

In June 1961 our 12 strong Electra fleet suffered a tragic loss. A night approach into Cairo was followed by a circuit, and an unduly steep descent while turning on to the final approach for runway 34. This resulted in contact with the surrounding sand hills, and complete destruction of the aircraft. Several fatalities occurred, but the cockpit crew survived – the F/E was actually thrown clear of the aircraft, and was found still strapped in his seat.

From the subsequent inquiry it was apparent that crew coordination had not been optimum. It was noted that the captain had been flying the required right-hand circuit on instruments from the LH seat. Since the airfield was therefore out of his line of sight it was the co-pilot's duty to maintain visual contact with the field. The captain's decision to commence a turn on to final was perhaps ill-judged as he had no visual contact, but his actions in then setting up a steep descent were fatal errors.

Both pilots had, at different times, been assessed by their instructors' as having a potential deficiency in visual judgment at night. Sadly their training reports had not been fully recognised as requiring further action. By pure coincidence they were assigned to the same flight, with unhappy consequences. These training reports had also mysteriously disappeared.

> *Footnote: The Electra tragedy led to a detailed fleet-wide inspection of all the aircraft. This resulted in the discovery of an amazing amount of debris within the fuel tanks: among the findings were a number of washers, odd rags and sponges, a screw driver, and even a small vacuum cleaner! Needless to say, Lockheed had many embarrassing questions to answer.*

The end of an era

My Electra days were now sadly drawing to a close. Almost my last flight involved a three day stop in Athens, and the crew decided to make it a memorable occasion. Apart from visiting the usual bars and restaurants in the neighbourhood of the Acropolis, we rented a car and headed for Delphi. Our arrival coincided with that of a thunderstorm, and tremendous claps of thunder reverberated through the mountain valleys. Our roadside hotel reception area had a lift which descended down the cliff face to the rooms. These looked out over a valley continually lit by flashes of lightning, while the windows rattled from the thunder. After a somewhat sleepless night we headed down to the car ferry, crossing the Gulf of Corinth to Corinth itself and then onwards, to stand on the bridge across the deep chasm of the Corinth Canal. Rather difficult to return to work after such an entrancing journey, brief though it was.

Observations in closing

Lockheed had been unfortunate in their timing of the Electra introduction; it was too near the arrival of the early B-707's and DC-8's, and of the Trident and Caravelle. The Electra, however, served KLM well for many years, and was eventually very saleable on the second-hand market. The early crashes in the USA had also severely damaged its reputation. Fifty year on, however, these aircraft are still flying – albeit in a different form. The Allison engine remains a very potent beast, and has been much developed – it is still the power plant of today's military Hercules aircraft. The Orion and all its maritime derivatives, is built around the same basic Electra airframe and (modified) wing structures, on which improved Allison engines are still installed.

This, the last of my propellers, had coincided with tremendous strides in the aviation world. No longer were ADF (Automatic Direction Finding) beacons the sole approach aids to airports. ILS (Instrument Landing System) installations were now available throughout the world. This aid was relatively unaffected by weather conditions, whereas the ADF beacon tended to point to the nearest thunderstorm, frequently a matter of some inconvenience.

Cockpit installed radar sets had also become the norm. They could give excellent pictures of thunderstorm activity in the distance, which often allowed for a gradual diversion around them with little loss of time. At close range, they could provide positive guidance for some last minute avoidance of the storm cells. They also had a useful function in identifying coast lines and islands, when one's navigation needed a little help!

ATC (Air Traffic Control) in all its many forms had been developed out of all recognition. The world was covered by a network of "airways", which in turn demanded continual improvements in navigation aids to ensure that aircraft were operated within their assigned airway. Radio receivers/transmitters had required duplication in the cockpit to make easier the constant change of frequencies needed in the vicinity of airports. One could now pre-set a radio to the next communication centre, then a later change to that centre became possible by a single switch movement. The radio no longer in use could then be pre-set to the next expected frequency etc. etc.

And now I was headed for true jet propulsion, my big propellers were going.

...........................they were to become miniaturized and multiplied!

My First Jet – DC-8

Douglas DC-8

*My DC-8 logbook has gone AWOL (absent without leave). The following stories,
therefore, cannot always be supported by reference to dates.*

Finding a date

Despite a missing logbook I am able to determine quite closely the date of my promotion to the DC-8 fleet. In the spring of 1964 I had made a last en-route flight with the Electra, accompanied by a crew that I knew well – in fact it had been something of an arranged gathering. After a fairly riotous two day stop in Athens they had presented me with a book, during a farewell party in the shadow of the Acropolis, detailing the discovery of Troy.

In August of the same year my library acquired yet another historical volume, "Forty Years in the Wilderness" by a well-known English traveller. Perhaps this choice of title had a double meaning? Apparently I was celebrating my fortieth birthday by undergoing a DC8 captain's check flight en-route!

Since I scarcely knew any of the crew I was greatly surprised, and embarrassed by this quite unexpected gift. I was even uncertain if the whole crew had been involved or just the cockpit members.

> *At the conclusion of my Lockheed Electra career I had logged approximately 10,000 flight hours in total, and some 1500 hours of simulator instruction. By the end of my DC-8 years the total flight hours had increased to only 12,000 hours, and my simulator hours by a further 800 …. over a period of six years this was an extremely modest increase in actual flight hours…. a true measure of my involvement in type office, and instructional affairs!!*

A change of controls

Viewed from afar, the DC-8 had always struck me as an extremely noisy and dirty beast, and this was certainly true of those aircraft which were fitted with the early versions of the Pratt and Whitney engines. Great trails of blackish smoke used to follow their departures, and the noise of their engines at full thrust seemed reluctant to diminish. Later models of the DC-8 had much improved engines – less noisy, reduced emissions, improved fuel economy and greater thrust.

My propellers had now become miniaturized – much smaller, but more numerous blades became a fan enclosed by an engine cowling. They were supplying air to a compressor which was then mixed with fuel, and ignited to produce jet exhaust thrust. The turbine engines of the Electra had now become real jet engines: the rearward thrust of these jet engines was to be my future driving force.

In terms of aircraft controllability, the difference between the Electra and the DC-8 was very marked. The Electra had responded smoothly and quickly to fingertip pressure, the DC-8 was very much a push and shove machine in comparison! And the great difference in the response from propellers, and that from pure jet power was very marked – a trap for the unwary.

Getting to know the DC-8

The cockpit was conventional in terms of pilot seat position, but the F/E was once again given a very extensive sideways facing panel aft of the pilots, similar to the Constellation layout. An additional seat (jump seat) was located behind the captain's (LH) seat for use by an extra crew member or an observer.

By tradition, the pilot actually handling the controls of an aircraft (PF pilot flying) had always sat in the LH seat – popularly known as the captain's seat. Before flight the captain would assign PF duty, and as a result the co-pilot could then be seated in the LH seat for a particular flight sector.

The introduction of jet aircraft brought with it a so called "fixed seat" policy. All pilots were then fully trained only in the seat from which they would always fly. There was to be no more interchange of seats. Fortunately, nose-wheel steering was available at both pilots' positions so that the PF (even if he was in the RH seat) would have full control of the aircraft on the ground as well as in the air.

Many co-pilots were initially unhappy with this new policy. They felt that a certain status had been lost when assigned PF duties. They were no longer sitting in the traditional captain's position.

The F/E's seat could be repositioned so that he was located between the pilots for take off and landing, and also for other phases of flight, when it was advantageous to do so. For normal flight regimes he would retire to his own panel and associated paperwork. I was not personally too happy with this

DC-8 Cockpit   (photo source unknown)

layout, as so much information was out of view from the right hand seat, and that was the seat I was so frequently to occupy as a flight instructor or en-route check pilot.

And some new toys

The basic flight instruments were familiar enough, though unfortunately somewhat smaller in size than the Electra. Some reading glasses were added to my personal equipment for night flights, and to my surprise the reading of maps and charts also became easier! Engine instruments were also noticeably smaller, and there were several different parameters to become accustomed to.

An interesting addition to the instrument panel was a Mach (speed) indication. Our high altitude cruise speeds were given as a ratio of the speed of sound, this being the most accurate indication of speed for a jet powered aircraft at altitude. A standard cruise speed would be in the region of .76M – safely away from the speed of sound, for which the aircraft was not designed. On flight test programmes, however, a shallow dive would be used to accelerate the aircraft to its design (structural) speed limit – .92M.

> *Mach reflects the name of an Austrian physicist who researched the characteristics of airflow, and the influence of temperature and pressure. The higher the ambient temperature the higher the speed of sound.............. this basic law resulted in early attempts to "break the sound barrier" taking place at sea level on a summer's day.*
>
> *At the normal cruise altitudes of jet aircraft the Mach number becomes the speed criteria, and a cruise speed well below Mach 1. is chosen. An increase of speed towards*

Mach 1. will result in a higher fuel consumption, since the effects of compressibility, and increased aerodynamic drag will start to intrude upon aircraft performance.

Navigational tools .... Doppler and Loran

Astro navigation had had its day. Cruise speeds were now so fast that the 15-20 minutes needed to take, calculate and plot an astro fix were near useless. The aircraft could be some 200 nautical miles past its astro calculated and plotted position. The DC-8, strangely enough, had been fitted with an aperture through which a periscopic sextant could be inserted. Since this really served no useful purpose it was rapidly downgraded to a smoke removal feature, opening the sealed aperture allowed air to escape together with smoke.

Doppler was a primitive form of computer which was, in part, a replacement for the professional navigator. Its name stemmed from its use of the "Doppler Effect" where relative motion between two bodies is sensed – in this case between aircraft and earth. It had to be pre-programmed by the pilot, but was completely independent of any ground based aids. It combined the Doppler Effect with data from aircraft sensors to display essential navigational information. Although generally reliable it had well known computer characteristics – garbage in, garbage out!

Two completely independent Doppler sets were installed in the DC-8. Since they were a replacement of the navigator, resulting in a reduction in crew members, the pilots were quick in demanding a salary increment, to become known as "Double Doppler" pay. How long this strange salary increment persisted I have no idea.

A not unexpected Doppler event occurred on a night flight to Accra, (West Africa). A passenger report was received stating that the pilot had been low flying for some ten minutes before landing at Accra.

Our investigation of this incident revealed that this had indeed occurred. The crew had used Doppler as the sole means of determining the point at which to commence descent from cruise altitude.

The Doppler information, for various reasons, was seriously in error. Descent had commenced too far out from destination, and it was only the illumination from a rising sun that prevented the crew from descending into the tree tops – some fifty miles from Accra.

For the North Atlantic and its bordering lands to east and west, a further navigational device was installed. This equipment was known as LORAN (Long Range Navigation), and had first been developed for pre-war use by the US Coastguard service in their ships. It was then used by RAF Bomber Command during operations over Europe.

Further development for use in civil aircraft led to a radar-like scope being installed by the RH pilot's seat. Radio signals were received from ground stations, displayed in a unique form on the scope, interpreted, and transferred to a special plotting chart – and then, with skilled luck, a position line was revealed. Since a minimum of two position lines, ideally crossing each other at right-angles, were always needed to obtain a "fix", another ground station had to be interrogated or some other form of radio bearing acquired.

My rules of survival

For a pilot there were several critical differences between flying propeller powered aircraft and jet powered ones. Although I was a newcomer to the DC-8 fleet, it was soon obvious that my background led to great expectations of a rapid progress through transition training. Not wishing to renege on those expectations, I made some careful preparations. Among these was to sneak into the DC-8 simulator during unused hours. I would then sit in the pilot's seat, close my eyes, and learn the position of every control, and every switch by feel alone. This exercise I would repeat from each pilot's seat, so that I became touch perfect from either seat. The simulator was very conveniently located sitting, as it did, next to the Electra one, and they were just down the corridor from my type office.

From conversations and reading I also began to construct a personal rule book, which I had no reason to alter as actual experience on the aircraft was acquired. The rules which I felt to be significant are summarised as follows:-

Rule 1 – Thrust response

Advancing or retarding the power lever on a propeller driven aircraft brought an instant change in thrust. On a jet aircraft the response to power lever movement was very significantly different, since there were no large propeller blades to bite into the air-stream.

During descent, for example, the engines would be in an idle condition – "spooled down". Advancing the power lever to increase thrust would be accompanied by several seconds delay before the engines accelerated, and produced the desired increase in thrust. This characteristic provided a world-wide upsurge in the number of (short) landing incidents during the early years of jet operations, and newcomers to established jet aircraft fleets were also frequently caught out.

> During a landing at Vienna a quite experienced pilot destroyed several elevated approach lights before landing on the runway. He had flown a steep descent path with the power levers closed, and the engines firmly "spooled down".

> Just before reaching the runway he advanced the power levers to flatten out his approach path…too late. He had forgotten the slow response from the spooled down jet engines.

The conclusion was obvious – never be caught near the ground in an idle thrust condition!

Rule 2 – Visibility in Rain

All my previous aircraft (apart from the Tiger Moth) had been fitted with windshield wipers, operated by electric motors. To my surprise, the DC-8 had no wipers! Instead, perforated metal tubes were located at the base of the windshield. These enabled a fierce blast of air (bled from the engine compressors) to keep the windshield free of rain.

A fine idea, but, if bleed air from the compressors was insufficient (engines spooled down) your windshield could become a rain-swept blur. This usually happened momentarily immediately after touch down (power levers closed), and before the engines "spooled up" again in reverse thrust.

> It did catch me out during a night landing at Beirut on a runway with a marked down slope. Commencing the landing flare, the rain suddenly became intense. The down sloping runway was delaying our touch down, and bleed air across the windows had ceased.

> I could increase power to regain visibility, but that would mean running out of runway. Vague glimmers of watery light, seen through peripheral vision, seemed to show us more or less on centre – but how high? The sole remaining option was perhaps to "dump" (retract) some wing flaps – the flaps were sneaked up a little, and after

*a second or two of almost complete blindness, the wheels touched with a solid
thump, a firm landing that was always the recommended technique on a wet runway!*

Immediate reverse wrapped us in even more wetness, but we had forward visibility again.

This was not a situation that I would wish to repeat in a hurry, but fortunately a down sloping runway of any significance was not met with too frequently.

Rule 3 – Beware of "Coffin Corner"

Jet operations at high altitude had introduced a new aerodynamic feature into cruise flights which became known as coffin corner. Cruise altitude with the DC-8 was generally in excess of 30,000 feet, and could be considerably higher at low aircraft weights. Since fuel consumption tended to decrease as cruise altitude was increased, pilots were much tempted to reach for the stars. This temptation could unexpectedly bring their aircraft close to a high speed stall condition – a situation which was not initially recognised.

An aircraft will stall when its forward speed becomes insufficient to maintain flight, and control inputs then become ineffective. Buffet (shaking of the aircraft) will occur, and height is inevitably lost until speed increases, and control inputs again become effective. All pilots are trained to recognise stall buffet, and to take appropriate action. This training, however, is carried out at relatively low altitude, and the stall speeds then encountered are very low – well below the normal operating speeds at higher altitudes.

A subtle increase of stalling speed also occurs as an aircraft climbs. The air becomes less dense, and the normal operating speed is then invisibly approached by an increasing stall speed. Aircraft weight is also an important factor. The greater the weight the higher the stall speed will be.

It is thus possible to reach a cruise altitude which is inappropriate for the aircraft weight. The low speed stall, increased by altitude and weight, merges with the cruise speed which is close to the high speed stall. The slightest air turbulence can upset this delicate balance, and stall buffet is likely to occur.

This buffet will initially be a gentle trembling of the aircraft, but unless immediate corrective action is taken, the trembling will increase to a heavy juddering. Immediate descent into denser air, with an increase in speed, is essential in order to restore safety margins. If the pilot fails to recognise the onset of stall buffet, and take appropriate action, an uncontrollable loss of altitude will occur before full aircraft control can be regained.

Several incidents of this nature occurred in the early days of civil jet operations, and were referred to as "jet upsets". Eventually special "coffin corner" graphs were produced which enabled the pilot to assess his margin of safety at high cruise altitudes. Since, however, safety margins could be rapidly eroded by in-flight turbulence it was also necessary to carefully consider forecast weather conditions.

*On a flight between Bangkok and Tokyo some 6000 feet of altitude was abruptly lost
in cruise flight. A cruise altitude had been selected which was excessive for the aircraft
weight. Moderate turbulence had been encountered, and the aircraft had stalled,
falling temporarily out of control.*

*Our investigation revealed that the effects of turbulence had probably masked the
onset of stall buffet. Other factors in the case showed, however, that the captain had
been grossly negligent in many respects. I was not surprised to hear that he was then
permanently demoted.*

Rule 4 – Know your fuel situation

Coming from piston engines I was quite amazed at the prodigious rate of fuel consumption on jet powered aircraft. I can no longer recall an exact figure, but the DC-8 consumed fuel at a rate of some 6 tons per hour. An economical fuel tanking policy was a Company recommendation. This minimized aircraft weight and fuel burn, which was sensible economics, but had to be treated with caution – fuel quantity tanked was ultimately the captain's decision.

Safe fuel reserves were inevitably an essential requirement, and the pilot always had the option of increasing the reserves when he felt such action was necessary. I also believe that the F/E who supervised the fuel tanking en-route had the habit of adding a little extra for "the wife and kids", regardless of actual circumstances.

When flying en-route with minimum fuel, an unexpected change in weather conditions or ATC (Air Traffic Control) requirements could raise fuel problems. Various means could be adopted to ease such a situation. At places like New York, for example, a combination of traffic density, and unexpected bad weather could result in delays for all incoming aircraft. Aircraft received instructions to "hold" at various radio beacons, and await their landing turn.

In some instances, a pilot getting very low on fuel would declare a "fuel emergency", and obtain priority landing clearance – in fact, jumping the queue. The impatient ones were discouraged from this practice by the arrival of an FAA inspector after landing. He would carefully check the fuel remaining before accepting that the declared emergency was a valid decision by the captain.

Only once did I feel the need to declare a fuel emergency. That was when inbound to Tokyo at a busy traffic period; we had encountered massive headwinds en-route, due to the unexpected movement of a typhoon. By the time we entered Tokyo ATC area, our fuel reserves were seriously eroded. Our options were simple, we either were cleared for a straight-in approach or we would have to divert immediately. To then be instructed to proceed to a holding beacon, and expect a 30 minutes delay before landing was not welcome news. I advised ATC of our intentions, and was "invited" to declare a fuel emergency …….. which I gladly did! Radar guidance for a straight-in approach, and landing was our reward.

> *Long after my retirement I read of a crash on Long Island, New York. The South American pilot had been unable to inform ATC of his extremely low fuel situation, since his command of English was extremely limited. Instructed to maintain a holding pattern, his aircraft eventually crashed due to fuel starvation.*

Rule 5 – Be familiar with the F/E's panel

Very occasionally the F/E would consider himself to be in a superior position to that of the pilots. These go-it-alone individuals were not always easy to spot, and this situation was made more difficult by the fact that a quite different crew were assembled for every flight departing home base. It then took several days to form a bond within the crew.

On a Schiphol departure for Madrid we had reached cruise altitude south of Brussels. As I left my seat for a quick visit to the loo, I noticed that a hydraulic pump had been switched off at the F/E's panel, an action which had not been reported to me. Returning to my seat I waited for a situation report from the F/E. Nothing happened!

> *Quietly seething with rage I called ATC on the radio, and asked for a return clearance to Schiphol. This was immediately given. The crew looked at me in astonishment ……………… "Why Skipper"?*

I explained to the co-pilot that the F/E had switched off a hydraulic pump – "because the system was losing fluid and pressure" said the F/E. In that case, I said, we would have been grounded in Madrid had we continued, as no spare pumps are available there.

Our return to Schiphol resulted in some 90 minutes' delay, while the faulty pump was changed, and then we set forth once again for Madrid. I never again encountered that particular F/E.

Flying the DC-8

First impressions led me to believe that the aircraft was very heavy on the controls, particularly at low speeds. The Electra could be flown with finger tip pressure, but now I seemed to require very firm hands. As experience was gained, my fingers seemed to acquire an additional strength allowing a return towards finger tip control.

Interesting devices were available to assist in slowing the aircraft down, in flight or on the landing roll. Descent from cruise altitude was normally commenced at about 120 nautical miles* from destination using quite a high speed. If the descent was started late for any reason, or if ATC require a more rapid descent, the flight spoilers could be extended. These were large panels that extended above the upper wing surface. The additional aerodynamic drag was very effective in slowing the aircraft down or increasing its rate of descent.

*Since navigational charts were mainly based on Mercator projections, all Western airlines measured distances in nautical miles. Indicated air speed readings were also given in nautical miles per hour.

For similar reasons the engines could be operated in reverse thrust. This resulted in the rearward jet thrust from the engines being deflected in a more forward direction. This was particularly useful after landing to assist in decelerating the aircraft. I soon noticed that most pilots found it necessary to have both hands on the control column during the final landing manoeuvres. This resulted in quite some delay before they reached for, and applied reverse thrust. The sooner it is applied after main wheels touch down the more effective it becomes, and that moment was being lost. It became a matter of self training to use one hand for landing and the other positioned to apply immediately reverse thrust at main wheels touch down.

Transition training was rapidly completed, and I was soon flying the routes as a co-pilot.

Heliopolis Palace – Crew Hotel

Heliopolis, shopping arcades

Heliopolis Palace (Cairo), Crew hotel

My eventual "captain's check" took me on a flight through Beirut, Ankara and Tehran – strangely enough on my fortieth birthday. With all aspects of training completed, including 3-engine ferry take-offs, I was now able to renew my acquaintance with the Far East routes.

I had missed flying these routes with the Electra due to pressure of other activities. I found that tremendous changes had been made. Modern landing aids (ILS) were now available at all major airports, together with greatly improved approach and runway lighting. Radio communication with ATC was decidedly better, but Asiatic English was still questionable at some locations.

Over the Bay of Bengal, however, a black hole in the communications network still existed. Quantas, Air France, BOAC, and many others, all filled the air with their call signs trying to contact Karachi or Calcutta.

Radio Operators Licence

Pilots Licence

MINISTERIE VAN VERKEER
EN WATERSTAAT

RIJKSLUCHTVAARTDIENST

No. LI/12353

14 mei 1965.

DE MINISTER VAN VERKEER EN WATERSTAAT,

Gelet op artikel 52 van de Regeling Toezicht Luchtvaart en mede
gelet op de beschikking van de Minister van Verkeer en Waterstaat dd.
6 januari 1960,no. LI/10400 **Rijksluchtvaartdienst;**

B E S L U I T:

I. met ingang van heden tot 1 oktober 1966 worden in de examencommissie
voor VERKEERSVLIEGER benoemd:

tot lid voor het theoretisch examen

W. DUINKER   te Leiderdorp

tot Plaatsvervangend lid voor het theoretisch examen

J. de HAAS   te Huizen

tot leden voor het praktisch examen (Vleugelvliegtuigen)

H.J. BEAUDOUX	te Groningen
F.S. ter BERG	te Amstelveen
A.W. BRISCOE	te Hollandse Rading
G.H. DETERMEIJER	te Paterswolde
K.A. van ESSEN	te Loosdrecht
J.J.F. GRIFFITH	te Huizen
C.F. HARGRAVE	te Blaricum
A.M. MEEUWSEN	te Paterswolde
P.M. ORANGE	te Huis ter Heide
J.H. SHANLEY	te Wassenaar

- 2 -

AAN:
de heer P.M. Orange,
Baarnseweg 18A,
Huis ter Heide.

410540-882r

Appointment as Government Examiner for Pilot's Licences

Contact with these ground stations varied from non-existent, to weak, to strong and fading! One aircraft might make contact, and then attempt to relay position reports from others. One could only hope that everyone would maintain their assigned altitude. This black hole situation continued to exist for the rest of my flying career – perhaps by now there is light in the darkness, or are mobile phones being used?

The somewhat startling increase in cruising altitudes, from my piston engine days, was not always a welcome change. I quite missed my relatively close inspection of the world's changing scenery, and there was much less to keep me busy. Automation was beginning to play an increasingly important role. I was almost pleased to find that jets did not always fly over the weather, towering cloud formations could still reach well above our cruise altitudes, and ways around or through them still had to be found, with or without the help of ATC.

Pre-ordained career moves

After several months of relative freedom as a route pilot, and a re-familiarization tour of the Far East area, it was time to rejoin the mainstream of events. Instructor training was scheduled on both the simulator, and the aircraft, and the type office had an empty desk prepared for me.

Senior figures in the instructional department again seemed to be non-national pilots, and I was often surprised at what seemed to be an unusually low ratio of national pilots among the instructional staff. Was there perhaps a small element of discrimination at work? On the other hand, I had come across several former instructors who were unwilling to continue in a job which involved so much simulator time.

Since the type office, and the simulator hall were located in the same building at Schiphol East I had easy access to both departments. As it turned out, this was probably too convenient as one was seldom "off-duty".

Type office and instructional duties

One of the more interesting aspects of type office duties was that all DC-8 test flights became our direct responsibility. These were always required after so-called heavy maintenance overhaul, which was carried out every two to three years. This involved a substantial amount of aircraft dismantling, so that every nook and cranny could be inspected for possible corrosion and metal fatigue. At the same time the opportunity was used to undertake modifications or to update installed equipment.

After some two weeks of round-the-clock work, the engineering department would declare the aircraft ready for flight test. The flight crew then commenced extensive ground checks of the aircraft systems before commencing the flight test programme, which usually involved some three to four hours flying in an area free from other traffic, frequently over the more northern areas of the North Sea.

Test flights of an aircraft were also called for after some less time consuming maintenance work. These might be, for example, after replacement of a major flight control system, or after a change of two or more engines. Such flights were of much shorter duration since they were directed at more specific features.

Engine changes always involved a climb to high altitude since it was necessary to shut the engines down in turn, wait for them to cool, and then see if they would successfully re-light (re-start) at altitude. Occasionally we had to return with a non-starter with perhaps not all the engines yet tested: returning with two non-starters was not popular.

My own life in these days had no set routine. It was a variable feast divided between office and instructional duties, interspersed with the occasional flight test. Since the office was in the same building as the simulator, some days were actually divided between the two requirements.

My companion in the type office, and on every single DC-8 test flight, was F/E Gerard Schoonman. We subsequently moved together on to the Boeing 747 project, thus establishing a working relationship that was to span nearly fifteen years. In the world of civil aviation this length of aircrew partnership was quite unique, and undoubtedly proved beneficial to our work.

Another valued member of the office work team was Jan Klein, a former F/E. Jan had been the Chief F/E on the Lockheed Electra, so we had already developed mutual respect and understanding. He had also flown the DC-8 for several years, but was, unfortunately, to become medically unfit for continued flight duties. He also joined Gerard and I when we moved on to the B-747 project.

The support of these two F/E's through so many of my type office and test flight years was an invaluable asset. They also became very adept at diplomatically correcting my written work, particularly when it was evident that I was struggling to understand the subject matter.

Three engined ferry flights

These were flights made in order to re-position an (empty) aircraft to a location where an engine could be replaced. Since they were made with an engine inoperative, the captain had always had special training, if possible the F/E would be an instructor, but the co-pilot could be a normal route pilot. A detailed crew briefing prior to flight was essential, in particular to ensure that the non-standard take-off procedure was fully understood.

Such flights also required close co-ordination, and co-operation between several different departments. All passengers and freight had to be off-loaded which was a particular headache for the airfield staff. The passengers had to be found accommodation or transferred to another flight, possibly with another airline.

A member of the cabin staff, which would have been off-loaded, would be assigned (or volunteer) to accompany us on the flight. His/her duty would be to monitor the empty cabin for any untoward events – and of course to keep us supplied with coffee.

The probability of a second engine failing at some point during such a ferry flight always entered into our calculations. The most critical time for a second engine failure would be during or shortly after take-off. With this in mind, our training was always made with an outer engine inoperative for the take-off, followed by a second engine failure at lift-off. The actual routing of the flight was also determined with care, ensuring that a good weather airfield was available within fairly easy reach.

> On one such ferry out of Madrid to Schiphol I was delayed for several hours.
> All normally suitable airfields in the vicinity of the route were fog-bound,
> precluding the possibility of a two-engine landing should the need arise.

The need for such ferry flights became less and less as engine reliability improved, and a pooling of spare parts and engines was made along the major routes. These were pools established by airlines using common equipment. In addition to engines, other critical components became steadily more readily available through the pool system.

Third party training and co-operation

As had taken place on the Lockheed Electra, on which I had trained pilots from Ceylon, so on the DC-8 KLM offered flight training packages to other airlines. Among our most regular customers were PAL (Philippine Airlines), and VIASA (Venezuelan Airlines), and some of their pilots were quite regular visitors.

With PAL and VIASA this co-operation also extended into the sharing of aircraft. This resulted, in amongst other things, one side of an aircraft being painted in KLM colours, and the other side in PAL or VIASA colours. This was highly successful in confusing the boarding passengers – wrong boarding pass or wrong airline!!

A Pre-view of the Trident

An interesting assignment in 1965 was a visit to the de Havilland factory at Hatfield in the U.K. I accompanied Capt. Chuck Ramsey of KLM's R & D department to make an in-flight evaluation of the Trident aircraft – already on order by BEA (British European Airways). Our brief was to examine in detail the cockpit layout, and to acquaint ourselves with its flight characteristics.

In command of the flight was Capt. Peter Bugge, deputy to de Havilland's chief test pilot Capt. "Cats Eyes" Cunningham. The aircraft itself was adorned, on wings and tail, with a variety of devices related to the particular test programme in progress. We departed Hatfield around midday, and after Peter Bugge had completed his test requirements I was given the controls. After gaining an impression of its general handling characteristics, and conducting a few stalls, we returned to Hatfield for an approach and landing. I found that the autopilot tracked the approach path with great accuracy, and that the manual landing was quite straightforward. During taxi-ing in, however, the offset nose wheel (it was not aligned with the centre line of the aircraft) was initially a little disconcerting.

In the cockpit we were greatly impressed by the arrangement of the glare-shield control panel. The glare-shield lies between the lower frame of the forward windows, and the main instrument panel. This location had previously been used to accommodate various knobs and switches which had not been successful in finding other homes. This area was now resplendent with the various controls for the constantly used flight guidance systems – a great step forward in cockpit design. Since, however, KLM had no further interest in this particular aircraft type there was no follow-up to our report on the visit.

The Lockheed Electra had been among the first aircraft for which a carefully designed glare-shield panel was included within the cockpit layout, and that was largely due to the influence of Frank Hawkins and Chuck Ramsey. That it was now part of the Trident cockpit design must have given them great satisfaction.

Note: Capt John Cunningham was a former RAF pilot who became renowned for his skill as a night fighter pilot in the defence of London. From those activities he acquired his nick name of "Cats Eyes". Newspaper reports at the time credited him with living on a diet of carrots!!

Inverted flight

Instruction flights were seldom routine, some unexpected event always seemed to be around the corner. This corner I rounded rather too quickly in the spring of 1967, and the event was recorded in newspaper headlines in both Holland and England.

At the time I was training two American captains from ONA (Overseas National Airways) on the DC-8. Having completed their training syllabus they were required to fly a "type rating" programme with an FAA (Federal Aviation Authority) inspector in the observer's seat. This particular individual had a nervous habit of constantly jingling a bunch of keys in his hand, but, despite that, was a very alert and observant person.

An essential part of the FAA check programme was a full stall and recovery with minimum loss of altitude. This was more demanding than KLM requirements, and in my opinion not a very wise manoeuvre with a large jet aircraft. The expected stall speed could be pre-determined from a graph, and in flight a *"sticker-shaker" would indicate approach to the stall. This exercise was carried out with the power levers (almost) closed, and the engines thus in a near idle thrust condition.

> *A speed sensitive device would cause the control column to shake, about 5 knots before actual stall occurred. This was intended to alert the pilot to the need for corrective action. In KLM training we took the aircraft only slightly past stick-shaker, so that initial stall buffet could be recognized. We then required a safe recovery with little emphasis on altitude loss.

> Recognition and immediate reaction we considered the key factors, altitude loss was a secondary consideration – quite different from the FAA philosophy.

The actual (full) stall speed on a DC-8 coincides with quite heavy buffering of the aircraft, and positive control is then lost unless immediate corrective action is initiated. This action entails easing the nose down, and applying power. Until the aircraft reaches the stall, however, it is essential that the pilot keeps the aircraft in a wings level attitude using aileron input as necessary.

After the first trainee had successfully completed his check programme he vacated his seat so that the other pilot could take his turn. We then repeated the programme until the stall exercise was reached. At 10,000 feet, with gear down, and wing flaps extended, we carefully approached the stall. As the aircraft slowed down the stick-shaker came into operation followed by initial buffet. As buffet increased a wing started dropping, and since insufficient corrective action was being applied, I called "my controls" to indicate that I was taking over.

As I commenced levelling the wings, applying power, and easing the nose down to regain speed, we encountered full and heavy stall buffet. At that same instant my seat broke loose, and I slid fully to the rear. In my fully stretched position I was unable to maintain a forward pressure on the control column, but could only ensure it was in a neutral and wings level position.

The buffet and vibration made the instruments initially unreadable, but as they ceased a glimpse of increasing airspeed prompted me to call for "reverse thrust" on the engines. Since I couldn't reach the reverse thrust levers this was immediately applied by F/E Anton Ton. The intention was to prevent a further too rapid increase in speed – after all, we had gear and flaps hanging down, and they would be vulnerable to excessive speed.

As the instruments again came into focus the altimeter was seen to be unwinding with alarming rapidity. The artificial horizon seemed to be almost a blank, until I spotted the *"sky pointer" marker in approximately a 150 degree position, indicating we were close to being inverted. Fortunately, I was able to roll the aircraft in the correct direction to regain a wings level attitude, despite my stretched position.

> * If the "sky pointer" is seen to move from its normal upright position, the direction of roll to return it upright is obvious. If, however, its movement has not been seen (as in this case) then the direction of corrective roll to level the aircraft is not immediately obvious, particularly when it is in a completely unusual position.

With wings level I was now able to reposition my seat, and recover from the dive towards a very cold looking North Sea. To avoid stressing the aircraft unnecessarily this recovery was very gentle, and full control was effected several hundred feet above the water.

The whole episode had lasted barely 15 seconds, but we had fallen at some 30,000 ft per minute – as registered on the flight recorder. Our speed had not exceeded 270 knots, though that was well in excess of our wing flap, and gear extended limit speeds. Not wishing for any further surprises we returned to Schiphol at low speed with flaps, and gear still extended. A thorough inspection of the aircraft after landing revealed no damage.

> *The subsequent investigation pinpointed a defective locking pin in the instructor's seat, and from the F/E's evidence an uneven spool up of the engines as the main cause of the incident. An uneven engine spool up from idle was a very common problem.*

I still vividly recall the reaction of the FAA inspector when level flight had been restored. "Gee fellows, that was real exciting"! Quite unperturbed he was still jingling his bunch of keys. It was only then that I realised he had never been strapped in his seat! His parting words were "Guess we'll have to do it over....... see you fellows tomorrow then". The following morning we did indeed do the stall exercise once more, but this time with a more successful outcome!

As a result of this incident we installed an "upset" switch in the simulator enabling us to train pilots in recovery from unusual altitudes. To our surprise, a considerable number of pilots had great difficulty with this exercise. Those who had the most difficulty were the pilots who had never undergone full aerobatic training. At the same time the FAA modified their requirements regarding stall training and recovery, and raised the minimum altitude for commencement of the exercise.

INSTRUCTEUR KREEG TOESTEL 450 METER BOVEN ZEE IN BEDWANG

gained — aircraft
above the sea in control

DC-8 van K.L.M.

fell as a stone

viel als steen 3 kilometer omlaag

= 30,000 ft per min !!

1500'
– later evaluated from the Flight Recorder (an automatic recording device) as 600 feet

Van onze Amsterdamse redactie

SCHIPHOL — Een DC-8 van de K.L.M. is gistermiddag omstreeks half vier bijna in de Noordzee gestort. Het toestel, dat op een instructievlucht was, viel van een hoogte van ruim drie kilometer tot 450 meter boven het zeeoppervlak.

● Met een K.L.M.-toestel van dit type gebeurde gisteren bijna een ramp. Vlak boven het zeeoppervlak kreeg de instructeur de DC-8 weer in zijn macht.

Newspaper report

And the aftermath

The rather violent movement that had caused my seat to slide fully back, and leave me in a stretched out position triggered off a back complaint.

> *In 2005 who does one sue ..... the airline or the manufacturer??*

As the months went by a steady increase in discomfort resulted ultimately in requiring medical attention. X-rays taken in Holland apparently showed no abnormalities, and various osteopaths and masseurs were tried without any noticeable improvement.

My friend, Frank Hawkins, was also suffering from a back complaint and was visiting a London specialist. Encouraged by his progress I joined his London expeditions, and we often travelled together – remarkable journeys, as his main discomfort was in sitting, and mine in standing!

My treatment in London showed no signs of success, and through family contacts I then was able to make an appointment with an orthopaedic surgeon in Harley Street – a Mr Williams. My appointment with him turned out to be a great surprise. I had previously known him as Lt. Col. Williams in Palestine during 1946. He had been at Arnhem as orthopaedic surgeon to the Airborne troops, and was then stationed in Palestine with a paratroop regiment. I was working with the same regiment, either dropping them from Dakotas or towing them in gliders, and even flying their gliders. I had occasionally dropped at his feet from a parachute jump, but fortunately without the need for medical attention. Our last actual (close) meeting had been behind a garden wall in the grounds of Jerusalem's King David Hotel on the day we were bombed out by the Irgun (terrorists).

This now was an opportune reunion, for he very rapidly diagnosed my back problem, and was able to organise a December '68 appointment for corrective surgery.

> *This surgery was to see the insertion of some stainless steel screws. They still ring the alarm at some airfield security checks!!*

My last duty at Schiphol was a DC-8 test flight, and that was on the day before I checked in to hospital. My recollections of regaining consciousness after the operation remain very clear. Trying to focus on the blurred image of a head looming over me, I mumbled "feel as though I've candled in". The reply came firmly back "not to worry, we'll get you a new chute". The nurses couldn't follow this rather strange interchange; it was later explained that "candled in" was a paratrooper's term to describe a parachute that failed to open.

My stay at the Middlesex hospital was enlivened by an exchange of telexes with Schiphol. The operations officers at LAP (London Airport) fulfilled a very useful post office function for this purpose. I had known most of them for many years, in fact from the days when we used to fly flags from the cockpit windows on arrival and departure. They were extremely dedicated and efficient individuals, always ready with advice, and tremendously loyal to KLM.

Many of them had been with the Company since the days when we operated from a wooden hut on the northern perimeter of the airfield. From that position there was a clear view of the gasometer that enabled one to line up on the approach path to runway 23 – the gasometer is still there, but 23 is now a taxiway. Their more modern quarters were now in the Queen's Building at Terminal 2.

The DC-8 begins to fade

As my DC-8 years slowly came to an end, and my back operation was retired to the history books, there still remained much to be done before my attention could become fully occupied with the B-747 project.

Reluctantly, I was pushed into a concentrated route exposure programme on the North Atlantic area. Previously I had always avoided these routes, even when a policy was introduced requiring that all intercontinental captains be world-wide qualified. It seemed to me that this was primarily a move towards simplifying the task of the crew assignment office, and not one that would improve the efficiency (and safety!) of flight operations. It was very strange to see a dedicated North Atlantic pilot struggling with the inefficiencies of the Eastern hemisphere, and with its seasonal weather characteristics.

My own route flights had steadily diminished over the years as other duties had taken priority. On the relatively few occasions that I did fly, it became a matter of commonsense (to me) to confine myself to areas with which I was completely familiar – for example, the Near and Far East. In these areas I felt confidently at ease, and venturing in to new territories held no appeal at all – particularly as there could be no regular exposure to them.

So off I set, as a co-pilot, to unravel the mysteries of Loran, and to become acquainted with all the many factors that make up "route knowledge". I even found it necessary to study a school atlas to gain some familiarity with the general geography of the American and Canadian west coast areas. One might be vaguely familiar with names such as Goose Bay, Boston or Windsor Locks, but to locate them precisely was something else altogether.

Finally, I was scheduled for route check flight followed by several flights as captain, and felt ready for the future. The DC-8 had been but a stepping stone in my career, but a very important and enjoyable one. Fortunately, I did not get my feet too wet, and could approach the Boeing factory in a fairly confident frame of mind.

Although I had been working on the Boeing 747 project since the beginning of 1969 I was not yet "contaminated". Only when simulator or flight training on a new aircraft commenced did one become contaminated, and at that instant the validity of one's pilot license became suspended until fully qualified on the new type of aircraft. A far cry indeed to the days of the fifties when one could be simultaneously qualified on several different aircraft types; two engines or four made little difference to the situation.

The long (or stretched) DC-8 passed me by. They had an excellent pilot (Capt. Nicolay) in the type office, and he and I frequently exchanged information related to our very similar work. I did go one day as an observer on one of their training flights with a senior instructor, and was rather horrified by what I saw. The instructor decided to demonstrate the flexibility of the long fuselage to his students, and sent them down to stand by the rear pressure bulk head with instructions to hold fast to a seat back. He then proceeded to apply aggressively rudder input, flexing the tail end in a sideways movement so that they could no longer see the cockpit door! .... my former respect for him was the only casualty of this episode.

...........................but memories are constantly revived

This rudder episode was recalled to my mind by the fairly recent crash of an A-330 in the New York area, apparently caused by the over enthusiastic use of rudder. The aircraft tail unit was then stressed beyond its design limits resulting in an in-flight break-up.

Modern airliners can be awesome in size, and particularly in fuselage length .... and lengthy objects will bend when encouraged to do so. Aircraft manufacturers recognise this factor by installing a *rudder "limiter" system. The mere fact that all large jet aircraft include a rudder "limiter" system in their design should, in my mind, be sufficient indication to their pilots that the rudder needs treating with the utmost respect. Perhaps they have never been taught the reason for its installation.

> *The actual travel of the rudder surface, in response to rudder pedal movement, will be automatically limited, when aircraft speed exceeds a certain value. The tail of the aircraft is thus protected against the possibility of being over stressed at high speeds.*

The correspondence in the aviation press that resulted from this crash was surprising in content. The manufacturer was blamed for lack of design information, and pilot training was criticised for improper instruction. The unfortunate crew were also blamed, perhaps in an attempt to shift the burden of responsibility – after all, they were beyond questioning.

From very early flying days I had been taught that the rudder was primarily for directional control during take-off and landing, and for use in the event of an engine failure, particularly at high thrust conditions. I found it quite disturbing to read that this basic principle had long disappeared from the training manuals.

The DC-8 required a very positive rudder input to retain initially directional control in the event of an outer engine failure at take-off thrust, and thus was provided with a quite large rudder area. Looking at more unusual aircraft, such as the De Havilland Comet or the Concorde, it will be noticed that their rudders are much smaller than those on more conventional aircraft. This is primarily the result of having their engines mounted far closer to the fuselage centre line. The asymmetric effect of any engine failure, and particularly of an outer engine at high thrust, then becomes substantially less, and requires a much smaller rudder deflection.

Memories of my near fatal "upset" were also revived by the crash of an Egyptian airliner into the Atlantic Ocean a few years ago. There was insufficient evidence to pinpoint an actual cause but the high rate of descent from cruise altitude was repeatedly commented upon. Since the rate of descent had been quite significantly less than that which I had experienced, such comment seemed to have little relevance. Whether this had been a belated "coffin corner" episode, followed by a failed attempt to recover from an unusual attitude, or a structural failure of some kind couldn't be determined.

Yet another failed attempt of recovery from an unusual attitude resulted in the disappearance of a Flash Airlines B-737 into the Red Sea, near a holiday resort on the Sinai Peninsular. This, however, appeared to have been compounded by a cultural problem. The very senior captain was not prepared to listen to the repeated warnings of his junior co-pilot.

Although my DC-8 career had been relatively brief, particularly in terms of hands-on flight experience, it was a period where the learning curve appeared endless. There always seemed to be a new experience to analyse for lessons which might have a future application. It was not a period which I could have missed in my career structure.

Paine Field, Everett. B-747: awaiting engines on the flight line

The Boeing 747 Years

Towards the end of the road

It had been a long journey from my days as an immature cadet pilot on Tiger Moth's in Rhodesia (Zimbabwe) to achieving the status of a captain on B-747's in Holland with one of the world's major airlines.

Along the way I had encountered many different situations in a variety of aircraft with vastly differing crews. Except for my RAF and early KLM days, however, my actual flying hours had been far less than those of the average airline pilot of the era. This was the result of so many years of involvement in instructional and office duties.

Actual flight hours recorded in his logbook, are but an imprecise measure of a pilot's hours of work. To them must be added the unrecorded duty time that takes place before and after any particular flight, and there are no limits on the clock time at which these periods of duty can commence or end. His natural body clock is frequently in complete disarray.

Today's airline pilot probably acquires actual flight time at a rate of some five to six hundred hours per year, and for an intercontinental pilot this will include some extremely long flights with rapid time changes. In former days on the Far East route, for example, our time changes were quite gradual, and more easily absorbed. During my early years with KLM I was accumulating flight hours at a rate of some twelve hundred hours per year, but by the time we had acquired our first flight simulator this figure had dropped to well below that being flown by the average route pilot, as office and instructional duties had taken first place. Over two thousand hours had been spent in the Electra and DC-8 simulators!

During my last ten years with KLM my actual flight time on the B-747 was often less than three hundred hours per year – a very slender accumulation for that day and age. Fortunately, it had been decided at an early stage of the B-747 project that I would no longer be an active member of the Flight Instruction department, but close contact would be maintained. The fact that our respective offices were at totally different locations actually made this contact somewhat loose.

It was late in 1969 that I was first sent to the Boeing factory near Seattle (USA) to get acquainted with my future, and with the leading people with whom I would become involved. This was the start of a ten year association with Boeing on behalf of KLM. After my retirement from KLM this association was to be continued on behalf of other airlines.

The World's Biggest

The B-747 assembly plant was at Paine Field (Everett) some forty minutes drive north of Seattle, and was claimed to be the world's largest building under one roof. A guided tour of the assembly lines was a significant feature of any visit. An intricate network of overhead rails carried cranes transporting parts to different assembly locations. Inside and outside the growing aircraft structures, armies of male and female mechanics, mostly equipped with pneumatic tools, made a deafening noise. They were all equipped with ear muffs, but the passing visitor really got an earful!

As the assembly line slowly moved along a structurally complete aircraft would finally arrive in front of the immense exit doors ready to be towed away for a visit to the paint shop, and the application of its airline colour scheme. Final fitting out would then follow before it reached the flight line to be readied for Boeing flight test.

At full production Everett would be turning out between five and six completed aircraft each month, and the supply of component parts had to keep abreast of that tempo. Various vital parts for the aircraft were manufactured at different factories around the USA, and then shipped to Everett to be united in the final assembly hall. In reality, therefore, the Everett plant was a gigantic assembly line to which all the different bits and pieces were sent.

Everett was but one of several Boeing plants in the Seattle area which turned out different aircraft types. Initial deliveries and training flights departed from Boeing Field much nearer to the city of Seattle. It was at Boeing Field that I saw the mock-up of the SST (Supersonic Transport), which was overtaken by the Concorde in the race to produce a supersonic airliner for the world's airlines.

At a later stage a more formal "delivery centre" was created at Everett itself to handle all B-747 customer departure flights. This did, unfortunately, create some difficulty with the essential process of filing a flight plan with ATC. Everything had to be done by telephone, and delays to departure time were not uncommon.

It is perhaps of interest to note that USA based airlines seldom engaged in any form of acceptance checking of their new purchase at Everett. A crew would arrive to collect the new aircraft, and perform some form of in-flight check on their way to home base. What then happened if discrepancies were found I have no idea – it was the overseas airlines, in this respect, that were the most demanding customers, and KLM was, of course, the most demanding of all!

The Flight Line

A walk around the flight line in 1969, where the completed aircraft awaited customer inspection, portrayed a rather unusual situation. Some twenty of the aircraft parked in neat rows were sporting different airline colours, such as Pan American and Delta, but they were completely without engines. In place of the missing engines were hung large blocks of concrete; apparently Pratt and Whitney, the engine manufacturer, was having production problems causing a delay on the flight line. Normally, the flight line would be keeping pace with the flow of aircraft from the assembly line, but the question of parking the nearly completed aircraft was now becoming a serious problem.

Appointment as an Engineering Pilot

In 1970 I was officially appointed by KLM as their B-747 engineering pilot, and a type office was created in the new Amstelveen (near Amsterdam) headquarters of the Company. It was from here that

KLM's new headquarters – Amstelveen. Author's office marked with an "x"

my future activities would be steered, together with those of F/E Gerard Schoonman. Also in the office was Jan Klein, a retired F/E, a most likeable and efficient person.

Early models of the aircraft were already in service. The "Jumbo" jet had astonished the world by its sheer size and capacity, probably to a greater extent that the Airbus 380 is likely to do in the near future. The media had had a field day. It had enjoyed frenzied feeding on predictions of crashes which involved horrific loss of life, and the inevitable end to production of the aircraft. Fortunately the media were soon turned to other more newsworthy events, and quiet was restored in the jumbo's jungle.

A Visit to the Bazaar

A great deal of managerial bargaining accompanies the purchase of a new airliner – a scenario with which I am not too familiar. Traditionally a manufacturer would produce a basic model of their new offer. Each interested airline would then examine the basic offering, and decide upon any changes required in order to fulfil their own particular requirements.

Many different Company departments were involved in this process. Operations were looking closely at the cockpit, the Cabin Staff were looking closely at pantry location etc., and Ground Handling had a host of their own unique problems. These changes, or options, were then put before the manufacturer for pricing. Depending upon what new engineering drawings or changes in construction were needed so did the price change.

The change deemed necessary by a customer could be many and various, and range throughout the aircraft. Number and location of passenger seats, number and location of toilets, providers of the fire

First KLM aircraft heading for the paint shop

detection system or of the radios and their controls were but a few of the possibilities. The resulting escalation of price, over and above the basic, could run into millions of dollars. KLM was no stranger to this process, but now they were to become more innovative in the market place.

An Innovation .... KSS

............................and later KSSU

KSS was created by an amalgamation of operational and engineering objectives between KLM, SAS (Scandinavian Airlines System) and Swissair. Some time later UTA (Union de Transport Airlines) joined the group for reasons of maintenance sharing. The initial intention of KSS was to be able to approach TBC (The Boeing Company) with a common specification for all the B-747's that the group then had on order and also for further orders. This specification would then be presented to TBC for costing.

This was a far more economic approach than had occurred in the past, when each individual airline would separately present (different) specifications, and be separately faced with individual costing. Together with this KSS agreement on specification (flight technical and engineering) came an agreement concerning the maintenance and major overhaul of the aircraft. Since KLM became responsible for all major overhauls of the aircraft, the flight testing of the entire KSS fleet would become the responsibility of the KLM type office flight crew.

A further intended benefit of the common KSS specification was that any aircraft in the fleet could be operated by any crew of those airlines, and without the need for extra training on aircraft "differences". Interchange of operating crews between major airlines was normally a complex matter, since differences between (what was essentially an identical aircraft) could be considerable. In theory, it would now become possible, for example, to replace an aircraft or crew shortage in one airline with a substitute from another. The discussions between the three KSS airlines became lengthy and tedious before a united front could be presented to Boeing.

Some Seattle Affairs

Reading in January 2005 that Airbus are making ready for an emergency evacuation demonstration, necessary for aircraft certification of their A-380 with five hundred and eighty three volunteers, recalls to mind a similar B-747 demonstration in the late '60's.

The FAA rules then, as now, require the evacuation of the maximum passenger load in just 90 seconds, with only half the normally available exit doors in use. Today this ruling is supported by the European JAR (Joint Aviation Regulations). This rule recognizes that a crash may occur which renders many of the doors un-useable, either due to fire or to fuselage distortion jamming the doors.

The escape slides could also be detached from the aircraft after inflation, and used as life rafts following a landing on water. Circular life rafts were also available, but they had first to be removed from their overhead storage bins near the doors.

...........................an evacuation demonstration

For the actual demonstration we were gathered in a darkened hangar, the massive bulk of a silent B-747 looming over us. At a pre-arranged signal the aircraft emergency lights came on, the doors flew open, and the emergency slides started to inflate and extend. As passengers started collecting at the doors the initial, almost horizontal extension of the slides, changed to a droop mode as they reached the ground. With extension very rapidly completed the cries of "jump-and-slide" filled the air, and the passengers were urged forward to provide a continuous flow of evacuees. They came sliding down the double channel chutes in rapid succession, finally followed by the cabin attendants.

The 90 second target time was comfortably achieved, and the excited participants made their way off stage, nursing a few cuts and bruises. It was an impressive demonstration, but probably not as impressive as the A-380 promises to be.

...........................and crew training

This evacuation drill was repeated by all crew members during their qualification training for the aircraft. For the cockpit crew there was a subtle difference. In the event that they might be unable to descend to the main deck for evacuation, then a roof hatch above the F/E's seat could be brought into use. Adjacent to the hatch were five handles connected to ropes of predetermined length. The drill was disarmingly simple – open the hatch, grab a handle, climb out onto the roof, and slide down the curvature of the fuselage to the ground. In theory, your thirty feet drop would be gently arrested just short of terra firma. I never met anyone who had been brave enough to try this procedure!

A VMU Test

Another fascinating event had been watching a VMU (minimum unstuck speed) test. This test determined the very minimum speed at which the aircraft could be made to leave the ground. It was not an operational speed in itself, but rather a datum point from which actual operational take-off speeds could be derived.

With a tree trunk strapped under the rear fuselage the aircraft was accelerated down the runway. As speed built up the aircraft was rotated, raising the nose, and pushing the tail down firmly against

VMU Test

the runway surface. Acceleration continued amid smoke and sparks until the aircraft became airborne in an extreme nose up attitude........VMU achieved!

...........................and some Seattle personalities

My earlier visit to Seattle had provided an opportunity to fly the No. 1 Boeing 747 with their chief test pilot Jack Waddell – Jack was a lanky Texan, complete with cowboy hat and boots. It was known that he had slow-rolled a Boeing 707, but whether he had shown his appreciation of the B-747 in a similar manner was only a matter of rumour at that time.

I found that handling of the aircraft on the ground took quite some getting used to. Its sheer size demanded very careful judgement of distances from potential obstructions. In flight, however, it was quite delightful .... very stable, but light on the controls and extremely responsive.

Our resident representative in Seattle at the time was George Malouin, who together with a team of KLM engineers was monitoring every stage of construction of our first aircraft. George was a fairly recently retired KLM captain with an outstanding technical reputation, and had continued his flying career with Condor, a German charter airline. Summoned from Germany by a member of KLM management he was appointed as our Seattle representative. For the KLM Engineering and Maintenance Division this was not a popular appointment since by long tradition all such appointments were their prerogative.

Unfortunately, George commenced organizing increasingly lavish parties (at KLM expense), and his replacement soon followed. Those parties did, however, provide an excellent venue for getting acquainted with Boeing personnel, which was to prove so advantageous in the following years.

KLM Acceptance Team – From left: F/E Gerald Schoonman, Ben Douwes (Engineering and Maintenance),
Jaap Veldhuizen van Zanten (pilot), Rob Knapp (Engineering and Maintenance), Author, Evert Homan (Avionics Specialist)

Final discussions with Boeing – Standing from left: Author, –, –, Jaap Veldhuizen van Zanten
Sitting from left: –, –, Louie Creyghton (KLM representative at Seattle)

Changing Seats

...........................and meeting Louie Creyghton

Throughout 1970 my B-747 office work had been interspersed with D-8 flights, the last of which was a Copenhagen flight in October. In November we were scheduled for B-747 training in Seattle, and it was off to the classroom. Joining me on this training programme were Jaap Veldhuizen van Zanten (pilot), Gerard Schoonman (F/E), and a selected group of senior pilots and flight-engineers. Our initial programme was to be classroom instruction followed by simulator training. Actual flight training would not take place until we actually owned an aircraft. To be flight trained on a Boeing owned aircraft would have been too expensive a proposition.

By this time Louie had become our resident representative. We could not have wished for a more supportive and energetic person, always ready with help and advice. In addition to his many other duties he always ensured that we had a fleet of Ford Mustang cars for travel to work, and for personal outings – Boeing went on full alert when Mustangs were reported on the freeway!

.... and the customer is always right!

New Year's Day 1971 saw the acceptance team of cockpit crew and KLM engineering specialists climbing aboard PH-BUA to commence the ground acceptance programme. Boeing was expecting it to be completed in a few hours, and not the several days that resulted! Ben Douwes (from the Engineering and Maintenance Division) was the leader of our team, and he would monitor and minutely record every detail of the tests that we subsequently conducted.

The discrepancies that we uncovered during our ground checks were all precisely recorded by Ben, and at the end of the day given to Boeing for their corrective action. They would work on such items

Ir. Bescamcon – handing over the aircraft keys after purchase of PH-BUA

overnight, and return them to us for re-checking the following morning. Coffee and sandwiches were brought on board so that any work interruptions were kept to a minimum. Our checks were actually based on a sequential list of our own devising, and this was later taken over by the Boeing team so that they could be better prepared for our rather demanding scrutiny in the future.

Once the ground checks were satisfactorily completed Boeing took us out to an elaborate lunch at a waterside restaurant. There were many aquarium tanks dotted around the dining room, mostly they seemed to be homes for slowly moving sea-horses, the first I'd seen!

In the air, the customer is still right

January 8th saw our aircraft ready for flight test. The Boeing test pilot Sandy McMurray and F/E Bill Spence would be in overall control of the flight, since the aircraft was still Boeing property, and we were still lacking in actual flight experience. With myself in the captain's (left hand) seat, and Gerard at the F/E's panel we were soon ready to go.

The actual flight lasted three and a half hours, working steadily through our programme which was guided by Ben from the observer's seat. There was a sequential flow to the programme, aimed at minimizing the time involved. Occasionally Sandy or Bill would interrupt to suggest a more efficient method of sequencing our actions, but generally they were quite content to observe our progress. Several unexpected faults were uncovered during this process despite the fact that Boeing had previously flown their own pre-delivery flight, which really illustrates the complexity of modern aircraft – check, and re-check were essential facts of life. At the extensive post flight de-briefing, with departmental experts in attendance, it was agreed that a re-flight would be necessary once the faults had been corrected.

It actually took a further two flights before we (the customer) was satisfied, and before telephones could be lifted to alert banks and financiers that a deal was about to be finalized. The transfer of some 125 million dollars from KLM funds to Boeing was imminent.

I had found that first acceptance test a unique experience, particularly the flying. The advanced capabilities of the various automatic flight and navigation systems were quite incredible. One had read about them, but this was now reality. The spread in operational speeds for such a large aircraft was also truly remarkable. An over-speed warning check (in a shallow dive) at close to the speed of sound would be followed by low speed stall checks in the region of 110 knots. At the controls one was scarcely aware of aircraft size or that one was manoeuvring some 250 tons of machinery around the skies.

> *We had considerably surprised Boeing by the very detailed nature of our acceptance checks, and they subsequently made use of our programme during their pre-delivery preparations.*

> *In later years I would apply a similar (but much shorter) technique before purchasing a new or second-hand car – much to the astonishment of the dealers, particularly when a gear box needed changing!*

The creation of Operating Manuals

.........................*crews, for the use of!*

Aircraft manufacturers had always provided their customers with a complete library of books related to the operation and maintenance of their aircraft. These were usually made available well in advance of the first aircraft delivery to the customer, and they were also provided with an ongoing amendment service.

Most European airlines had, however, a well developed history of presenting operational information to their crews in a readily recognizable in-house format. This greatly simplified the process of training, when crews were moved to a different type of aircraft. In some companies the use of the native language would also be a requirement.

The operational data supplied by Boeing to KLM was thus our first task in the field of preparation. Several volumes of excellent manuals and detailed checklists for every phase of flight had to be adapted to the customary KLM format – both in operating philosophy, and in Anglicizing much of the American wording. This requirement occupied a great deal of our office time in that first year of preparation.

There were inevitably critical comments on the fruits of our labours, but at least it showed that we had some interested readers!

...........................and now the number game, in round figures

This leviathan of the skies was to be a new numbers game for the operating crews and for the operational staff. With an empty weight (no passengers or fuel on board) of some 160 tons, and a maximum take-off weight capability in excess of 350 tons, its capacity exceeded anything previously encountered. Within its wing tanks about 150 tons of fuel could be loaded, but that was initially consumed at a rate of almost ten tons per hour if the aircraft was heavily laden.

Cruise altitudes were dependent on aircraft weight, but would be in the region of 35,000 feet. The cruise speed was defined as a percentage of the speed of sound (Mach 1), and would normally be .780 Mach for optimum fuel economy. These were base line numbers, and reflected the astronomical purchase figures (in 1970) of around a million dollars for a single engine, and some 125 million dollars for the aircraft itself.

...........................and the numbers game related to salaries

...........................the old Midas touch!

The "numbers game" proved costly to the major airlines in another field – that of flight crew salaries. An increase in aircraft size and capacity brought with it an increase in the field of pilots' responsibility, or so ran the historical argument. It was a line of reasoning that had begun when aircraft were first flown for hire and reward, and by now had become unstoppable. It had always seemed to me a somewhat spurious argument – glad though I was to accept the winnings.

To me, flying an aircraft with some three hundred passengers on board was really no different from flying one with only thirty. Was there even a difference between a full plane, and one only partly full? The piloting technique was unaltered, the rules were the same, and so where was that increase of responsibility?

One reads, with some degree of scepticism, accounts of pilots deliberately avoiding towns and villages in their dying aircraft. Self preservation is an overwhelming human instinct, a last struggle towards open fields or woods would seem vastly preferable to impacting against hard bricks and stone.

The direct sense of increased responsibility would have been much more apparent to the cabin crew, faced with the seemingly endless rows of seats and anxious faces. In a similar fashion the ground handling staff would be confronted with vastly increased numbers of arriving and departing passengers, many with urgent personal problems to be solved in a double fast time.

Over the years salary rises tended to become significant events, and could be assured of attracting some media headlines. They would routinely accompany a promotion, but at other times, would result from union negotiations. Since they were normally backdated a useful lump sum resulted, enabling a fulfilment of that very human activity of "keeping-up-with-the-Jones". My B-747 winnings were very useful in the purchase of a new car – an MGB.GT, which is still with me thirty-three years later with nearly 400,000 miles on the clock.

...........................*things were made to last in those days!*

Flight training

With the acceptance and final purchase of "our" aircraft, flight training could at last begin. This was mainly carried out at Moses Lake airfield, a traffic free location some twenty minutes flying from Seattle. My own instructor was Boeing captain Max Shinn, who firmly guided me through the comprehensive programme – some ten years later I was to employ him as a captain for Garuda Indonesian Airlines.

Several senior KLM flight instructors were also trained at this time, but full completion of the required KLM training programme had to await the successful acceptance of our second aircraft, and we were back within a month to deal with that.

Finally, home with the shopping

The day of our homeward bound departure finally dawned, and a large crowd of well-wishers assembled to wave us farewell. Checklists were completed with unusual care, and we taxied out to the departure runway. With the last checks completed, the engines were spooled up (partly accelerated), and as the brakes were released advanced to full take-off thrust settings. Acceleration down the runway to take-off speed was quite rapid, and we then were up and away for a ten hour flight – taking us over the frozen landscape of northern Canada, Greenland and Iceland, and eventually over Scotland and the North Sea to position on the approach path to Schiphol (Amsterdam).

We had been listening to the Schiphol weather broadcasts for some hours, alive to the possibility that our arrival could be delayed by fog. Fortunately, the fog was starting to lift as we drew nearer, and we finally landed in misty conditions on the morning of January 31st 1971. This was the start of a new chapter in the long history of KLM.

The arrival hall at Schiphol was a seething mass of official welcomers, sightseers and families of the crew. Guided through the throng we found ourselves before cameras in readiness for a TV and radio interview, not too welcome after a long and tiring flight.

PH-BUA arrives at Schphol 31/1/1971

While the welcome was still in progress the aircraft was unloaded, and quietly towed away to hangar 11 to commence its PDM programme, and also provide a chance for the ground staff to become acquainted with their new charge.

Party Time

The PDM (Post Delivery Modifications) was a regular feature for all newly delivered aircraft. Some ten days were then spent on the installation of equipment which was standard in the KLM fleet, but which would have been too costly to have installed at the factory. It was also a useful training period for the many ground mechanics who would be responsible for its future maintenance. With the PDM complete it was passed to us for another test flight. Evidently the engineers were supremely confident, as the aircraft was scheduled for the opening flight to New York that same day!

Chief Pilot 747 – A W Ravenhill

Fortunately, all went well, and after landing we were able to park the aircraft at the departure gate at Schiphol Central. It immediately became the centre of activity as it was readied for its inaugural flight to New York in the capable hands of the Chief Pilot, Capt. Ravenhill. During the flight it became apparent that an error had been made in programming the inertial navigation system. Happily the crew were able to resolve a quite confusing situation, and continue with the flight as planned.

The Winds of Change

With the introduction of the B-747 on the route network far reaching changes began to evolve. The sheer size and range of the new aircraft promoted variations in the operational cycle that could scarcely have been envisaged by the pioneers of old. Their old stamping ground of the Far East was probably to show the greatest evidence of these changes. On the North Atlantic the premier destination remained New York, but this was still an out-and-back flight for the crews; a short night stop in combination with a five hour adjustment to the body clock was no small strain on crews and their families.

...........................in crew complement

In Constellation days the crew complement had included one stewardess. By the time that the DC-8 came into service four to six stewardesses were considered normal, but the newly introduced B-747 was decorated with a minimum of ten. This startling increase in numbers was not only due to the passenger potential, but also to the legal requirement that each emergency exit door (ten on the main deck) be manned for take-off and landing.

These dramatic changes in crew complement, leading to several personal moments of embarrassment, "were you in my crew"? were matched by significant developments on the ground.

...........................and the world of commerce

For example, the UAE (United Arab Emirates) was created in 1971 leading to an explosive development of the Gulf States. In particular, the growth of Dubai was phenomenal as skyscrapers started their soaring journey to out rival Hong Kong. Its pre-eminence as a centre of local trade had now become international. Even our old sand runway at Sharjah was now fast disappearing under concrete, although the old fort was retained as a museum. New housing estates began to appear on the sandy wastes surrounding the growing town centre, and endless piles of builders' rubble dotted the landscape.

These labour intensive developments throughout the Gulf demanded more workers than could be supplied from local sources. The sub-continent of India and the Philippines became major sources of recruitment – and therein lay major traffic changes for the airlines. Places such as Baghdad and Calcutta started to disappear from the timetables as the world of commerce reviewed its priorities.

...........................and the latest fashions!!

Bangkok was also now facing a revival as a Far East crew centre, and the vastly increased number of crew members passing through led to the need for a dedicated crew hotel – an hotel which could accommodate the twenty-four hour demands of a crossroads position, with crews transiting to and from Australia and Japan, arriving from home or returning there. The hotel could accommodate four entire 747 crews at any one time, while still retaining a few rooms for emergencies.

The changes that now encompassed crew stopovers in Bangkok were quite revolutionary. The hotel tennis court and swimming pool were scenes of fashion spectaculars: each new season in the fashion world produced ever more revealing bikinis and tennis apparel. The crew bar, presided over by Jimmy, was a central meeting point for newly arrived crews to greet old friends already in "residence". Delicious (free) snacks were constantly available for those disinclined to partake of a more staid restaurant meal.

The majority of the hotel staff were long term local KLM employees, or would become so in the course of time. They had seen similar jollities before, though certainly not on such a grand scale. They must also have been fully aware of the not infrequent assignations made between crew members, but their discretion on such matters was incomparable.

It was sad to hear in later years that further changes in the operational scenario brought about the closure of this fondly remembered crossroads in an historical route pattern. It is to be hoped that the local staff were well treated in the process.

> *For the local staff, this preview of Western customs was a foretaste of the mass tourism that was soon to envelop the whole of their green and pleasant land.*

The ever listening ears!

Over the years KLM Flight Watch (located in the Amstelveen Head Office) had grown into a very efficient organization, staffed by people who had often had experience of being station managers along the routes. They were thus well versed in the problems that could be encountered when an aircraft became unserviceable. A twenty four hour watch was maintained on KLM aircraft the world over, and this was also co-ordinated with Maintenance Control at Schiphol East.

Crews could thus establish radio contact with home base on designated frequencies from virtually anywhere in the world. If a flight technical or operational problem was involved then either Gerard or I could be directly linked into the problem for advice; middle of the night telephone calls were not unusual!

The F/E's had received R/T (Radio Telephony) training, allowing them to use an on-board radio for these contacts. They also used this contact to call directly Maintenance Control prior to arrival at Schiphol, and give a summary of the aircraft's technical condition. This allowed preparation to be made for any necessary work prior to the aircraft's next despatch.

Closely linked into this system was our Despatch Deficiency Guide, which was carried on board. This listed a vast number of items in every major system of the aircraft which were required to be operative for a departure. The key issue was always the matter of airworthiness – could the aircraft be safely operated with a particular deficiency or perhaps it could be operated only with special limitations? Some items could be held over for later corrective maintenance, and a despatch allowed, but very careful consideration was always needed.

Occasionally, uncertainty would exist for the crew experiencing a problem, and the final decision on whether to despatch or not would be made by Gerard or myself. In this context I sometimes used my personal knowledge of the crew concerned and their capabilities in arriving at a decision. Not always an easy task.

Keeping Abreast of Events

...........................and pooling resources

Throughout 1971 deliveries of new aircraft continued apace. In total I collected seven new ones from the factory, and most required three test flights before our stringent requirements were satisfied. The opportunity to fly some line services (passenger flights) constantly eluded me, apart from a mid-summer flight to London. That was where it had all begun twenty-three years ago when I had flown to Amsterdam as a newly enrolled KLM pilot; now I was being greeted by staff who had handled my Dakota, Convair, Electra and DC-8 flights over the intervening years.

As the year progressed, a not unexpected problem started creeping around the corner – our early models of the Pratt and Whitney engine were showing signs of unreliability. To improve the accessibility of spare parts, and particularly that of engines, a pool arrangement with other airlines was in existence along the routes. Despite the outward similarity of the aircraft, however, they could be very different beasts under the skin. Electronic equipment could be different, various pumps could differ, and certainly engines could come from different manufacturers. Nevertheless, it was a useful resource.

> *The "pool" allowed any partaking airline access to the spares stock of parts. The user would then assume responsibility for replacing the borrowed item. A borrowed engine could, of course, take a long time to replace.*

Three Engine Ferry permutations

The early seventies saw a considerable number of engine failures along the route, due to the lack of reliability in the newly developed high thrust engines. The required ferry flight operations that resulted were very similar to those we had used on the DC-8. Should things go wrong, however, the consequences could be much more severe, but now we had the additional support of a full-flight simulator in which to perfect our procedures and techniques.

Since the North Atlantic airports, at that time, were all within reach of local assistance, it seemed that the Far East network would be the most likely area for ferry operations. It was thus decided that only two ferry captains should undergo the necessary training programme.

..........................and simulator support

Probably the key feature in the simulator training was a take-off with an outboard engine inoperative, followed by an inboard engine failure (on the same side) shortly after lift off. Very quick and positive use of rudder, sometimes supported by aileron, was needed in such an exercise in order to counteract the severe asymmetric effect.

A take-off roll would be commenced with balanced engine thrust – one engine on each wing at full blast. As forward speed built up, the thrust of the third engine would steadily be increased, balancing its asymmetric effect with increasing rudder application. Should a second engine fail while getting airborne in this unusual condition a very rapid increase, or reversal, of the existing control input would be required – depending on whether the asymmetry had increased or vanished?

In the cockpit, a demanding situation could develop which required sound crew co-operation, and careful handling of the several checklists involved. Several variations on this training programme were perfectly feasible, but all obeyed the cardinal training rule "on every take-off an engine failure must be expected".

A three-engined ferry was originally assumed to require but one take-off and landing. In practice, however, these operations had often to be conducted through two or even three airfields – primarily because a pool engine was no longer available at a convenient location.

For some of the longer ferry flights that arose, special clearance was required from Head Office. The designated ferry pilot would then travel as a passenger to the stranded aircraft. If he was already somewhere along the route then an urgent re-scheduling of other captains became necessary to cover his absence from the normal scheduled services.

One (engine) out

..........................and three to go!

In 1972/73 both my home and office events were frequently disrupted by the need for a ferry operation. Some of these turned out to be my first, and (so far) only chance to catch a glimpse of my favourite territory – the Far Eastern routes.

Many of our pool partners were operating with General Electric engines, and our Pratt and Whitney's were becoming increasingly difficult to replace when the need arose. In consequence my passenger journeys could be to Karachi or Delhi, and then a ferry through Beirut to Schiphol or to Bangkok, for a ferry through Manila to Tokyo. Sometimes the journeys were much shorter, and a ferry from Lisbon, or from Athens were comparatively uneventful affairs.

These flights were fortunately without undue incident, but it was always with a sense of relief that three fans (engines) were still turning at final touch down. It was not until 1976 that I made the very longest of my many ferry flights from Singapore to Amsterdam with an overnight stop in Dubai – a total of just over fifteen hours on three engines. None of this, of course, exempted me from regular refresher training on the simulator.

The "5th Pod" arrives on the scene

While Pratt and Whitney was paying urgent attention to the improvement of engine reliability, Boeing was busy developing (and certifying) a so-called 5th pod configuration. This involved the creation of an under wing attachment point upon which a spare engine could be hung, allowing its transportation to any destination on a normal passenger service. The influence of this configuration had surprisingly little effect on actual aircraft handling, and thus no extra crew training was required. Several performance factors (especially fuel consumption) did, however, demand adjustment.

> *From an historical point of view this was not a new development. Spare engine carriage had first been used in the 1920's by the RAF in Mesopotamia (Iraq). The territory was then a British Protectorate, following the collapse of the Turkish Empire, and the RAF had the main role in policing the turbulent tribes.*
>
> *This they did by dropping leaflets, followed by bombs when necessary. A forced landing in potentially hostile terrain required a rescue mission. If an engine was involved this would be flown out strapped to the fuselage of the rescue aircraft, between the wheels. A mechanic would accompany the rescue aircraft in place of the second crewman.*

Hang Your Trophies on the Bedroom Wall

...........................automation is here!

My bubble and periscopic sextants were long gone, and my hand-held Dalton computer was now slipping from my trembling fingers. INS (Inertial Navigation Systems) had now replaced the need for heavenly bodies, and stretches of the imagination. The Mercator's plotting charts had been reassigned to wallpaper duties, and no longer displayed my imaginative calculations, and my pencils, erasers and dividers had long been consigned to the rubbish bin.

INS was the "in" thing. Feed it with your departure point and your destination, assuage its hunger with desired routing information in explicit terms of latitude and longitude, and it would guide you with a faultless hand. Feed it garbage, and it would respond in kind. Available for instant display were the direction and speed of the prevailing wind, together with the drift angle and groundspeed. The time and distance remaining to the next en-route point, or to any other place on earth, could be provided with unerring accuracy. We had three of these devices in the cockpit, and each one could easily surpass any of the navigational skills that we had previously acquired.

...........................so the navigator is replaced, and what about the pilot?

Our first B-747 was equipped with two AP's (Automatic Pilots), either of which could be coupled to the INS or to a radio beam for automatic navigation of the aircraft. Coupling to speed and height requirements was also a standard feature. Although one AP was sufficient for all flight phases, including approach to landing, two had to be engaged if a fully automatic landing was the intent.

With two engaged constant internal discussions took place between them, and if any disagreement occurred one would disengage – auto-land was then a no no!

With our fourth aircraft (PH-BUD August 1971) a third AP was installed, as was the case on all subsequent aircraft. The objective of this more complex installation was to increase the success rate and accuracy of auto-landings by having all three AP's coupled to the pertinent localizer and glide slope beams. As a result, the disengagement of two AP's had to occur before an auto-land attempt became invalid, requiring a manual take-over by the pilot for landing or go-around (overshoot).

The three AP systems also included, available at the touch of a button, an automatic go-around capability if visibility for landing was considered insufficient. This feature, together with an improved ATS (Automatic Throttle System), provided for a safe climb-out flight path. Once again the ultimate objective of these devices was the lowering of the landing weather minima. The accountants calculated that the avoidance of a few weather related diversions would soon reimburse the installation costs: I hope that they were right; the operational and maintenance costs must have been very high.

...........................but perhaps the pilot is not so easy to replace

The three AP channels added considerably to the number of items covered in our aircraft acceptance programme. Not only was another important feature added to our ground checks, but an increase in flight time also resulted; each AP channel had to be processed through its several modes of engagement, before working through the various sequences of multi channel engagement.

On flight test the automatic go-around feature was a particularly stressful testing area. From near touch-down, the activation of this mode resulted in a tremendous acceleration of the unladen aircraft. Extremely nimble fingers were then required to re-programme the entire AP system into an airfield circuit, approach and landing mode once more – and without forgetting the correct sequencing of landing gear and wing flaps. The intent of this frantic activity was to retain AP control throughout, ending up with a fully automatic landing followed by automatic braking ..... yes, that too!

Although far from what would be normal operational handling, this method of testing did determine the proper functioning of many modes of the AP system, or otherwise, in the approach, and landing phases of flight.

> *It was interesting to note that Airbus introduced a totally new philosophy regarding auto-throttle control during flight. The actual power levers would remain stationary, and only the engine parameters shown on the instruments would reveal that engine thrust was varying. It is a strange development to read about, and pilot reaction has been very varied.*

And now, whose turn is it for landing?

The advent of an automatic landing system, particularly the triple AP installation, introduced another problem into our operations – and this time a very human one. The need, and desire of a pilot to gain, and retain expertise in the actual manual landing of his aircraft was now in conflict with the demands of the automatics. To build up statistical data of system accuracy and reliability, and to provide maintenance with appropriate data, a regular flow of information was required from the operating crews. Detailed forms had to be completed after each auto-land attempt. If this information was lacking, then so was the mandate for lowering the weather minima for landing.

With long range aircraft the number of landings had become far less frequent, and an equitable division of these was still needed between the two pilots. It was a simple matter of maintaining good proficiency, and of satisfying the human lust for "greasers" (soft landings). Into this communal situation had now been thrown an intruder, the auto-land mode of the AP system! Who would lose out?

It was therefore not unnatural that a degree of silent opposition arose to a policy of "auto-land whenever possible". To be but a monitor of events in the final phases of a flight did not sit easily on the pilot's shoulders, and, after all, he had become but a monitor for the climb, cruise and descent phases of the preceding flight. It actually became necessary to keep records of the auto-lands attempted by each individual pilot, and have a quiet talk with the less enthusiastic ones.

The operational use of the "go-around" function was not used in my time since the existing weather minima did not require it. It was, however, included in a simulator training session, during which each pilot became qualified to operate at lower weather minima. For actual en-route operation at lower weather minima it was required that both pilots be qualified through the simulator training programme.

Turmoil in a Troubled World

The introduction of our B-747's on the route network, and my own reappearance on the scene, coincided with a new dimension introduced into the aviation scenario – terrorism and hijackings. New threats from this source were constantly making headlines, and self-appointed experts on the matter were full of opinions and recommendations for counter-measures. Probably the most significant opening event to the decade was the 1970 simultaneous hijacking of American, Swiss and British airliners. They were forced, by Palestinian militants, to land on a desert airstrip in Jordan. After evacuation of their occupants, and unsuccessful negotiations, the aircraft were destroyed.

...........................including a KLM hijack!

Our own hijack occurred in 1973. En-route from Tokyo to Amsterdam a B-747, laden with Japanese tourists, was hijacked by armed militants. Several nerve-wracking days of flights between different airfields followed, many refusing permission for a landing. Eventually, under the able command of Capt. Jack Risseeuw, a landing was made in Malta. Under the leadership of Dom Mintoff, the Maltese Prime Minister, meaningful negotiations were opened. After a last exhausting flight these negotiations resulted in the release of the passengers and crew at Dubai.

...........................and looking for solutions

World opinion, as usual, was divided over the most effective response to this new peril in the air – in modern idiom, aircraft were soft targets. Most airlines agreed to the introduction of security guards on board, some requiring that they be armed, but others refusing that ultimate step. These measures took time to introduce, selection and training of suitable personnel had to be made, and rules of engagement had to be considered prior to their implementation.

With differing national characteristics between airlines, and matters of national pride involved, the requisite rules and regulations seemed to lack any cohesive purpose. Despite all the difficulties, however, security guards gradually began to appear on the scene, and would be at the aircraft doors to scan the boarding passengers. During flight they would occupy vacant seats at strategic positions around the cabin.

Crew numbers again increase

..........................as we are joined by Security Guards

So it was that my own crew members became increased in number by the on-board presence of at least two security guards, and they operated to the same flight schedule as the rest of the crew. All too frequently several of these guards were individuals quite inexperienced in the ways of the world, and totally unfamiliar with air travel, whether it be of a national or international nature. From our rather jaundiced view point it appeared just as well that they were unarmed.

Many of these new companions, quite naturally, took every opportunity to explore the new worlds to which they now had access. Since their duties were more tedious than onerous, it was almost paid holidays; particularly when there was the added bonus of so many nubile stewardesses, and the renowned Bangkok fashion parades.

The presence of more senior members among this contingent was, however, a comfort and they assimilated well with the regular crew members – as did some of the younger ones.

Changing of Faces

In the course of the years two new configurations of the B-747 joined our growing fleet. One was a part freighter part passenger version, commonly known as the "Combi". The other was a stretched upper deck version, into which the earlier aircraft were converted. Initially this was a "mini" stretch; the full stretch to over-head the wing was to come later.

A combi had also appeared in our DC-8 fleet, but then the freight compartment was in the forward end of the fuselage. This had left only a narrow passageway between the cockpit and the passenger compartment making inter-communication rather difficult. In the 747 the freight compartment was in the rear of the main deck, allowing normal access between cockpit and cabin.

The passenger seating was reduced to about two hundred requiring fewer emergency exit doors, and therefore fewer cabin crew. At the same time, however, the potential freight load was increased to fifty tons, and quite a surprising variety of cargo could be carried.

..........................and fewer girls!

The introduction of the Combi, along the route, particularly on the Far East, had a significant effect on crew composition. The crew of a standard configuration aircraft would disembark at a slip station to await the arrival of the next aircraft: if this was then a Combi probably six of the stewardesses would be reassigned to other flights, or sent home as passengers.

A further development complicating this situation was the introduction of revised work-and-rest regulations for each category of crew. Only the two pilots would have identical turn around schedules, and on some flights they would be the only crew to leave and return to Schiphol at the same time. The solitary F/E had his own schedule, and the cabin crew a different one entirely. Perhaps I was exceptionally unlucky, but I seemed to have frequent changes in crew when I was out on this route.

I believe the team spirit and crew unity suffered as a result of these necessary changes, and certainly the ability to recognise my own crew during a stop-over at a slip station was greatly diminished.

Above and below: Named after KLM's founder, Dr Albert Plesman. A stretched upper deck aircraft

........................all about a Stretch

In contrast to the Combi the stretched upper deck configuration allowed for a potential increase in the number of passengers carried. From immediately behind the cockpit the upper deck was extended further rearwards towards the wing. The original five seats and bar now became a compartment seating some forty-five passengers, equipped with toilets and a pantry. The pantry had a lift which connected with the main galley below. In later versions of this stretch the original circular staircase was also removed, and replaced by a straight version.

Introduction of the "Combi's"

...........................and fewer girls at party time!

The Boeing development of an aircraft in which the main deck was divided into separate compartments for passengers, and freight became universally known as the Combi. The rear fuselage was fitted with a large door for the loading of freight on pallets; the floor was strengthened and also fitted with rails to permit sliding of the pallets into position.

Initially, some of our early aircraft were returned to the factory to have this extensive modification done, but a few later aircraft were received straight off the production line in this configuration. With a reduced passenger accommodation fewer exit doors were required and this, in turn, led to a reduction in the number of cabin crew required.

The introduction of the Combi along the routes had an immediate impact on the crew turn-around schedules, since the standard aircraft configuration became intermixed with the Combi ones, variations occurring as load requirements dictated. Cabin crews could therefore be reduced in number while en-route because the next aircraft to arrive was a Combi.

The former team spirit and crew unity suffered considerably under these new circumstances, and to be able to recognize instantly members of my own cabin crew at a slip-station was not an accomplishment that I ever acquired. The catwalk display at Bangkok also seemed to undergo a subtle change; perhaps the audience had become too transitional.

Recordvlucht van KLM-jumbo

Van onze luchtvaart-redacteur

SCHIPHOL – KLM's nieuwste passagiersvliegtuig van het type Boeing 747, de Charles A. Lindbergh, is zaterdagochtend op Schiphol aangekomen na een record snelheidsvlucht uit Seattle aan de Amerikaanse westkust.

De Britse gezagvoerder Peter Orange en zijn bemanning voerden de vlucht uit in 8 uur en 13 minuten. Dat was 36 minuten sneller dan de vorige kortste tijd waarin zo'n overtocht van de vliegtuigfabriek naar het KLM-nest werd uitgevoerd. De afstand van 8150 km werd met een snelheid van gemiddeld 1000 km afgelegd.

„Allemaal precies volgens het in Seattle opgesteld vluchtplan", aldus Orange. Het toneel was kort voor het vertrek gedoopt door de oceanograaf Jon Lindbergh, zoon van de beroemde vlieger Charles Lindbergh die in 1927 met de Spirit of St. Louis als eerste alleen uit de Verenigde Staten over de Atlantische Oceaan naar Parijs vloog.

Met de Charles A. Lindbergh onder het registratienummer Ph-BUL heeft de KLM nu tien brede-romp-

★ *Gezagvoerder Peter Orange (55) voerde alle elf afleveringsvluchten (inclusief die van het op Tenerife verongelukte toestel) uit van de voor de KLM bestemde Boeings 747. Na in de Tweede Wereldoorlog bij de Engelse luchtmacht te hebben gevlogen, kwam hij in 1948 bij de KLM. Daar boekte hij in 30 jaar 15.000 vlieguren. Sinds 25 jaar is hij gezagvoerder.*

vliegtuigen Boeing 747. Volgend jaar komen er nog drie van zulke toestellen bij.

Newspaper article following delivery of PH-BUL

At long last, a return to the East

It was not until 1974 that other duties finally permitted a proper return to my favourite territories of the Middle and Far East. Prior to this I had only been permitted fleeting visits through the need for one-off appearances on three-engine ferry operations. My few route flights, since the introduction of the B-747, had been only to New York since these allowed more regular access to office, and availability for test flight duties. As more time at last became free I was finally able to request a Far East flight.

Much had changed during my absence from the route, and more changes were still to come. But for now I was able to depart Schiphol with a fifteen strong crew, innumerable passengers, a state-of-the-art aircraft, and a schedule which included stops at many almost forgotten stations. And it was still possible, after ten days en-route, to return to Schiphol with the same crew which allowed a measure of crew bonding.

...........................*through Beirut and Dubai*

Beirut had again become a major crew slip (change of crew) station. The Riviera Hotel on the Corniche provided a convenient centre for leisure activities, which were many and various until later restricted by the threats of war. A bowling alley at Alhambra was a favourite gathering point, as were the tennis courts a short walk behind the hotel.

For me, however, it was Dubai where I found the greatest changes. The former fishing and trading port was growing out of all recognition. Although skyscrapers were springing up alongside the Creek, its quays were still crowded with dhows and water taxis. The visible cargo on the dhows had now become, however, cars, refrigerators and TV sets, destined for other ports in the Gulf, or for destinations as far afield as India. Apparently there was also a roaring trade in gold smuggling.

A night arrival into Dubai from the north was preceded by a descent towards a distant glow of light on the horizon, which eventually was seen to be the burning gas emitted from an off-shore oil well. This provided a convenient marker just sixty miles out from Dubai. Finally, one could discern the city lights, and the less prominent ones of the airfield. After landing we were usually parked alongside other earlier arrivals – nearly always a row of six or seven jumbo jets, so dense had the international traffic become. As we left the aircraft, our walk to the terminal building took us under the noses of these towering monsters – always a rather eerie feeling.

The crew hotel was the Sharjah Carlton on a wonderful beach-front location, just 20 minutes drive from the city centre via the Clock

B-747 – Repairs en-route

Tower at the end of the Creek. The hotel was a busy meeting point of crews returning home, with those headed for eastern destinations. The swimming pool area was something of a focal point, and resulted in quite a few sunburnt bodies during the long summer months. During the cooler winter, when it was emptied for cleaning, it also provided deep shelter from the cold winds while the winter sun could still be enjoyed. The sea was best left to those who enjoyed sea snakes and jellyfish for company, but their companionship was usually extremely short and rather painful!

...........................through Singapore or Bangkok, and onwards to Tokyo or to Sydney

Further east saw crew slips in Singapore or Bangkok, the re-exploring of local areas of interest or enjoying the tennis courts. Nostalgic visits to Raffles Hotel (Singapore) still provided evidence of its colourful colonial past, and Boogie Street demonstrated the more modern (and discernible) era of the transvestites. Manilla was but a brief commercial stop en-route to the seething metropolis of Tokyo for a brief night-stop before returning to the crew slip station at Bangkok.

A Single Room at the Sheraton?

...........................and time to relax!

Over the years it had become the custom for each crew member to be allocated their own room at hotels en-route, despite the fact that some of these hotels had now become extremely luxurious. Even the most junior pilot or stewardess would now find themselves the sole occupant of a remarkably spacious room, and would also receive a daily allowance which covered reasonable expenses in such an establishment. Reasonable expenses were naturally considered to be a meal from room service or in the hotel dining room. Good luck to those who had sufficient energy to walk around the corner to a far less expensive eating place; open air booths at the "Car Park" were a favourite destination. This saving on meal expenses was a useful addition to shopping money!

Any of these rooms provided ample space for the entire crew to hold a party, a party which was sometimes joined by crew members from other airlines. Before a firm stop was put to the practice, some of the supplies needed for these gatherings originated from the aircraft. Perhaps, surplus give-aways for passengers, which would otherwise have been appropriated by local cleaning staff.

At the time our stewardesses were on a five year contract, after which their flying days were over. It was said that among the reasons for this limitation was the fear that they would become too accustomed to the luxuries of life found along the routes – making their return to a more normal life that much more difficult!

An unhappy catalogue of wide-body errors in the aviation world

...........................both human and mechanical

As B-747 operations, and those of other wide-body aircraft, spread around the world so did an increase in the number of incidents and accidents associated with them. Although many airlines had GPWS *(Ground Proximity Warning Systems), and an aural stall warning system installed, the installations of TCAS **(Traffic Collision Advisory System) was yet to come.

> *GPWS gave an aural and visual warning, in the cockpit, when the aircraft
> approached the ground too closely in otherwise normal flight conditions.*

> **TCAS gave an aural and visual warning, in the cockpit, when a potential state*
> *of collision existed with other airborne traffic.*

An early wide-body accident had demonstrated yet again the need for a proper division of attention in the cockpit, a factor which never seemed to be entirely absent. A Lockheed Tristar descended gracefully under autopilot control to a watery grave in the Everglades (Florida), while the entire cockpit crew were engaged in attempting to find a solution to a landing gear problem.

In very different circumstances another watery grave was encountered. An Air India B-747 plunged into the Indian Ocean after a night take-off from Bombay, when the AHI's (Artificial Horizon Indicators) of both pilots failed. Cross checking between them failed to reconcile the problem as the standby horizon had not been included in their comparisons – the F/E had, however, seen the vital difference, but his warnings went unheeded by the pilots.

> *The writing is on the wall when the concerns of a third crew member are not*
> *addressed. Should the crew co-ordination receive more attention in training, or should*
> *the third man become redundant in a modern cockpit?*

> *Neither of these options appear relevant to some Far Eastern cockpits where the*
> *captain can equate with God – flight into a visible mountain is not an item for*
> *discussion, even with the second crew member!*

In 1974 a Turkish Airlines DC-10 crashed near Paris with the loss of all on board. The cause was eventually revealed as the result of an improperly locked lower fuselage cargo door. Its subsequent in-flight failure caused an explosive decompression leading to a floor collapse with fatal damage to various connections to the aircraft control surfaces.

As a direct result of this tragedy, all wide-body aircraft were required to install internal pressure relief venting between cargo and passenger areas, thus excluding the possibility of a floor collapse in the event of an explosive decompression. The location of hydraulic pipes, and other connections with the control surfaces was also reviewed. At the same time, exhaustive tests were carried out on the design and functioning of the door locking mechanisms, and changes made to render them foolproof.

In the same year, a Lufthansa B-747 went down shortly after take-off from Nairobi, with many casualties. Extension of the LE (leading edge) flaps had been overlooked, as had the necessary check on their indicator lights. As a result the aircraft actually left the ground in a stalled condition, from which recovery was impossible. This (avoidable) accident led to much soul searching among all the B-747 operators, ourselves included. Reassurance was needed that their own checklists and, operational procedures would forestall the repetition of any such similar event.

And then came Tenerife

In 1977 our own terrible tragedy (and that of Pan Am) occurred at Tenerife on the Canary Islands. A runway collision, in poor visibility, between two laden B-747's resulted in the loss of over five hundred lives. There were no survivors from the KLM machine, and only a handful from the Pan Am one – devastation was total.

I considered myself fortunate to have been unavailable (I was out of reach in the simulator) for despatch to Tenerife with the KLM investigating team, and the necessary inspection of the carnage. Later, however, I was sent to Washington for the prolonged NTSB (National Transportation Safety Board) investigation. There we listened to constant replays of the CVR's (Cockpit Voice Recorders) from both aircraft, and the recorder from the control tower, and endeavoured to determine the exact sequence of events. I found it very difficult to hear continually the last words of the KLM captain, who had been a good friend of mine over several years. His final tone of voice convinced me that he knew what had gone wrong.

This visit also involved several interesting trips by the Lockheed Electra shuttle service to New York, and then by helicopter to the roof of the Pan Am building for a meeting with our lawyers on the 42nd floor. These meetings were largely a matter of discussing the progress of the investigation.

There was considerable concern at the time over the amount of information being unaccountably leaked to the press. The source of this leak became apparent when I was talking with an NTSB official in his private office. There was suddenly the sound of our CVR being replayed which was located inside the sealed and guarded incident room. The sounds were coming through the air conditioning ducting!!

..........................and the lesson plan still uncompleted

Much has been written about this terrible tragedy, and endless opinions voiced as to its cause. Blame has been shifted from one party to another, but a cautious division of any blame would seem to be more appropriate. From among the many definitive factors involved, two warranted very immediate attention, namely, the need to limit the possibility of runway incursions, and the need to improve communication between Controllers and aircraft crews. Although English was the internationally recognized language for use between control and aircraft, its worldwide use is still either faulty or indeed absent.

A third factor was recognised as the need for improvement in crew co-ordination, and this was ultimately to receive attention in Crew Management training. It took many years for this particular training to find its way into the syllabi after many years of discussion.

Today, over a quarter of a century later, some of these immensely important recommendations are still lacking in universal application. Runway incursions are still an all too frequent occurrence, and as evident at Milan in the very recent past, result in needless loss of life. Some Latin countries are also notorious for their use of native languages, denying the "foreign" pilot much essential information regarding the whereabouts, or intentions, of other aircraft. Paris is particularly noteworthy in this respect, with numerous incidents directly related to matters of language.

When Air France voiced its concern over this problem by issuing an order requiring its pilots use only English for air/ground communications, a strike of its pilots resulted!!

(Tenerife) .... "say again please" ! ....

I must admit to some surprise when I first heard the rapid staccato-like utterances of Air Traffic Control in North America, they grabbed my full attention. Language has always been something of a problem in communication between aircraft, and those who provide instructions to them, but it was hoped that Tenerife would make a turning point in this respect.

One of the saddest accidents that resulted from this difficulty happened not too many years ago. A South American aircraft was inbound to New York with minimum fuel reserves when traffic delays were encountered, and inbound aircraft were then assigned to holding points at different locations. A "holding" required the aircraft to proceed to the given location, and then fly a race-track pattern at an assigned altitude while awaiting further clearance. The South American aircraft had insufficient fuel reserves to deal with a lengthy hold, and attempted to advise ATC of this. With a poor command of English the captain was unable to alert ATC to his increasingly alarming situation, even after losing an engine from fuel starvation. The aircraft finally crashed on Long Island with all fuel exhausted.

Declarations of a "fuel emergency" in the New York area were not uncommon, somebody would always attempt to jump the queue! The authorities soon found it necessary to send an FAA inspector to board any arriving aircraft who had declared a fuel emergency. He would carefully inspect the fuel remaining status to determine whether the declaration had been valid. If not considered valid a hefty fine coul result.

...........................fuel exhaustion will always be with us

Even in 2001 an Airbus 330 landed on the Azores with empty tanks after a lengthy glide following complete fuel exhaustion. A masterly demonstration of airmanship on a powerless aircraft did not, however, excuse the circumstances that caused such a predicament. Do I hear the inevitable comment? .... if only there had been a third crew member!

As world-wide traffic increased in volume so did the traffic delays at the major airports. In this respect New York could be particularly difficult, with quite frequent visits to the various holding points. Even on departures it was not unusual to find oneself in a lengthy queue on the taxyway, patiently awaiting one's turn to move along. There was usually ample time for the cabin crew to serve a few drinks, while we idly watched the continuous stream of lights in the sky which marked the incoming traffic. These were all distanced at precise intervals by radar control, and the runway had to be vacated as quickly as possible after landing since the next aircraft was close behind.

...........................and the beginning of history

We were some seven years into our 747 operation when Boeing called an inter-airline meeting. The intent was to review the operational difficulties that had been experienced with the aircraft, and those now occurring. It was interesting to note that a new generation of 747 pilots was appearing on the scene – both from the airlines, and from Boeing itself. Many questions raised for discussion were all too familiar to us – they had been raised and solved many years before. We were already in a period of historical revision!

Variety is the Spice of Life!

One of my several returns to Seattle was with an aircraft due for a modification programme. It was mid-winter, and Paine Field (Everett) was snugly blanketed with snow, but runways and taxyways had been sufficiently cleared for operation. On landing we used reverse thrust which resulted in the runway lights being covered with a further layer of snow as we passed by. In making a 180 degree turn on the runway I then managed to misjudge the location of its edge, and sank my outer wheels into soft ground to become firmly stuck. Boeing were apparently at full alert for such an event because within minutes we were greeted by the flashing lights of a rescue vehicle, and a tractor was being attached. With little difficulty we were pulled free in an undamaged state.

I heard no more of this embarrassing incident so presumably it went unreported to the powers that be. It had been my sole self engendered incident with a KLM aircraft in some thirty years; the Gods had been kind to me, and I could well afford a round of drinks that evening!

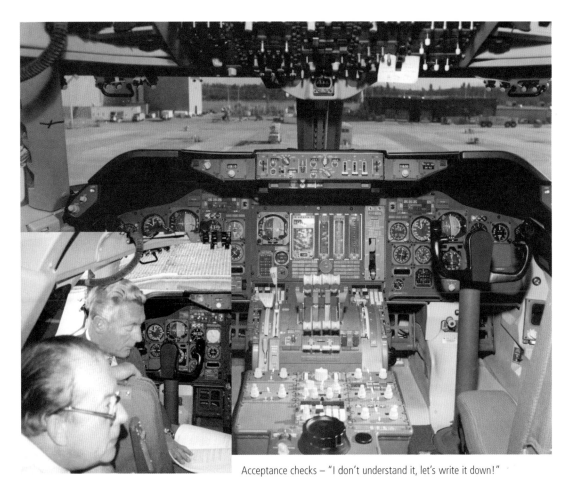

Acceptance checks – "I don't understand it, let's write it down!"

Awaiting acceptance checks

...........................on a Wing and a Prayer

Awaiting an incoming flight from Mexico at Mirabelle Airport (Montreal) we were eager to get home. As we completed our pre-flight preparations the message came in that a re-fueling truck had damaged a wing leading edge. From ground level the damage appeared to be no more than a dent in the surface, but closer inspection revealed that the outer skin was in fact broken. Since the outer skin covered a porous honeycomb structure which gave the critical curvature to the leading edge we had a potential problem – moisture could penetrate, freeze and expand to spread the damage. Flight cancellation became inevitable, and the passengers were re-booked on other airlines.

Contact with Schiphol and with Boeing soon led to the conclusion that an on-the-spot repair could be made with a team of Boeing engineers. But first the aircraft had to be moved from Mirabelle to Dorval, an airport just twenty minutes flying away, which had appropriate hangar accommodation.

A temporary repair was needed for the short ferry flight, and this was effected by the Boeing team which arrived from Seattle. It amounted to a large patch firmly strapped over the damaged area, and we were assured that a low-and-slow flight was perfectly safe. With just cockpit crew, a volunteer stewardess and the repair team, we set forth – very slow and very low! Even so, the patched wing showed discernible bulging.

With repairs complete, we were directed to Chicago to uplift a full passenger load for Amsterdam. Departure from Dorval was on an extremely foggy morning – our clearance to enter the runway for take-off was abruptly cancelled as we were actually beginning to enter; as I stood on our brakes a landing aircraft passed uncomfortably close to our nose with a deafening roar!!

...........................anyone for a swim?

Happily cruising along to Chicago at our assigned altitude the stewardess entered the cockpit. Expecting some coffee we turned round to see that she was dripping wet! Breathlessly she told us that water was pouring down from the ceiling, the F/E immediately went back and returned some time later with the information that the overhead water tank had sprung a leak, and that its contents were now well spread through in the cabin area.

On arrival at Chicago it was evident that a lengthy drying out process was needed, so the waiting passengers had to be re-routed or accommodated overnight. An all night drying out process followed, together with an inspection for possible damage, before we were finally able to set course for home.

...........................or a sail through Amsterdam?

In August 1978 we were off again to Seattle, this time to collect PH-BUK which was a stretched upper deck model. This featured an extension of the upper deck area from behind the cockpit towards wing. It increased the passenger accommodation from eight seats, and a small pantry to forty-five with a dedicated galley, connected by a lift to the main pantry below. For use in an emergency two exit doors were installed for the passengers, and a crew exit door immediately behind the cockpit. These doors were each equipped with automatically inflating slides.

It was very strange leaving the cockpit to be immediately confronted with more passengers than we had carried on a Constellation, and going downstairs this confrontation continued section by section in the main cabin. It was hard to realise that all these fellow-beings were encased in a fragile aluminium structure some 35,000ft above the earth, and in an outer air temperature

PH-BUK arrives at Schiphol   (photo source unknown)

of minus 60C. Since this whole cocoon above the earth was primarily under automatic control, there was little doubt that the cabin crew were the most active persons abroad!

The aircraft acceptance programme was definitely one of our smoother ones, only two test flights were required in strong contrast to the previous aircraft which had required four separate flights. That had been due to a very slight skin deformation in the area of the pressure vents associated with the airspeed readings, resulting in a difference between the captain's and the co-pilot's indicators.

But BUK was destined for an unusual future. After twenty-five years of faithful airline service it was sold to Aviodrome (Holland's national air museum) for a token one Euro, but Aviodrome had to fund its transportation costs. Runway dimensions at Aviodrome (near Lelystad), insurance problems and the Dutch licensing authorities all combined to prevent an airborne arrival; the sole remaining option was dismantling, and transport by water. Not too difficult a feat for Dutch engineers, with their vast experience of salvage and water borne transportation.

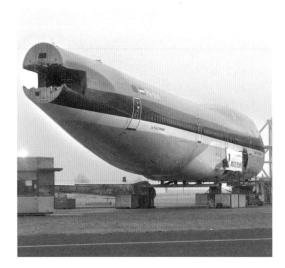

PH-BUK sailing through Amsterdam

This dismantling at Schiphol took quite some time, but eventually the engines, wings and tail were removed, and carefully loaded onto pontoons/barges for their water-borne journey to Lelystad. The subsequent pictures of this fleet negotiating various bridges and locks, and transiting the canals of Amsterdam were quite unique – a "jumbo" serenely sailing past Dutch canal side houses.

...........................*Seattle again*

In May 1979 I departed for Seattle to conduct my last B-747 acceptance and delivery for KLM. With the end of my KLM career in sight, this last journey to Seattle was quite a significant occasion. To everyone's surprise, the acceptance of PH-BUM required four test flights before it was satisfactorily concluded. Nevertheless, Boeing marked the occasion with a party on my behalf (neither they, nor I, realising that I would be back just over a year later), and readied our aircraft for delivery by pasting on its nose the legend – "PETER ORANGE".

KLM was not best pleased with that, and the sticker was rapidly removed after our Schiphol arrival.

Boeing's farewell to the author

.........................what happened to my flight leave?

As May drew to a close I realised that my scheduling records showed well over two hundred days of flight leave owing to me, since on return from a route flight I was normally the next day in the office. There was very obviously no possibility of taking this leave, so I rather naively suggested that perhaps I could receive extra pay in lieu of!

The suggestion was not well received, and the only feasible solution was to quietly make my last flight, and then just as quietly disappear on leave for some sixty days. So off I went to Dubai for an unannounced last KLM flight, and this time without the escort of a second co-pilot. It was a very strange feeling to realize that this at last was the end, and that now I had to seriously set about my future.

Closing Up Shop

As August 1979 loomed ahead of me, I began to realize that my days were numbered – that my 56th birthday would spell the end of my thirty-one years of service with KLM. The sad failure of a twenty-five year old marriage had already occurred, and an amicable divorce was now in process. The three children were embarked on their own careers, and the world ahead began to look a rather empty place – but there were still airplanes, and even jobs for elderly pilots!

I explored several possibilities, the most interesting being with SIA (Singapore Airlines), with GIA (Garuda Indonesian Airlines) or with an old acquaintance – Steadman Hinkley who was setting up a new B-747 operation in Jeddah (Saudi Arabia). .... but more of that later.

...........................test flights continue

In the meantime 1979 saw the emergence of some of our aircraft from heavy maintenance – an in-depth inspection process lasting several weeks, and involving extensive dismantling for inspection and refurbishment. Unfortunately, our test flight programme uncovered numerous problems, and both BUD and BUG required over six hours of test flying before we found them acceptable for passenger service. This was no improvement over the SAS and SWR aircraft that I had flown the previous year after heavy maintenance by KLM.

One unusual test flight was made for the sole purpose of evaluating a newly issued In-flight Smoke Evacuation procedure. This introduced the previously untried procedure of opening doors whilst in-flight. While the aircraft was pressurised it was physically impossible to actually open any of the cabin doors since their initial movement, after unlocking, was inwards.

We therefore de-pressurised the aircraft, and activated some smoke generators, after which a rear exit door was unlocked, and moved slightly inwards, and then secured with rope. On the same side of the aircraft an over wing exit door was then unlocked, moved slightly inwards, and also secured with rope.

The aerodynamic noise level increased significantly, but the cabin was free of smoke in a very short time as air flowed from one "open" door to the other and exited overboard. The procedure thus became a new entry on our Emergency Checklist.

...........................shorter flights en-route

My en-route flights had again become very restricted, but a very convenient weekend trip to Dubai and back was quite frequent. Occasionally a Mexico flight could be fitted into my timetable, but that was the longest. The Far East trips demanded too long a time away, and they had also begun to lose their attraction for me. I think this loss of allure was mainly due to the constant changing of crews en-route, and also to the fact that some of the newer generation of cabin crew made me feel very much a "foreigner". My past KLM life had not facilitated a proper acquisition of their language, and this, quite understandably, was not understood or appreciated.

I fully agree with those who say that to live in a country for so long, and never become fluent in the language is unacceptable, but that was the unfortunate result of airline life – and particularly of my own rather unusual involvement in that form of life.

My Dubai flights were inevitably accompanied by a second co-pilot. These were enthusiastic pilots awaiting their turn for more advanced training. In the meantime they had only received limited air-work training on the 747, qualifying them to be at the controls during en-route climb and cruise flight only. I had great sympathy for these rather frustrated individuals, and (with great reluctance) surrendered my seat to them at an early stage of a flight, allowing them to build up their handling experience. Those who then nonchalantly maintained a climb under autopilot control got short shrift – a precision climb hand flown on instruments is invaluable practice.

Athens (Greece) occasionally played a part in my en-route mini dramas. During a flight from Schiphol I was alerted by KLM Flight Watch that there was possibly a bomb on board, and "what were my intentions"? – "proceeding Athens" I replied. Together with the purser, and without disturbing the passengers, I made a thorough search of the pantries and toilets without finding anything unusual. On reaching Athens we were given immediate landing clearance with instructions to proceed to a parking area well away from the terminal buildings. Once there, everybody was rapidly disembarked, and the aircraft left to the tender mercies of the Greek emergency services – apparently the only thing they found were some nice meals in the pantries!

On another occasion we had an indication of a possible landing gear malfunction, when positioning for final approach to land. Discontinuing the approach we re-cycled the landing gear, but the potential fault persisted. I then requested a low fly past over the Control Tower, to allow ground observers a chance to detect any fault. Since I had not been given any height restriction my fly past was very low indeed, and the usual binoculars were not needed – since nothing faulty could be seen during this close inspection we made a normal landing, as gently as possible

...........................a KLM party!

A quite unknown event for a retiring pilot was a farewell party, but this was organised on my behalf by the office staff in Amstelveen. It was well attended by my immediate superiors, and even Sergio Orlandini (KLM President Director) put in a brief appearance. Among several gifts was a beautifully researched photo album recording my entire flying career through the RAF and KLM.

But the most surprising gift of all was from the department which I had so frequently criticised, the Engineering and Maintenance Division. This was a fan blade from a CF-6 engine mounted on a wooden base and bearing an inscription reading –

Farewell Presentation

> *In appreciation of your support and continuous belief in us over the years.*

........................and now behind the scenes

In preparing for my future, several possibilities were being examined. Within KLM itself a serious attempt was under way, by pilots nearing retirement age, to raise the pension age of 56 by several years – the objective being 60, which was already common in the USA. Unfortunately, this attempt was undermined by our own pilots' association and thus made no progress. The more junior pilots could only regard an increase in the pension age as a block to their own promotions – the fact that they would also eventually benefit was disregarded. It was evident quite soon that raising the pension age was unlikely to succeed, and I thus applied for a position with Singapore Airlines.

After a successful interview with their Chief Pilot, I was accepted by Singapore Airlines subject to completion of their lengthy training requirements. My extensive experience at the Boeing factory seemed to be of little interest to them. Two other possibilities arose at about the same time; Garuda Indonesian Airlines (GIA) approached me regarding the introduction of their B-747 fleet which was then on order. They indicated that I would be responsible for the acceptance/delivery of their aircraft, the control of their training programme, and the production of operating manuals. It sounded very attractive and quite challenging.

Another possibility arose through previous contact with Steadman Hinckley, the owner of an American company which operated non-scheduled flights – Overseas National Airways (ONA). Many years previously I had been involved in the DC-8 training of some of their pilots – a particular connection being the stall incident over the North Sea.

Anyway, ONA was now setting up a subsidiary company named United Air Carriers Inc. (UACI), for operations in Saudi Arabia. A B-747 had been leased from Korean Airlines for this project, and a number of pilots had received B-747 training.

...........................and gaining a partner!

Since Steadman also required a senior KLM stewardess, I approached the few that I knew with the offer of a short term change of environment. The choice fell on Elly Hoving, and within a week she and I were in London interviewing cabin attendants from other airlines who had applied for a job. Retired KLM pilots, or some about to retire, were also on my shopping list.

..........................so, farewell KLM from Jeddah

August 1979

A 1996 reunion of the KLM acceptance team

The Pilgrim Trade

Gathering in Frankfurt

After our recruitment activities in London, Elly and I flew to Frankfurt to join the UACI crew members already there. We now had the impressive titles of Operations Consultant and Cabin Staff Supervisor, and had also managed to negotiate fixed salaries paid monthly in US dollars. Other UACI flight crew were paid per flying hour, and any period of inactivity was thus most unwelcome to them – their take home pay took a severe nose dive!

Our new colours

Most of June was occupied with training activities for those new to the aircraft, and the completion of maintenance on our Korean B-747 in Le Bourget Paris. Finally I went to Le Bourget (my first visit since Electra days) to collect our aircraft, rather appropriately registered HN-7447. Somehow, Korean flight crew licences were obtained, and all that remained was a diplomatic clearance allowing us to proceed to Jeddah. In the meantime we enjoyed some tennis, and got better acquainted with our new team mates, who were not best pleased with this period of idleness.

My Korean licence

We also had time to undertake a little local exploration; on one occasion we had parked at a local beauty spot, gone for a long walk, and returned to find a window in our car smashed. Everything that we had carefully concealed under the seats was gone – driving licenses, passports and UACI identity cards… the lot. Our respective embassies were extremely efficient in replacing our passports, so no lasting harm was done.

Elly awaiting engine start

Two former KLM pilots arrived to join us and, Capt. Bill Hobbs (UACI Chief Pilot) rightly insisted on them receiving some "differences" training on the aircraft. The considerable difference between airline cockpits, of the same basic aircraft, could be quite extensive. Instruments could differ, and even their location on the panels could be different. Radio control panels would be different, and their interconnection with the various instrument displays would also be unfamiliar.

With no simulator available, and no permission for flights in the Frankfurt area, this training would have to be done in Jeddah.

As the delay in obtaining our clearance had no visible end in sight, the crews that had assembled in Frankfurt were sent home to await a recall. That left just Elly and I to watch over our silent monster, which was parked at quite a remote location on the airfield. At intervals we would obtain transport out, stairs would be obtained, and we would climb on board and generally check things over. Starting up the

A truly international cabin crew

APU (auxiliary power unit) we would exercise various systems, and run the air conditioning system to clear the rather stale air. We would also gaze with wonder and some concern, at the very cramped installation of 490 seats.

Steadman Hinckley (the Chief Executive of UACI) finally arrived with our diplomatic clearance to operate on behalf of Saudi Arabian Airlines; all future flights would now carry a Saudi flight number. On July 1st we departed Frankfurt on our six hour flight to Jeddah, opening a new chapter in my aviation experiences. Our total number of crew members on board was probably around thirty, so that there were plenty of empty seats to be found. Elly spent a great deal of the flight getting to know her new charges, who mostly originated from Greece and Thailand, and improving their familiarity with the on-board equipment. The remainder of our cabin crew were already in Jeddah, together with some Arabic interpreters, awaiting our long delayed arrival.

Settling down in Jeddah

Our arrival in Jeddah coincided with one of the warmer days at 42°C, and the long queues at customs and passport control were far from welcoming. Elly and I had eleven bags between us, which the customs pounced upon with great joy – each of my many manuals and note books had to be very slowly and carefully examined, in case prohibited "girlie" magazines were hidden in their depths. After careful and prolonged scrutiny of our passports and visas we finally made it to the exit, only to discover a few members of our crew were still missing. It was quite some time before they reappeared, and some of the Thai girls were in tears after quite a fierce interrogation.

We were initially accommodated in quite a smart hotel, though rather uncomfortably close to a government building of some description – the nearby streets seemed to be constantly thronged with armed police and soldiers. We soon discovered that the hotel swimming pool was strictly segregated – men only in the mornings, and girls only in the afternoons. The "security guards" were only in evidence during the afternoons of course!

Waiting for pilgrims

..........................*midnight with the Sheiks*

My first night in Jeddah came to an abrupt end at 23.00 hours. The telephone rang demanding my immediate presence at an airport meeting with the management of Saudi Airlines. Arriving at the airport I was hurriedly conducted to a conference room to face an impressive assembly of fully robed sheiks. After an exchange of courteous greetings it was soon apparent that the subject of discussion was my request for a training flight. They quite rightly pointed out that they had "wet leased" a B-747, which meant that the crew were trained and licensed on the aircraft.

It was with some difficulty that I found myself trying to explain that not all B-747 aircraft were identical, as each airline tended to have its own version. Some of our fully qualified B-747 pilots, I explained to them, were quite unfamiliar with the instruments installed in the Korean aircraft – in the interests of safety; I thus felt it necessary that they had a brief flight exposure to the essential differences. Could this not be done on the ground, they asked. Only if we had a representative flight simulator, I replied. Very well, we will consider the matter, and let you know tomorrow.

The following evening there was a repeat performance of questions and explanations, and finally permission was granted for a training flight of no more than two hours duration. With that settled I collected the two former KLM pilots for "differences training" and the entire cabin staff; we had discovered that some of them had extremely limited experience of actual flying .The training flight was thus accompanied by a running commentary covering the noises made by landing gear movement, flap movement, in-flight spoilers and reverse thrust on landing. During this session Elly also discovered that some of the girls were too small to be able to reach the overhead bins where life rafts were stowed; this matter would have to be borne in mind when their positions were assigned during passenger flights.

...........................waiting for flight schedules

Our flight schedules were soon arranged, and each flight carried a Saudi Airlines flight number. My own flights were always with Elly as my purser, so frequent reports reached me of any unusual events in the cabin. Since we were operating with "dry" pantries there was never a problem with alcohol, but seating the larger build of passengers could be very difficult as the seat installation was so cramped.......and we were indeed carrying 490 passengers on every flight. These flights were quite regular between Jeddah, Riyadh and Cairo, with the route to Cairo taking us over the southern tip of the Sinai Peninsular, across to Luxor, and then north along the Nile.

...........................who made that landing?

It was at Cairo one night that I made the heaviest landing of my career, so heavy in fact that I requested a "Heavy Landing" inspection! Elly had arrived in the cockpit, convinced that my co-pilot had made the landing, to ask "what went wrong?" My red face told it all, and we went down to soothe the passengers. Several overhead bins had opened, and distributed their contents on unprotected heads – but not a word of complaint, "we are safe, Allah He's saved us" was the general cry, even from one elderly gentleman mopping up blood from a head wound. No first aid was required, and certainly no doctors, they all just happily stumbled down the steps!

Seemingly, in my anxiety to produce a perfect landing I had completely forgotten the well-known down slope on the runway in use. After easing up the nose into the landing attitude I had sat there awaiting a smooth touch down. Surreptitiously the runway surface got further and further away from my wheels until we actually lost flying speed, and literally fell onto the runway!

...........................caterpillars into butterflies!

On many of our flights into Cairo, and also into northern Europe destinations, we were treated to some quite interesting transformations en-route. Ladies of indeterminate age would board the plane in Jeddah fully enshrouded in typical Muslim dress, and then start queuing for the toilets as soon as we had cleared Saudi Arabian airspace. On re-emergence the Muslim dress code had completely disappeared to be replaced by Western style apparel – jeans and tight fitting blouses! The rest of the flight would see them devoted to caring for their nails, and the selection of appropriate jewellery.

On return flights to Jeddah this transformation was reversed. How they managed with passport pictures we never discovered, but the empty bottles to be found in the seat pockets after their departure seemed to suggest they probably had solutions.

Exploring Jeddah

Off duty periods demanded a certain caution in dress, as we had no wish to walk around town in our uniforms. We were warned to beware of many things, particularly of the so-called Religious Police. These wore no uniform, but walked around in pairs looking extremely important; without warning they were liable to stop you, demand identity papers, and commence a fierce interrogation. Improper dress, lacking in sufficient modesty, was always a sure show stopper.

Fortunately, Elly and I escaped their attention during our wanderings around the old town exploring the souks, and admiring the intricate carving on the window shutters and fragile balconies. The wood work was sun-bleached with age, but still fulfilled its essential screening effect. The occupant of a house could comfortably view the out side world without being seen, not so very different from those mirrors outside the windows of town houses in Holland !

In taxis we demurely sat in fore and aft seats to avoid attention, and prayed that the driver would avoid any accidents. Local law also decreed that the passengers shared the guilt with the driver if an accident occurred, and all went to jail until the matter was resolved. We had one such event with a crew bus; it was stopped once by the Religious Police because male and female crew were sitting side by side, and was then stopped again because of a collision. The driver and the entire crew were promptly removed to jail, where they had to be fed by "friends and relatives". This seriously disrupted flight schedules, and much pressure had to be exerted by Saudi Airlines to secure their release.

A return to Heliopolis

Saudi Airlines decided to station us for several weeks in Cairo; we then found ourselves in an extremely smart hotel in Heliopolis – an excellent change of venue for all concerned. Freedom of dress and behaviour, and unrestricted access to alcohol was a welcome change from the strictures of Jeddah.

Much to our mutual surprise, we also met with KLM crews who used the same hotel, and splendid reunions with old friends were quite a regular occurrence. The airport, at that time, was always a scene of utter chaos with endless crowds shuffling through the dirt, and officious staff shouting at the unfortunate passengers. To get anything done, within a reasonable period of time, required endless bribes – only the ATC staff, locked away out of sight, seemed to be immune to this system.

A stay in Riyadh

Our next brief stationing was in Riyadh, again in a very smart, but very restrictive hotel. The swimming pool was strictly male-only at all times, and off duty dress code was firmly enforced before one could even leave the hotel.

By now I was quite well acquainted with the DIY (do it yourself) mode of operation required by this type of flying. In KLM, and other major airlines, there was always dedicated staff to make flight-plans, load sheets, and to arrange ATC clearances – the pilot was merely needed to fly!

But now, even external pre-flight checks of the aircraft, together with the F/E, had become my responsibility. It was a whole new way of life, and I needed a special pass to enable me to attend to pre-flight check needs.

With a few days off, Elly and I made a brief visit to Holland, In Frankfurt we rented an Avis car for the final drive. It turned out to be a Volvo and to my amazement, I could find nowhere to insert the ignition key – a helper from the desk showed me the key hole down by the gear lever, which seemed a very unusual location. On returning to Riyadh a few days later we found that the entire crew had left for Jeddah, complete with aircraft – we were stranded. Since there were no local flights that evening, our empty B-747 was sent up to collect us............travel in style!

Warming up for the Hajj (pilgrimage to Mecca)

As the pilgrim season got under way, the airport at Jeddah became a forest of large jet aircraft tails from around the world – a mass of colourful decorations and national emblems. Many of them we failed to recognize, and some looked too decrepit to safely fly. The town was crowded with pilgrims; in spotlessly clean white robes, fending off the persistent attentions of those beggars who had managed to evade the police. There seemed to be some sort of warning system in force – a few individual beggars would hover on the outskirts of the crowd, and shout a warning when the police approached, a rapid exodus (even of the "disabled") would then follow.

I had heard tales of the Hajj in Douglas DC-4 days, when pilgrims had attempted to light a campfire on the aircraft floor. Elly had flown a Hajj season with KLM from a base in Morocco, so we had some idea what was in store. Our flights departed from Jeddah empty, and were destined for places like Damascus, Dubai or Karachi, there to collect a full load of pilgrims, and speed them on their way to Mecca.

..........................anyone for Mecca?

The loading of pilgrims on our flights for transportation to Jeddah and Mecca was seldom a matter of routine. Some five hundred hopeful Hajji's* (those seeking pilgrim status) would gather in a seething mob at the aircraft steps. Under the rather brutal control methods of the local soldiery, males and females would be separated, since the females had to be loaded first. They would come streaming aboard endeavouring to reserve seats for their husbands who would be following; this process involved much shouting and struggling – but worse was to come! A gunshot signalled the release of the males, who came clambering up the steps in a frenzied mass – and then came the frenzied search for their partner. Since their ladies were heavily veiled, it was a complete mystery to us how reunions ever took place – on some occasions they obviously didn't, and much shouting and screaming took place before the right partner was found.

A Muslim acquires the title of Haji when a pilgrimage to Mecca has been made.

The soldiers, negligently waving their weapons, would also try to come on board, but these I stopped at the open door, pushing their rifles aside. Another problem arose when the main deck seats were full. The surplus passengers absolutely refused to go upstairs, apparently believing that up there was too near to Allah. Elly would call me down from the cockpit to exercise my captain's authority in getting the upper deck utilized. It all took a great deal of time and patience before we were actually ready for departure, and later in the flight it was not uncommon to find that we had stowaways on board, they had been hiding in the toilets.

From the cockpit point of view a fairly normal flight pattern would follow but the cabin staff had the utmost difficulty in trying to serve some refreshments – particularly when some of the more devoted followers of the Muslim faith started unrolling their prayer mats in the gangways, and demanded to know in which direction Mecca was located. It was also standard procedure to announce when we were passing in the vicinity of Mecca, and this triggered off a mass change of clothing. Clean robes and veils etc were dragged out of the overhead bins, and in aisles and on seats a communal

Loading for Mecca

change of clothing took place, the discarded items being returned to the luggage in the overhead bins.

This costume changing event unfortunately took place very near to our top-of-descent position, which made it almost impossible for the cabin staff to clear up the cabin, and get everyone seated for landing. We soon learnt the wisdom of (secretly) moving the position of Mecca by about a hundred miles.

Disembarking the passengers was somewhat more orderly since they were under our direct control.

We also soon learned, moreover, that more than a cursory glance at the voluminous robes of the ladies was essential. They could easily conceal a life-jacket (several went missing) or other item of aircraft equipment, we occasionally came across one of our coffee pots for sale in the souk! Once everybody was off, the aircraft was closed, and locked by the airport authorities, and no cleaning of any sort took place until our next departure. Over a period of time the interior acquired an aroma of its own, which was far from pleasant until we could activate the air-conditioning system to disperse the worst of the smell. The toilet areas were in a terrible state, since their proper use was quite unknown to many.

Once the pilgrims from all over the world had reached Jeddah, and continued onward to Mecca by road, we returned to the more humdrum routine of Cairo and Riyadh flights until it was time for the Hajji's to return to their home countries.

A Meeting in Jakarta (Indonesia)

In the moderately restful interval between the inbound and outbound Hajji flights, Elly and I took off for Jakarta where I had a meeting scheduled with Capt. Koesjinatin, the Operations Director of Garuda Indonesian Airways. With the construction of their four B-747's getting near commencement they wished to finalize their introduction programme, and the crew training requirements.

It was agreed that pilot training would primarily be done by Boeing, and also that of the Flight Engineers but that I was to monitor both classroom and flight instruction. My further attention was to be given to the production of Operating Manuals and Checklists, until such time as the aircraft became ready for acceptance – for which I would have to prepare a ground and flight acceptance programme. It was also to be my responsibility to recruit further expatriate pilots, and train them to the required standard.

Altogether, a very busy future lay ahead in Seattle, and I was thankful that I had much KLM documentation as background support. With regard to Elly, Capt. Koesjinatin was willing to offer her part-time work in Seattle but could make no promises as to her further employment once we were in Jakarta.

We flew back to Jeddah in ample time to partake in the pilgrims' return, and I immediately advised Steadman Hinkley that our period of employment was coming to a close – he had always been aware that we were on a rather temporary basis. Both parties had, however, achieved results. Elly and I had, in modern parlance, become an item, despite the difficult environment, and Steadman had got his B-747 operation off on a sound footing. I did warn him, however, that his aircraft was probably beginning to suffer from severe under floor corrosion, in the vicinity of the galleys and toilets, due to the continual delays in cleaning..

> *"Our" aircraft, HN-7447, was later shot down by Russian fighters. A navigational error, arising from improper (unmonitored) settings to the flight guidance system, had allowed the flight to stray over Russian territory.*

Homeward bound Hajji's

Departing from Jeddah with a full load of passengers in the Hajji season was a remarkable event. The main problem lay in the vast number of aircraft arriving and departing, with many on very similar routings – or even to the same destinations. "Slot" times were introduced for departing flights, and if you were not ready to start engines, and taxi out for take-off at your given "slot" time................then hard luck...........you had to wait for a new "slot" time which might, or might not, be given that day! Unless one had a very serious technical problem, entailing flight cancellation, one kept to the given "slot" time, irrespective of the situation in the cabin.

On occasions, passengers were still squabbling over seats as we entered the runway for take-off, and the best that could be done was to push them on the floor. There were, unfortunately, some circumstances where normal rules and regulations just had to be ignored. One unfortunate crew, of another airline, missed their slot time due to a boarding delay. They and all their passengers were held on board for over six hours until a new slot time became available, and no further aircraft servicing was permitted. I didn't hear whether crew duty time became involved............

Passenger boarding was done in a far more efficient fashion than we had previously experienced, and the soldiers looked as though they knew what they were doing. There was still the division of male and female passengers, but recognition of each other on board seemed to have improved which resulted in quicker seating. The fact that there seemed to be an occasional surplus of passengers after the doors were closed was seldom a surprise, solutions were always found.

Around Christmas 1979 we had been able to move out of the hotel into modest apartments, which allowed a great deal more freedom of movement – having to shop and prepare meals gave the whole venture a far more homely atmosphere. The flying hours of our UACI colleagues took an unwelcome nose dive when we experienced a technical problem which demanded an engine change. The only place where we could obtain a new engine was back in Frankfurt, and I was the only pilot qualified to operate a three-engine ferry flight.

So off we went to Frankfurt, with an intermediate landing in Rome. I had with me as co-pilot a captain who had been qualified on DC-8 ferry operations, and since there was very little difference in procedure, I invited him to make the take-off out of Rome. That take-off was a near disaster...........he was evidently sadly out of practice!

And off to ventures new

In early May we said goodbye to our UACI friends, struggled through the extensive exit procedures from the country, and set forth for Seattle. We were armed with a letter from Garuda that gave their full support should we require any form of assistance. Since the world, and particularly the USA, was now demanding credit references and credit cards for every sort of transaction this letter proved extremely useful. Neither Elly nor I had ever held a credit card, and had quite some difficulty in obtaining them from our banks in Europe.

Volcanoes in Seattle

A Wedding en-route!

Before we returned to Seattle, armed with Capt. Koesjinatin`s instructions, Elly and I had some ten days to ourselves, and we decided to put into action the plans which we had been slowly formulating. We had decided to get married, and the only question was where and when. We were also quite definitely agreed that it had to be a low key event, and the most appropriate place seemed to be with my elder sister and her husband in Barbados. They were delighted with the idea, and promised to put all the necessary arrangements in hand.

So our travel itineraries took us from Jeddah for a brief stop in Holland, and then to Barbados prior to our final approach into Seattle. In Barbados everything went according to plan, and apart from a few minor legal hitches, it was a wonderful day to remember – my sister and her husband had given us a wonderful start to our new life............... we were no longer an item, but a proper couple with an unusual thirty year age difference......... twenty-five years later that difference is still there, but perhaps a little less obvious!

And a landing in Seattle.

Our return to Seattle in May 1980 was a total surprise to our many friends in the area, but there was immediate help in finding us accommodation away from a hotel environment. We eventually rented an unfurnished top floor flat in an apartment block, overlooking quite extensive gardens. Renting furniture etc was very simple, despite the fact that we had not yet got credit cards – my letter from Garuda was like a magic wand. Acquiring

Garuda's first – headed for the paint shop

a telephone was merely a matter of walking into a shop, selecting a model, taking it home, and plugging in to a wall outlet..........hey presto, on line! Bedding, towels and kitchen utensils appeared with amazing speed, on loan from our friends. Car rental was also essential, and for quite a period of time two cars became necessary.

Almost immediately my daily journeys were to the Boeing Ground Training school to make a start on producing the necessary operating material for the crews that would be arriving for training. I was in for quite a surprise when they did arrive – a few quite senior captains, but many extremely young looking co-pilots and F/E's. Most of the captains had international experience of some sort, but the co-pilots were straight from inter-island experience in Indonesia on Fokker Friendships or DC-9 aircraft. Their knowledge of the wider world was virtually non-existent.

Meanwhile, Elly was busying herself putting the finishing touches to our apartment, and typing out the material that I was producing – not an easy job as so much of it was of a technical nature. We took several trips out to the assembly plant at Everett, about a forty minute drive, and saw our first Garuda aircraft approaching the end of the assembly line...........already time to start thinking about an acceptance programme, and this time I was completely on my own!

...........................The first Garuda aircraft is ready for acceptance

Since these Garuda aircraft were updated versions of the earlier ones that I had accepted for KLM, there were many new features for me to become familiar with – mostly within the different modes of the flight guidance systems..........automation was forging ahead. When I finally started the ground acceptance the senior Garuda F/E joined me, fresh out of ground school and simulator training. He turned out to be a great help, and we ran quite an efficient programme together. Elly, together with a member of the Garuda staff, went meticulously through the cabin, checking out emergency equipment, and the proper functioning of toilets and pantries.

Standing next to us on the flight line was a brand new KLM aircraft awaiting the arrival of an acceptance team from Schiphol. Great reunions when they finally

Ready for acceptance checks

arrived, and several grand parties resulted. There was also considerable rejoicing over the fact that Elly and I were now a married couple, even though it was an unexpected development to some. Anyway, it was highly convenient having them next door on the flight line as I could always turn to their various experts for helpful advice when the need arose – which it frequently did.

Our first flight with PK-GSA took place on the 25th June, and lasted a mere three hours, so well had Boeing prepared the aircraft. The following day flight training commenced for the Garuda crews, which mainly took place at Moses Lake, and I returned to endless office duties. The Boeing instructors

Acceptance Flight. PK-GSA

Acceptance Flight. PK-GSA. Author, Sandy McMurray (Boeing pilot), Bill Spence (Boeing F/E)

soon found that some of the co-pilots needed more time than they had anticipated, and I was frequently called upon to make progress checks – to me, some seemed to be rather nervous or over-eager to make good..........a question of culture, and *"loss of face" was perhaps arising ? A talk with their senior captain appeared to improve matters, but similar problems were to arise in the future in which both captains and co-pilots would be involved

> *"Loss of face" was (is) a western description of a situation that frequently arises
> in dealings with Asiatic cultures. To "lose face" is to lose status among one's fellows.
> In aviation it can become a grave problem in crew unity. A pilot will "lose face"
> if he fails any form of check. A captain can even "lose face" if he listens too readily
> to his co-pilots or F/E's advice or warnings.

...........................an expedition to Montana

Shortly after that initial training session I packed my bag, and together with crews that had just completed simulator training, we took "our" aircraft off to Glasgow (Montana), where Boeing had arranged for our unrestricted use of an airfield for training. I was now properly back in the RH seat as a flight instructor, and quite enjoying this change of venue.

This period of training became a very intense week of continuous work, which also gave the new aircraft a real shake-down, and some quite rough handling. I was quite amazed at how the aircraft responded, there were absolutely no teething troubles that I can recall. I also had the opportunity to give two senior Garuda captains some training in the RH seat, which would enable them to fly as check pilots en-route in the future.

...........................and here comes number two!

We then had to hurry back to Boeing field where PK-GSA had to be prepared for its delivery flight to Jakarta via Tokyo. While that was taking place, I returned to Everett to commence work on our second aircraft, which was now ready for acceptance checks.

This aircraft turned out to be a little less "clean" than the first one – or was I getting my hand in again? – And eventually required two test flights totalling five hours of problem solving. Overall the whole programme was proceeding smoothly, and Elly was able to take time off and have flying lessons in a Cessna. She was frequently seen in the Everett area, and the Boeing pilots named some of her rather uncertain manoeuvres "Elly Stalls".

First delivery flight – Capt. Bill Zoethout (ex KLM)

...........................and still more training

About this time some job seeking pilots began to appear for interviews and flight checks; they were being sent to us through a well-known crew recruitment agency. Since the Garuda pilots themselves seemed to be a more sensitive collection of individuals than the typical American or European pilot, I felt that considerable care should be exercised in the selection process. Some very competent pilots were rejected on the basis of attitude, but how could one tell them that? One group of Scandinavians failed to meet my standards of flight competency, except for one.........and his most recent experience had been in helicopters!! But he refused to stay if the others were not accepted...........since I was not prepared to accept group pressure, they all returned home.

Meantime our first aircraft had departed for Jakarta with a crew change in Tokyo, and I had made myself unpopular in certain quarters by not selecting an ex-KLM pilot for the actual arrival into Jakarta. In my opinion, all the crew leaving the aircraft in Jakarta would be in uniform, and none of the on-lookers would know who was actually at the controls.................and that was the way it turned out, even the F/E was hailed as captain, after all he also had four (thinner) golden rings!

The selected captain for that final stretch had actually been a former colleague from our Jeddah days, he had decided to leave the UACI operation, and join us in this new venture. Capt. Don Hoyt was later to spend a great deal of his time in Tokyo, giving simulator instruction to the Garuda crews on a JAL (Japanese Airlines) flight simulator.

Finishing off with a Big Bang!

Before our final departure from Seattle we were treated to a media display which seemed intent upon spreading alarm and despondency throughout the region. Seismologists had detected rumbles in the bowels of a sleeping giant – Mount Helena was about to blow its top, and devastation would be widespread. There were several very isolated and picturesque mountain tops in the State of Washington with year round snow cover at their summits, but Helena was by far the nearest to the city, and its sprawling residential areas.

Widespread preparations were made to meet the threat, and every possible Boeing aircraft was flown away to safer areas – those that remained were cocooned in dust proof sheeting. Cheap filter masks for one's face could be bought at every drug store, and naturally these were also available for pet animals. Filters were also available for every air inlet on most cars – Elly`s Toyota being an exception, of course.

In the end Helena blew at the predicted time, but it was something of a non-event as far as the city was concerned. Devastation on the mountain slopes from ash, mud slides and larva flows was far reaching, but thanks to a change in wind direction there was only minimal dust fall-out over the Seattle area. We could trace our names on the top of the car, but that was about all.

A final round of farewells

Our Seattle sojourn was almost over with the fourth aircraft nearing readiness for acceptance. This went off quite smoothly, though it did take two test flights to complete. There then arose the matter of my own proficiency, since my annual check programme on both the simulator and the aircraft was due. Fortunately there was a Boeing flight instructor available who doubled as an FAA (Federal Aviation Authority) inspector. So I underwent the necessary checks (successfully) under his eagle eyes.

There then came a few more pilots applying for jobs to be processed, and I took them over to the airfield at Moses Lake for some circuits and landings, and general flying. Two of them proved satisfactory, and so travelled with us out to Jakarta.

We then had a final round of farewell parties, and were able to return the many household items which had been loaned to us. It would be many years before we saw some of these folk again, but many of them visited us in Jakarta after visiting Garuda management, and we were able to repay some of their hospitality.

..........................and a last delivery flight

We would be flying the last delivered aircraft, PK-GSD, on its delivery flight as far as Tokyo, and from there we would travel as passenger to Jakarta. Since I had never flown westwards out of Seattle, or approached Tokyo from the north, I had to borrow an atlas to familiarize myself with the lay of the land and the sea, in these northern latitudes.........the Aleutian Islands and the Bering Straits were familiar names, but not their exact locations. It was a good thing that I took a sneak pre-view of the intended routing, as my Indonesian crew's geographical knowledge was a great deal less than mine –at least I was able to answer some of their questions with a show of confidence.

Our passengers on the flight were mostly various Indonesian dignitaries who had seized on the chance of a free ride home, and so Elly had enough to keep her fairly well occupied. The actual flight took us well over ten hours with very little scenery to attract our attention. In many ways it reminded me of those Mauritius flights so many years ago, but now the navigation was so totally different, and demanded so little effort .....we were in the computer age !

It was during this flight that I suddenly realized that my travels would henceforth be in the company of Muslims. A quiet voice suddenly whispered in my ear "which way to Mecca, Captain"?

Somewhat startled, I turned around to find the second F/E holding his prayer mat ready. "Just a moment" I said, and started leafing through our books to find the coordinates (the latitude and longitude position) of Jeddah – knowing full well that we would not have Mecca information, but feeling that Jeddah was close enough.

With these, I then showed him how to type them in to our third INS (inertial navigation) computer, first making sure that this computer was not connected to the autopilot system. That done, the distance and direction of Mecca could be immediately displayed. He was immensely grateful, and carefully aligned his prayer rug very precisely, making his abeyances in the correct direction. To tell him that that direction would change, as our flight progressed, I felt might confuse the issue.

Our Tokyo arrival was on time, and within the hour we were refuelled and on our way to Jakarta, and the opening of a new chapter in our lives.

10th September 1980.

Our new colours

Sunset in Indonesia

Hotel Borobodur

On arrival in Jakarta we were initially installed in the Hotel Borobodur, one of the many glitzy hotels that shielded the less salubrious parts of the incredibly crowded city. Meantime, Garuda housing department was rather belatedly endeavouring to find us more permanent accommodation in the form of a rented house.

In the hotel there were also many Boeing pilots who had been sent to assist in the introduction of the aircraft and Garuda crews, along the route network. Their assistance was essential for several weeks, but as was always the case with factory pilots, some problems were also introduced. Their standard American style* of operating procedures for any aircraft type did not always match with European procedures – which Garuda had long adopted – and was thus somewhat confusing for the crews flying with them. It was purely a matter of philosophy, but quite difficult to deal with.

Indonesian licence

*For example: In KLM the co-pilots were trained to the same standard as the captains. Handling of the power levers during the take-off run was always done by the PF (pilot-flying), and he could be the co-pilot. In the USA the captain always handled the power levers, regardless of who was PF.

A first view of Hong Kong, and some later ones

Within the first week I was assigned a flight to Hong Kong on a route exposure training flight for two Garuda captains. It seemed inappropriate for me to declare my innocence, at this early stage, by revealing that I myself had never actually been to Hong Kong. Instead, I gathered an armful of appropriate maps and charts, and settled down to some concentrated study. Every feature of the area was carefully examined, and all the unfamiliar names committed to memory.

The weather for the flight was in one of its kindest moods, and we had a grandstand view of the whole area, and of the critical features that I had committed to memory. But I was still astonished by that final approach to the runway which brought us so incredibly low over a housing complex, and the need for a final smart manoeuvre down on to the runway threshold..... The landing roll-out with water on either side was quite relaxing after all that!

I made several subsequent visits to Hong Kong, which occasionally involved a night stop allowing some modest exploration of this teeming Asian power-house. One flight was memorable since it was a check flight for a Garuda captain. I was required to declare him qualified (or otherwise) on the route and the airport. Unfortunately the result was "otherwise", and he failed his check – some weeks later he passed a check under the supervision of another expatriate captain.

The critical feature of this event was that the Garuda captain had "lost face" by his failure. The following year he was appointed as Chief Pilot on the B-747, a position that gave him a desk in my office. He turned up at the office to announce his appointment, and also to say that he felt too embarrassed to be able to work from a desk in my office. Somewhat startled, I asked why that was.........his firm response, "you failed me on a check flight to Hong Kong last year." The matter was discussed and I thought resolved, but a certain tension remained for ever after in the air. I had an uneasy feeling that unseen knives were at work throughout the remainder of my Garuda service!

A new home in Cilandak, Jakarta.

We were eventually able to agree with Garuda upon their offer of an unfurnished bungalow in a residential area of Jakarta. It was quite compact, set in a walled garden with a swimming pool, and came with two young servants. It was only later that we discovered the roof leaked badly, but fortunately not in critical areas, and that no other ex-pats were within easy reach. With a company car and driver, however, we seemed to be moving up in the world.

From Cilandak, it was some thirty minutes drive into town, and forty minutes from my office at Kemajoran, the old airport which was now primarily a maintenance base. Neither of these journeys was very pleasant, the appalling traffic conditions in a humid atmosphere laden with diesel fumes left me quite exhausted by the time home was reached.

Our home actually lay very close to the flight path into Halim Airport, and this we found quite interesting. I soon acquired an air-band radio from Hong Kong, and once this was set to the correct ATC frequencies Elly was able to monitor my progress on training flights, and listen out for my final landing clearance – she claimed to be able to tell from my tone of voice how the training session had gone!

..........................and visitors galore!

We were hardly settled in before a succession of visitors started descending upon us. Boeing was making ongoing attempts to sell Garuda more aircraft, and their representatives were frequent visitors for a beer or a meal. They were also very generous in inviting us out for an evening, but we felt it more appropriate to get them away from their quite constant hotel life.

There were also the ex-KLM pilots that I had recruited, and they and their wives were quite regular visitors. Just to complete our guest list, there were a couple of ex-KLM pilots flying with Singapore Airlines, and if they had a night stop in Jakarta we were the chosen port of call. Their final departure from Halim Airport would usually include a flashing of landing lights and a word of thanks, for the benefit of our radio, before they changed ATC frequency after take-off.

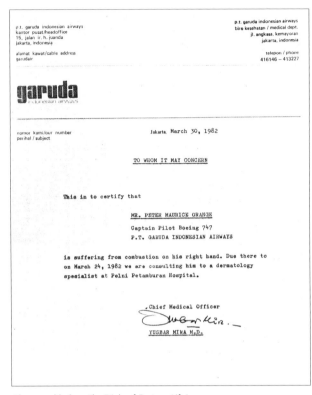

Above and below: The Trials of Eastern Life!

And a rather familiar work environment

My initial work pattern was in many ways very similar to the one that I had been used to in KLM, although the hours were quite different. Up at 06.00hrs to await my driver, and in the office at 07.00 hrs was the normal sequence allowing a relatively cool drive – the offices closed at 15.00 hrs, which then meant a hot and sticky drive home in the traffic hour. In between times my driver would return to Cilandak if Elly needed to go shopping or visiting.

The creation of Operating Manuals was nothing new to me, but this time it was without the advantage of discerning proof readers – something I sorely missed. It also demanded an unusual degree of priority in my work; we were actually flying this new aircraft along the international routes............ perhaps with some incomplete paperwork?

En-route training

The en-route training (route exposure) was carried out by both Boeing pilots and the expatriate ones that I had recruited. I had the greatest admiration for the manner in which they handled these very difficult assignments. For example, a young Garuda co-pilot would turn up for a flight to London. A departure from a warm and humid Jakarta in shirt sleeves was quite normal, but it later turned out that he had no uniform jacket along, and not a single item of warm clothing for a European winter.

He would have some idea of where London was located on a world map, but the route to be followed in order to reach it was very often an unsolved mystery. And in reaching that far off destination there would be countless different ATC regions to pass through, and each region would

The author with a Garuda crew

have its own version of the English language, and its own subtle manner of issuing a clearance. Those expatriate captains that flew with them had an extremely difficult job, which they performed with resounding success.

Unfortunately, two minor incidents occurred during these stressful flights, and both were with expatriate captains in command. On each occasion the check pilot had, quite correctly, been in the observer's seat monitoring checklist handling and engine starting. Each time there had been an inadvertent brake release by a pilot at the controls, necessitating some quick avoidance by the ground crews. The check captains stood accused, and I had to fight hard to prevent their instant dismissal by Garuda.

..........................*and basic flight training.*

My own flying was to a great extent limited to giving flight experience to new crews fresh from simulator training in Tokyo, where we had the use of a JAL (Japanese Airlines) flight simulator operated by our own instructor – Don Hoyt. After the completion of simulator training it was normal airline practice to allocate some four hours of in-flight training to the pilot being qualified on the new type of aircraft, followed by en-

In the RH seat again

route flights with a route instructor. When his proficiency was judged to be adequate, he received a final assessment by a check pilot.

My expected (by management) four hours of flight training was a non-starter........... those hours frequently doubled, or in one case tripled, before a student could be passed along to a route instructor. And in this uncomfortable scenario the question of "loss of face" was just around the corner:...........management answers to any questions I raised concerning extended flight training time inevitably brought the same response...."continue until you are satisfied, Captain." .... Cost was apparently secondary to the insidious question of "face".

Since these youngsters were being abruptly exposed to a very large aircraft, it was quite natural that handling difficulties would occur, and that the development of new visual judgement criteria would take time. In dealing with this rather unreal situation my patience was taxed to the limit. I must confess that I had never before flown a B-747 in the manner of a primary trainer, and my own fluency and accuracy in its handling improved considerably.

It was after some of these weary and lengthy sessions that Elly would hear my tired voice on our air-band radio asking Halim Tower (ATC) for a last landing. Tea time by our pool could then be anticipated, or dinner preparations commenced.

How about some home security?

We had no less than three silent night time burglaries at Cilandak, at least one occurring when Elly was alone in the house. Standard drill on such occasions was to lock the bedroom door and keep quiet, never mind what was lost. I naturally requested security guards from Garuda, when I was scheduled for an overseas flight. This they initially refused, but relented when I cancelled my assignment on a flight to London unless guards were at our door before I left from home. Seemingly I made my point, and security guards then turned up before every subsequent overseas flight.

How effective these guards would have been was an unanswered question – apparently they spent most of the night sound asleep under the sheltered walk-way in front of the bungalow. A pile of cigarette butts was at least evidence of their passive presence.

Tales of Australia

My few flights en-route took me via Bali to different Australian destinations, to Perth, or to Sydney via Melbourne. Sydney was of particular interest since there was a three day stop over, which allowed ample time for swimming at Bondi Beach, exploring the Harbour Bridge area, or visiting relatives I had not seen for many years. The Sydney flight was so attractive that I felt it would make a nice break for Elly.

Bali

Approaching Garuda for a staff ticket, I immediately ran into something akin to a brick wall. Tiring of these difficulties, we went along to see the KLM representative, Mr. Ten Cate. He immediately had a KLM staff ticket made out for Elly, entitling her to travel first class on my scheduled Garuda flight to Sydney........problem solved! We had an excellent few days in Sydney, and even managed a guided tour of the Opera House before lunching on sandwiches in the Botanical Gardens.

...........................and a need for handcuffs!

Australian regulations required all flights in their airspace to carry a pair of handcuffs, rather far fetched I had always felt, but now I was to see the reason why. On our way from Bali to Melbourne, with the stunning scenery of the outback far below us, I suddenly noticed that a rear door "open" light on the F/E's panel had illuminated.

Not alarming, since the light in fact showed the door was only unlocked – somebody had moved the handle. In a pressurized aircraft (which we were) it was physically impossible to open the door as an inward movement had to be made before it could be swung outwards, and any inward movement was prevented by the pressurization.

At almost the same time as I noticed the warning light, the purser arrived in the cockpit to tell me that a couple of passengers were drunk and making trouble, including trying to open a door. With some concern, I carefully checked our flight details with my two "student" pilots, and alerted the F/E to careful instrument panel monitoring.

That done, I gave the fire axe to the purser warning him that only the blunt side should be used should the need arise, pocketed those welcome handcuffs, grabbed the fire extinguisher, and headed for the aft cabin.

There was quite an uproar in progress, alarmed passengers trying to get away from the drunks who were exposing their persons; they seemed to be under the impression that the nearest toilet was through an opened rear door. Many people were also engaged in trying to protect the door from further attacks.

I found that the simplest way to gain attention was a couple of noisy bursts from the fire extinguisher, and it also provided a compelling threat to corral the miscreants within a seat row. We soon managed to handcuff one of them to a seat support, and the other we bound hand and foot with a length of escape rope.

Back in the cockpit I alerted Melbourne ATC to our problems, and requested a police presence at our arrival. At the arrival gate we were greeted by two truly massive Aussie policemen, festooned with every imaginable gadget of crime prevention or attrition. With all the other passengers disembarked, they strode purposefully down the back, and reappeared with the two very sorry looking victims of everyone's wrath.

Bali-high flyer tried to step outside

The captain of a Garuda Boeing 747 handcuffed a passenger into his seat yesterday after he tried to open a rear door while the jumbo was flying between Bali and Melbourne.

It is impossible to release an emergency exit or door during flight, but a spokesman for the airline said the man's action had caused "considerable alarm" to other passengers.

Garuda said the man was one of a group of five passengers who had joined the flight in Paris, four of whom became drunk on the sector to Melbourne. None of the group was Australian.

The airline said one of the five men was arrested on arrival in Melbourne, and two of the five, who were booked to fly with Garuda to Sydney, were ordered off the plane and told to make other arrangements.

The spokesman said: "As soon as the handle was pulled on the door a warning light alerted the captain, who went to the rear of the plane to investigate.

"He found the passenger still standing beside the door and immediately confined him to a seat with handcuffs.

"There were other unpleasant incidents. Another member of the party had walked about the cabin exposing himself, and a third member had fallen over a seat while drunk."

Garuda's spokesman described the incident as "rare, but of a type which can happen to any carrier."

From a Sydney newspaper

Much paper work resulted, which also had to be repeated at Sydney, before we were released at Melbourne to continue our flight. The local papers managed a short report on the incident the following day. The final outcome of the story was, however, rather unwelcome. It transpired that the guilty two were staff passengers from another airline, travelling on a free pass..........one wonders how they got home, and whether they still had jobs when they got there.

Mt. Galunggung blows its top

On the 24th of June 1982 we were again treated to an awesome display of the forces of nature, but on this occasion the expertise of man was called upon to avoid an airborne tragedy, all brought about by an unpredicted volcanic eruption.

Flight BA 009 was a Boeing 747 on a night time flight from Kuala Lumpur (Malaysia) to Perth in Western Australia, and was passing over head the Jakarta area when sudden turbulence violently disturbed the smooth tenor of the flight, and curtains of static electricity flickered eerily around the aircraft – St. Elmo's fire. The engines started surging, and smoke drifted through the cabin.........the crew was struggling with this totally unknown situation when all the engines completely stopped.

The aircraft descended to an uncomfortably low altitude before the crew were able to restore part power on two engines, and set course for Halim (Jakarta) to make an emergency landing. The ILS (Instrument Landing System) for the landing runway was inoperative, thus preventing the crew from using the autopilot to help with the approach to landing.

The crew had managed to alert their London headquarters to the situation, and that message had been passed along to Boeing in Seattle who, in turn, alerted their service representative in Jakarta.

Jim Barber (the Boeing rep.) picked me up on his way to the airport, and we watched in awe as the shadowy outline of the B-747 felt its way down on to the runway, its landing lights produced only the faintest of glimmers in the dusty atmosphere.

It was an unforgettable sight, the cockpit windows so blasted by volcanic ash that very little visibility remained, the nose and wing leading edges blasted free of paint, and the cabin choked with dust. Inspection soon showed that every filter in every system needed cleaning or changing.

The crew had done an impressive job, particularly the pilots and the flight engineer.

The whole incident was due to a lack of warning by the meteorological office and by Air Traffic Control, that a cloud of volcanic ash from the eruption was drifting across the airways. This essential information was so slow in being released that a Singapore Airlines B-747 got caught in the same dangerous cloud the following day. Although the results of this second encounter were less severe, an emergency landing in Halim still became necessary.

And I nearly blow mine!!

Two Australian pilots, who had flown for SIA (Singapore Airlines) were passed to me for flight assessment after applying for employment. In take-offs and landings of a varied nature they performed reasonably well, and I recommended that they receive an en-route check flight.

A few days later I was assigned to a Dubai (UAE) flight and return, which would call at Singapore and Bangkok on both the outbound and return flights. An ideal flight for the purpose of checking on a pilot's performance, and so................would I please take the two Aussie candidates along!

On the first stretch into Singapore I gave the captain's seat to "Jack", thinking that this would be an easy ride since he was fully familiar with the area, and qualified on the B-747. My feeling of relaxation in the RH seat slowly eroded as I watched his handling of the autopilot system when we neared our first destination.

Cleared for approach to the landing runway by Singapore Control, I watched as "Jack" prepared for an automatic approach – he was intending to disengage the autopilot close to the runway for a manual landing. Settled on the approach "Jack" unknowingly pressed a wrong button, and the autopilot disengaged, as a result both an aural and a visual warning were activated. "Jack" cancelled the warnings and watched the continuing approach (no longer automatic!) in quite a relaxed fashion. As we slowly drifted off centre line he commented that the autopilot didn't seem to be doing a very good job; that's because its not on autopilot, I quietly responded.

With no other traffic around, and with the consent of ATC, I had allowed this uncontrolled approach to continue longer than I would normally have – vainly hoping for some recognition of error by "Jack". When this was not forthcoming, I took over and realigned the aircraft for landing.

On the second stretch of the flight to Bangkok I put "Bob" in the captain's seat, hoping for a more positive performance. The flight went well, and we were then ready for the final Bangkok to Dubai sector with "Jack" once more in the captain's seat. As the flight smoothly progressed I left my seat, giving it to "Bob" while I went for a walk through the cabin.

Returning to the cockpit, some twenty minutes later, I was horrified to see that both pilots had their seats fully in the aft position, and their feet resting on the central pedestal...................."who is flying the aircraft?" I enquired. An unhurried, and apparently unconcerned, seat restoration to normal flight positions resulted while I occupied the observer's seat ....I had no thoughts of again leaving the cockpit on this flight.

The remainder of the flight to Dubai and return proceeded without incident, until we reached Singapore once more – and again "Jack" unaccountably repeated his previous error of cancelling autopilot warnings without realizing that the autopilot was, in fact, disengaged.

After arrival at Jakarta I had no hesitation in telling them that they had both failed their check flight, and that Garuda would not be employing them. Apart from "Jack's" mishandling of the autopilot, I could not accept a situation where neither pilot was in a position to instantly assume manual control of the aircraft should the need arise. This decision they refused to accept.

Some days later I was called for an interview with Garuda's vice-president. He needed a full report on the flight that I had made with the Aussie pilots as apparently they were threatening to sue the airline for misrepresentation, or something. End of story, as far as I was concerned, I heard nothing more about it.

Would you like an Airbus?

At sometime in 1982 I was asked to go to Toulouse to handle the acceptance programme of the Airbus aircraft (I don't recall the particular model, probably the A-320) which Garuda had on order. At that time I was not an Airbus fan – side stick controllers replacing time honoured control columns, an endless array of computers which apparently told the aircraft what to do, even if that was against the pilot's wishes, and automatic control of engine power with no corresponding movement of the power levers (throttles) etc.

Since I was already looking forward to a return to Seattle, and the acceptance of new B-747 aircraft, I had little hesitation in politely turning the offer down.................... big mistake, a little more knife sharpening could be softly heard! But apart from anything else, I didn't really feel capable of rapidly acquiring all the detailed knowledge of the new technology that would be necessary – this was now a new age of technical advancement, streets ahead of the venerable B-747 that I knew so well.

Tension in the humid air

Garuda started preparations for their first Hajj operation to Mecca with B-747's, and very wisely insisted that all the potential pilgrims be pre-assembled in camps for a few days. Once there, they underwent some instruction on the basic facts of air travel with particular attention being paid to the proper use of toilet facilities – basins were for the washing of hands only! Normally the aircraft, of any carrier, would need to have its interior completely refurbished after a Hajj operation. By this arrangement Garuda managed to minimize the destructive results of pilgrim traffic.

During these preparations I was asked by the Chief Pilot (rather reluctantly) to review his planned schedule. I immediately noticed that it was planned on a High Speed operation, which would involve the aircraft flying somewhat faster in cruise flight than was normally the case. Although High Speed resulted in a modest decrease in flight time, the increase in fuel consumption was quite significant, and an economic penalty thus arose – but economics was someone else's problem.

To my astonishment I noted that the fuel consumption figures in his planning had not been adjusted to show the results of flying at High Speed cruise. Arrival at destination would be with near empty tanks, and therefore no reserves. Despite an inevitable (second) "loss of face" when this error was pointed out, I had no option but to do so. I noticed that the finalized schedules were based on normal cruise speed, with a refuelling stop in Karachi.

And a death on board

The one flight that I made during that particular Hajj season had two particular points of interest.

The pre-instruction policy that had been insisted on had really paid off; the aircraft interiors were remarkably clean. I was also able to see that the death of a pilgrim after the Hajj was completed was not a very sorrowful event.

Returning from Jeddah with a full load of jubilant Hajji's, one of the cabin attendants came to tell me that a pilgrim had died. With a refuelling stop to make in Karachi this was not quite the right moment; if we advised the authorities of this, which was what we would normally do, the aircraft would be impounded while the bureaucratic community became immersed in their paperwork.

The simplest solution, and the one that we adopted, was for yet another pilgrim to be sound asleep carefully draped in a blanket. Since none of the passengers were allowed to disembark, this simple deception easily passed the cursory head count made by a turbaned policeman.

Safely back at Jakarta, smiling companions carried the deceased from the aircraft; he had made the pilgrimage, he was a true Hajji, but his time had now come! The proper arrangements were then put in hand made by the authorities and by his relatives.

Tension returns

Seattle was ready for our return, and travel arrangements had to be made. I requested that Elly be allowed to join me on the trip, and this was initially approved. When I then actually went to collect our tickets there was not one for her, so I naturally asked for an explanation. It took several days before

I was called for an interview, and was then told that it had been decided not to send me to Seattle............ would I please brief the Chief Pilot on the procedures!

..........................*the wheel had turned full circle, a lost face was being restored!*

The Writing on the Wall!

As 1982 drew to a rather weary close it was evident that the paint being used on the wall was of an indelible kind; even my loyal driver (Sudjoko) was accused of being more loyal to "The Captain" than to Garuda. Despite my protestations to the Head of Transport, he was abruptly replaced and never seen again. Transport then had to be requested from a car pool, making life very difficult for Elly.

On an assigned flight to Sydney, which was to be a route check for a senior captain, I did myself no favours by refusing to accept his pre-flight gift of a case of whiskey. A chapter dealing with the problems of "face" had not been included in my manuals! This, in my opinion, was not a subject that had any place whatsoever in aviation.

During this particular flight, however, I happened to get in conversation with a passenger who turned out to be the director of a pilot training school in Adelaide (Australia). He was most interested in my varied flying experience and offered me a job, subject to the approval of his Chief Instructor. On a later Sydney flight I flew over to Adelaide, and had a satisfactory interview and check flight at the training school which resulted in a job offer.

At about the same time I was informed by Garuda management that my office services were no longer required by the airline, and that I was being demoted to the status of a route pilot only. As Elly and I discussed these, not unexpected, developments by the side of our swimming pool (which was still a muddy yellow colour from volcanic ashes) we came to the conclusion that it was time to move on.

I had become uncertain about the Adelaide venture, it was ab initio training that I would be embarking upon, and that was a very long way back in the memory bank; much book work learning would be involved before I could function properly. Elly was also uncertain about even more years overseas since her elderly parents were becoming increasingly frail. In the end we decided to resign from our increasingly difficult situation in Garuda service and head back to Europe.

Even this didn't prove easy as Garuda was prepared to give us only economy class tickets back to Amsterdam, and refused to help with our household possessions. The fact that I was now no longer a Garuda captain appeared to be a key issue.

We rather reluctantly turned once more to Mr. ten Cate for air freighting our household possessions back to Amsterdam, and then to the UK. He also immediately issued us with two first class KLM staff tickets for the journey on any flight that we cared to take. After all that kindness I didn't like to trouble him about our two cats, which Elly was determined would accompany us. So I made the round of different airlines enquiring about "airline staff discount prices" for two cats in under floor class! British Airways direct to London turned out to be the best deal, and off they went for six months' quarantine near Heathrow.

And so it was a final last packing, with quite an emotional farewell to our young servants who had been so intensely loyal and efficient. My last contact with Garuda was the quite unexpected appearance of two captains who came to thank me for all my efforts, and to wish us good luck.

A Last Look Around, remembering my very last flight as a Captain

My very last flight as a commercial pilot was to Sydney, via Bali and Melbourne. I arrived in Sydney in a somewhat sombre mood, unsure how to spend the next two days. The Indonesian crew always disappeared on their own mysterious errands, often laden with parcels. The only evidence of their presence would be a dark figure stepping aside in the hotel corridor, quietly murmuring "Morning, Captain", or the smell of their extremely pungent cigarettes.

Since this was to be my last visit a little exploring seemed to be in order, and I set off to re-visit the hotel in which we used to stay thirty years ago. It had of course, long gone, and was replaced by a towering glass fronted office block.

As I wandered around the streets the vastly changed nature of Sydney's inhabitants began to unfold; every race, colour and creed seemed to be represented. Restaurants of many exotic origins abounded, shopkeepers were Greeks or Indians, taxi drivers hailed from Thailand or the Philippines.............where had the good old Aussie gone? He was still around, ANZAC Day was the proof; it was then they appeared in their thousands to remember the sacrifices of the Australian and New Zealand troops at Gallipoli in 1916.

Tiring of the noisy city I took a ferry boat ride through Sydney harbour to Manly Point, just watching the shore line scenery slide by until sleep overtook me on the return trip, to be reawakened by the blast of ships' sirens as we entered the docking area. And then it was time for a last ride out to the airport in a crew bus, one blonde head among a dozen very dark ones.

Out of Sydney on a north-north westerly heading we were cruising over the dramatic scenery of the Northern Territories at 35,000 feet, and my mind was beginning to drift. Through force of habit I was alert to every slight variation in the behaviour of the aircraft, but a drift had started in my mind .... this had all begun with a view of the world receding away from me......then I could

see where we had been, but not where we were going – perhaps just as well in 1941. And finally I had arrived up front, to spend the rest of my flying days watching the world approach me head on, and what spectacular watching that had been. And the future? .....that was to be watching the world pass sideways, from a cabin window.

But now we were over the Timor Sea, and it was time to commence my very last descent into Den Pasar, Bali. Leaving Bali I lined up on the runway for the very last take-off in my career – not a thought that actually registered at that moment as routine took over. It was a mere ninety minutes flying time to Jakarta, just right for a last look around. Again, I studied those towering and menacing clouds lining the

My Last Approach

horizon, occasionally lit up from within by lightning flashes, and their tops in constant motion as they seemed to boil in the fading sunlight. Was it from these majestic forms of nature that those Indonesian craftsmen had derived inspiration for god-like carvings, some of which had such frightening appearances?

And then it was time to start that last descent into Halim for a final landing……. this had better be good! I surprised the co-pilot by switching off the autopilot as we commenced descent, but I wanted the "feel" of this last twenty-five minutes of flight. A good approach, but the landing could have been better…….. getting out of practice already? And all too soon it was engine shut down, a last look around that familiar cockpit, and away to greet Elly with a bunch of flowers from Sydney. It was not unexpected that officialdom prevented her from coming to the aircraft stairs – but it couldn't prevent a wave from the balcony.

Saying it with flowers

A last look at Seattle

Feeling that we deserved a good holiday, we flew a few weeks later from Amsterdam to San Francisco, rented a car, and had a wonderful leisurely drive up the West Coast to Seattle. After memorable reunions with old friends we gratefully accepted a KLM invitation to travel back to Amsterdam on the delivery flight of a new B-747.

……………*that very neatly rounded off quite an extensive aviation career*

Passengers on a KLM delivery 1983

In Conclusion

Sadly the mists of time have almost erased many of the memories and sensations of actual flight, particularly those of the propeller driven days. Long gone are those feelings of awe associated with uncomfortably close views of menacing mountain peaks, of the more distant views of arid deserts, or the timeless tranquillity of seas upon a desert shore.

Bad weather approaches, to a hoped for landing, had been something of an art in the propeller days, given the very imprecise nature of both forecast and actual weather reporting in those times. A broken cloud base, flooded paddy fields, a road or railway track were isolated clues in helping to define an arrival.

In contrast, the jet age ushered in the days of much greater accuracy and precision in reporting of weather conditions. The hushed stability on a jet approach, in weather approaching landing minima conditions, was accompanied by a surety that a landing would result. I can hardly ever recall a missed approach and overshoot (go-around) from a jet approach. Up to date weather reports and advanced aircraft technology had virtually eliminated the old "look-see" method of operation, and its often token observance of published weather minima for landing.

I sincerely believe that the crews of my generation had far more challenging and interesting careers than the crews flying today. Time away from home was probably a great deal longer, but overseas life was a great deal more interesting, with longer crew slips at exotic locations. Actual flights were generally far slower, and time changes thus more easily accommodated, except on the North Atlantic routes.

So............ good luck to those who follow my wings aloft.

Appendix

Each aircraft type in the KLM fleet had its own type office. This office, among its many other functions, would produce Crew Bulletins at intervals which alerted flight crews to any significant events concerning their type of aircraft. To attract more interest these bulletins were occasionally written in an unusual form. The Flight Safety Foundation (USA) somehow acquired two examples of these and published them internationally – what about my copyright? – and these are given below.

Parable of the Straight and Narrow

A few months ago an airline captain brought his jet in for a night landing in a rainstorm. Prior to his departure from home base, he had been warned of deficiencies in the destination airport's runway lighting, of the upslope of the runway and to expect reduced visibility in increasing rain intensity in the area. Despite these pre-warnings, however, the captain had a problem. He came in too fast, a bit high, could barely see out the windshield, ran into a sudden crosswind, was sitting too low in his seat to see much of the runway during the flare-out, and he touched down on one side of the runway at an angle to the non-existent centreline. The jet ran off the runway and travelled some 800 feet before being brought back on the concrete, hitting three concrete runway light foundations in doing so.

This incident prompted a supervisory pilot of the airline to author the following "Parable of the Straight and Narrow".

"The Lord was troubled in His mind as He pondered on the ways of mortal man. And foremost in His thoughts lay the problems of His birdmen – those men to whom were entrusted the care of so many of His faithful, and to whom the guidance of their aerial machines was a devious and tricky task. And the Lord in His troubles gazed upon the world of His creation and saw thereon the rusty wrecks of countless aerial machines. Sadly He said unto Himself: 'Unto them (my birdmen) have I given wisdom and understanding and for their guidance prepared the Book of Flight Techniques. For their common good prepared I many lessons, showing unto them the perils of the wilderness that lie before the runway and beyond the runway. And furthermore have I created devious perils upon the runway surface that they may learn therefrom the proper manner in which to halt their cumbersome machines. All this have I done for their enlightenment and thereafter have I prepared Feasts at Many Bars, in which may be found the relaxing temptations with which they (My birdmen and their helpers) must also contend.

'And yet (said the Lord unto Himself) one thing have I not done – for them must I prepare a lesson which showeth those perils lying beside the runway'.

"And forthwith the Lord called out with a loud voice for the servants of His Aerial Ministry. And these servants (with neatly folded wings) being assembled, they received the following instructions from the Lord. 'Go forth to an airfield of your choice and prepare the circumstances for My lesson'. And the servants took note of their Lord's commands in the following manner:

- let there be darkness upon the earth;

- create thunderstorms of scattered nature;

- let the wind be devious in its ways and strength;

- cause the approach lights to be without sufficient power;

- let there be no glide path angle assistance for the birdmen;

- let the runways lights be dim and let some be removed;

- let there be a hollow in the runway at the sacred point where the aerial machine seeks the ground;

- let the birdman's throne be low in height, so that as he seeketh contact with the runway, the darkness of night envelops him;

- let the aerial machine have a pneumatic rain removal system so that the birdman's window become blurred as he flareth for landing.

"And these things, being done, the Lord was pleased and commanded His servants to observe with care the lesson thus prepared. And so it came to pass that the aerial machine approached, being skilfully guided by the birdmen to avoid the perils before the runway. And lo! the birdman flareth his aerial machine at the sacred spot as described in the Book of Flight Techniques. But well prepared were the servants of the Lord; the darkness was blurred with rain, the runway lights were scarcely discernible to the birdman's anxious eye and the runway dipped mightily beneath him. Thus, carefully the birdman sought to brush his wheels against the ground and the aerial machine floated over-long, And then did the servants of the Lord give a mighty puff and behold, the aerial machine responded with a sideways drift, its wheels seeking the rough and stony ground. And thus it blundered through the perils beyond the runway edge until the birdman could regain the narrow path of true salvation.

"Thereupon did the Lord command His Minister-in-Chief to pronounce words of warning and wisdom for the guidance and salvation of all birdmen. For the lesson of the Lord showed the perils of reluctance to firmly place the wheels upon the ground and to ride in a floating (above the runway) aerial machine. And the Minister-in-Chief uttered solemn words of wisdom to guide those birdmen who would follow the straight and narrow path; and the scribes of the Minister noted His words thus:

> "at all times strive mightily to set your aerial machine upon the runway at the sacred spot prescribed in the Book of Flight Techniques (chapter 2.3.8 Verse 01);

> "elevate your throne so that you may survey at ease all the wondrous creations of the Lord;

> "alert well your senses to the insidious attack of a side-ways drift, and remember well that such aggressions can be fought only with a lowered wing – kick not solely upon your rudder".

"And all these things being done the Lord was well-pleased and commanded a day of rest for the servants of His Aerial Ministry. And the birdmen of the Lord laboured mightily to stay upon the straight and narrow path which He had shown them".

The Gospel according to St. EGT*

*EGT – The exhaust gas temperature is one of the most important parameters
concerning jet operation. The cockpit dial is marked with temperature limits.
If these limits are exceeded then the turbine blades are likely to be damaged.

.... and from His heavenly abode the Lord pondered upon the ways of mankind and upon the beauties of the earth of His creation and His wisdom and understanding were great. And observing the multitude of His creatures and the beauties that surrounded them, He summoned a meeting of all His Angels – and spoke thus:

"For the lowliest of My creatures let there be wings of steel and fire that supporteth caverns of vast size and space. And let there be placed therein beauteous maidens to wait upon their needs. And let there be couches of comfort and stools of convenience and when all this is accomplished let these aerial machines transport My creatures to every farthest corner of the earth. And these machines shall be entrusted to the care of My special Birdman – and they shall spread their wings over every land and every tribe therein, and none shall be deafened nor assaulted with noxious odours".

And thus the Angels of the Lord set forth and descended upon that land known to all men as America, for their dwelt many tribes of great wealth and skill. And unto the tribe of Boeing, in the far land of Washington, the Angels spoke thus:

"Let there be gathered all the adults of your tribe and let there be created in this rocky and forested land a vast cave. And within this cave shall ye build with great care and skill giant aerial machines to transport all the peoples of the Lord. Let its dimensions be such that all mankind will gaze with awe upon the fruits of your labours – and your labours will be to the greater glory of the Lord".

And this being done the Angels of the Lord sought out the tribe of Pratt and that of Whitney, for they were famed amongst men as craftsman of uncommon skill in harnessing the power of horses. And unto them the Angels of the Lord spoke thus:

"Let there be created engines of tremendous power, that shall draweth the mighty chariots of the tribe of Boeing unto the heavens of the Lord. But beware that your skills are steadfast and true, that none may be imperilled by plagues of imperfections. And above all – harken well unto the sound of thy machines and let them not impurify the airs, for then shall the curse of all mankind fall upon thy heads."

And so the Angels of the Lord sought out the tribes of all the Birdmen, and unto the Lord's special tribe of KLM, they spoke thus.

"Let there be created temples of wisdom and learning. Let there be machines of instruction and simulation and let thy Birdman be so drilled and tested that none may endanger the lives of the Lord's creatures entrusted to their care. For unto them shall be entrusted wondrous chariots of the sky, and therein shall be encompassed all the tribes of the earth. And take heed, lest sins of omission and complacency overwhelm thee – for perfection can be found in no man, nor in the things of his creation".

And all this being done the Lord was well pleased. And thus it came to pass that all was fashioned according to His wishes and the prophets of doom (and they were many and numerous) were confounded, all men stood in awe of the Almighty and the prowess of His creatures.

But the Birdmen of the Lord suffered great trials and tribulations and their many skills were stretched upon the racks of imperfection and adversity. And many a time there arose great surges of bitterness and frustration within their spirits – for unto them were offered not only the hymns of praise but also the laments of woe and these were many and numerous for great were the errors of the technicians of the tribes. And so it came to pass that the steel of their sinews was dulled, their nerves overwrought and the edge of their alertness blunted to the Devil's touch. And then the Lord besought a test and an awakening, a trial by fire to purify their souls – and the trial ran thus:

Unto the fair city of Montreal, in that land known as Canada, came a mighty chariot of the air. And the Lord caused a multitude of malfunctions to plague the craft and divert its Birdmen. He plague's the APU, disconnected a generator, caused failure of the pressurization and bedevilled the autopilot. But His Birdmen were alert and wary and combated these evils with skill and fortitude, and thus came well satisfied unto the given place of alightment (runway 06L). And then allowed the Lord a gentle storm to blow; and the northerly winds were encumbered with snow, and the night darkened and the surface of the land grew slippery beneath the feet of man. But the Birdmen of the Lord cried in praise "Autoland" – and indeed set foot upon the earth in soft comfort at the most propitious spot.

And this being encompassed, and being wary of the treacherous surface beneath their wheels, all engines were set unto reverse – as prescribed within the gospel of the AOM. And lo! – The Lord set torches within the bowels of No. 4 engine to further test the skills of the Birdman engineer. And he respondeth well with a cry of "overheat" and rapid shut-off action. And so the Birdman pilot placed all engines unto a restful reverse, and eased with care his mighty chariot into the street of narrow turns. And then decreed the Lord His final trial for, unobserved, the Birdman engineer attended no more unto the engines and the pilot Birdmen's eyes were strained against the elements without. Thus, unseen and unheard were the torches of fire thrust within the bowels of No. 3 engine – and thus the heat arose unheeded until a pilot Birdman cried aloud in belated recognition of this distress, drawing back the engineer from the remote wilderness of a myriad winking eyes, on panels to the rear. But alas! – the bowels of No. 3 were sore strained and stressed, and the tribe of Pratt and that of Whitney were returned the black sheep of their family. And the lesson of the Lord was hard and fearful, for it touched upon the pride of men and upon the riches of their tribe. And the Birdmen of that tribe were filled with sorrow and alarm and unto them with strident voice and wrathful tones spoke the Patriach Ray thus:

"Heed well the lessons of this day for he who ploughs the furrow of adversity needs team-mates at his side. Let none depart the assignments of his task without due warning to his fellows. When the elements of nature and the frailties of man turn their hand against you let no man point his hand and say, "the engines went unguarded"!

AMEN

Footnote

The incident related above was certainly not one of complacency, but rather misdirection of attention during a still critical phase of engine handling. While the succession of events may have pressured the engineer into leaving the forward panel at an inopportune moment, no criticism can be levelled at the pilots for being fully occupied with external events.

In searching for a remedy the following suggestions are offered:

• if a pilot 'feels' the engineer requires alerting, call "coming out of reverse";

• if an engineer finds it essential to leave the forward panel, he should call "watch the engines", or words to that effect.

This incident resulted in a cancelled service and a fifth pod operation. Due to weather conditions and the need for specialist attention the required **borescope inspection took some 24 hours to accomplish. The fifth pod operation and subsequent engine change caused delay to other scheduled services.

> *Note: This international publication came to the attention of the engine manufacturer, enabling him to reject an insurance claim since a crew error was involved.*

> **Borescope – A visual inspection of each turbine blade by a telescopic magnifying device which allows an inspection without dismantling the engine.*
> *A slow and laborious task.*